China's Expansion into
the Western Hemisphere

China's Expansion into the Western Hemisphere

Implications for Latin America and the United States

RIORDAN ROETT
GUADALUPE PAZ
editors

BROOKINGS INSTITUTION PRESS
Washington, D.C.

Copyright © 2008
THE BROOKINGS INSTITUTION
1775 Massachusetts Avenue, N.W., Washington, D.C. 20036
www.brookings.edu

Library of Congress Cataloging-in-Publication data
China's expansion into the western hemisphere : implications for Latin America and the United States / Riordan Roett and Guadalupe Paz, editors.
    p.   cm.
    Summary: "Analyzes the history and motivations of U.S.-China-Latin America relationship. Focuses on China's growing economic ties to the region, including Latin America's role in China's search for energy resources. Highlights the geopolitical implications of Chinese hemispheric policy and sets recent developments in the context of China's role in the developing world"— Provided by publisher.
    Includes bibliographical references and index.
    ISBN-13: 978-0-8157-7553-9 (pbk. : alk. paper)
    1. China—Foreign economic relations—United States.   2. United States—Foreign economic relations—China.   3. China—Foreign economic relations—Latin America.   4. Latin America—Foreign economic relations—China.   5. China—Commerce.   I. Roett, Riordan, 1938–   II. Paz, Guadalupe, 1970–
    HF1604.Z4U636 2008
    337.5107—dc22
                                                     2007048434

Typeset in Minion

Composition by R. Lynn Rivenbark
Macon, Georgia

Printed by R. R. Donnelley
Harrisonburg, Virginia

Contents

Acknowledgments

We owe our thanks to the many individuals and institutions that played a role in the completion of this volume. Our deepest gratitude goes to the Tinker Foundation, whose generous support made possible the two-year SAIS project on China and the Western Hemisphere that culminated in the publication of this volume. We especially thank Renate Rennie and Nancy Truitt for their participation and support throughout the project. We are also greatly indebted to the individual authors for their valuable contributions. Several other individuals played a key role in the preparation of the final manuscript. Special acknowledgment goes to Frank Phillippi for his able editing assistance and generous patience. Charles Roberts once again played a key role in producing superb translations of the chapters originally written in Spanish and Portuguese.

We would also like to thank the participants of the three workshops conducted in Washington, Beijing/Shanghai, and Buenos Aires, in particular Peter Brookes, Alejandro Casiró, Lucio Castro, Sergio Cesarín, Daniel Erikson, Antoni Estevadeordal, Stephen Johnson, David Michael Lampton, Thomas Lovejoy, Rodrigo Maciel, Thomas Mesa, João Batista do Nascimento Magalhães, Renee Novakoff, Martín Pérez Le-Fort, Fernando Petrella, Susan Kaufman Purcell, Roberto Russell, J. Stapleton Roy, Julia Sweig, Sergio Toro, Lia Valls Pereira, Manfred Wilhelmy, and Zheng Bingwen. For their research and project assistance, we are indebted to Emmanuel Guerisoli, Sarah Johnston-Gardner, Amy H. Lin, Anne McKenzie, Susana Moreira, and Mariano Turzi. For their invaluable feedback, we owe special thanks to the anonymous reviewers of the preliminary manuscript. Finally, we would like to recognize several individuals at the Brookings Institution Press who were not only instrumental in the publishing process but also a pleasure to work with: Christopher J. Kelaher, marketing director and senior acquisitions editor; Mary Kwak, acquisitions editor; Susan Woollen, art director responsible for the cover design; and Janet Walker, managing editor. To all other individuals who played a role in the production of this book we also express our gratitude.

China's Expansion into the Western Hemisphere

RIORDAN ROETT *and* GUADALUPE PAZ

1

Introduction: Assessing the Implications of China's Growing Presence in the Western Hemisphere

At the outset of the twenty-first century, China is a rapidly rising global presence. Assessing the implications of its growing economic, political, and security influence is a difficult but critical endeavor because of the potentially serious consequences of misjudging China's intentions and the true scope of its power.[1] China's self-proclaimed "peaceful rise" has led to several major intellectual debates about the changing international landscape, including whether U.S. hegemony has begun an inexorable decline.[2] Among the most salient debates is whether an emerging multipolar international system, with an increasingly powerful European Union (EU) and Asian bloc, will have a destabilizing effect on the current world order founded on U.S. hegemony.

At a time when the United States is concentrating a great deal of attention and resources on the war on terrorism, China has made important inroads in expanding its influence abroad, particularly in developing regions such as Southeast Asia and Africa. Another relatively recent development in China's "going global" strategy is a new interest in engaging Latin America. China's expanding diplomatic and economic ties with the region, the backyard of the United States, have awakened new concerns in U.S. policy circles. Skeptical policymakers in the United States view China's new presence in Latin America as an opening salvo of a larger diplomatic offensive by Beijing to challenge U.S. interests in the Western Hemisphere. A more benign viewpoint considers China's expanding ties with Latin America more of an opportunity than a threat and a natural manifestation of its growing need for commodities and energy resources.

The chapters in this volume provide a variety of perspectives on the implications of China's growing international presence. In part I Chinese and Latin

1

American scholars offer different views on China's foreign policy, its geopolitical drivers, and the repercussions of deepening Sino–Latin American ties. Part II focuses on the economic and energy security aspects of the China–Latin America relationship. What is the impact of China's economic rise and growing regional engagement on Latin America's development and economic prosperity? What can Latin America learn from China's economic successes and what can losers do? How will China's drive to satisfy its long-term energy needs affect Latin America? In part III the authors analyze China's growing influence in Southeast Asia and Africa in an effort to provide a broader framework of analysis, namely: Can Latin America draw lessons from China's role in other developing regions? Part IV offers some conclusions about the implications of the changing landscape in Sino, U.S., and Latin American relations drawn from the various viewpoints presented in this volume.

Overall, this volume seeks to answer several key questions. Is there any reason to believe that China's economic and commercial interests in Latin America will endanger the strategic relationship between China and the United States? What do the countries of Latin America expect to gain from the expanding economic and diplomatic role of China? Finally, what are the implications of growing economic and diplomatic linkages between China and the Western Hemisphere for the traditional perception of U.S. hegemony in Latin America?

To better understand the current dynamics, this chapter examines the linkages in Sino, U.S., and Latin American relations. As a first step, it is important to recognize the asymmetrical nature of the triangular relationship, an asymmetry resulting from U.S. primacy. Even if U.S. hegemony in the Western Hemisphere is deemed unquestionable, the preeminence of China's economic and diplomatic ties with the United States over its ties with Latin America plays a key role in China's pragmatic approach to greater engagement with the region. Similarly for Latin America, the United States will continue to be its most important export market in the foreseeable future. Nonetheless, China's growing presence in the region presents interesting opportunities, though not without costs in certain sectors. All of these factors must be taken into account when analyzing the prospects for deepening ties between China and Latin America.

China's Strategy: Peaceful Rise?

One of the central reasons China's rapid economic ascent is of concern to the rest of the world is its impact on the price of commodities and on global currency and credit markets. China's growing geopolitical influence is also of increasing concern—in particular to the United States and other developed nations—given the implications for the existing world order. As Xiang Lanxin states in chapter 3, China has "launched a diplomatic offensive" to assuage international fears of a potentially destabilizing geopolitical effect from China's growing power and to convince the world that China is merely following a "peaceful rise" path. Although the official Chinese government view—presented in chapter 2 by Jiang Shixue—contends that China is, indeed, simply pursuing a global strategy, this claim is generally disputed in subsequent chapters with the argument that geopolitical concerns are the primary drivers of China's foreign policy. That said, there is also general agreement among the authors of this volume that China's current international strategy does not appear to be revisionist in nature but, rather, to be characterized by pragmatism and caution and led by necessity and opportunity.

As Robert Devlin explains in chapter 6, China's successful economic diversification and upgrading strategy has been aided by several important policy factors: long-term strategic planning and goal setting; placing priority on the development of local capacity and on sound fundamentals such as competitive exchange rates, high savings and investment rates, education, research and development, among others; and a proactive state that plays a role in horizontal and vertical interventions as needed. This approach to economic development is increasingly viewed as a potential model for other developing regions to emulate.

China is also becoming more sophisticated and influential on the diplomatic front, as Joshua Kurlantzick notes in chapter 9. Several chapters in this volume underscore one of China's most effective diplomatic strategies: forging strategic partnerships through the promotion of South-South cooperation in multilateral forums. In Africa, for example, China has benefited from the largest single bloc of votes in multilateral organizations. As Chris Alden notes in chapter 10, African votes have been crucial in several areas of interest to Beijing, including securing the vote to hold the 2008 Olympics in China. China's diplomatic influence is also increasingly aided by tools such as humanitarian aid, foreign direct investment (FDI), soft power, symbolic diplomacy, and a foreign policy free of conditionalities. This no-conditionalities approach, what Alden calls a policy of no political strings, has led to fears that a Beijing consensus, countering the principles of the so-called Washington consensus, could be emerging. As Alden explains, this foreign policy model is based on noninterference in domestic affairs of states and the promotion of sovereign integrity, which appeals to many developing countries, including pariah states. China has been widely criticized for explicitly employing this approach at the expense of sound business practices, respect for human rights, and good governance.

China's foreign policy in the twenty-first century clearly will be determined by varying combinations of considerations: security, trade and investment, natural resource needs, and geopolitics. Thus far Chinese efforts have focused on win-win rhetoric of promoting world peace and harmony, South-South economic and diplomatic cooperation, and political stability in Asia, its sphere of influence. As Kurlantzick points out, an interesting aspect of China's foreign policy has been a tendency to successfully reach out to nations whose bilateral relations with the United States are strained. For example, China made an overture of greater cooperation and aid to the Philippines after President Gloria Macapagal-Arroyo pulled Philippine troops out of Iraq in 2004 as part of a deal to win the freedom of a Philippine hostage, an arrangement that led the United States to withdraw its economic assistance to the country. At the same time, China is careful not to incite new tensions with the United States. Although China's economic dependence on the United States is an incentive to diversify its economic relations, Sino-U.S. relations will continue to be of paramount importance in the foreseeable future.

The China-U.S. Relationship

Despite ongoing skepticism in some U.S. political circles, the strategic ties between Washington and Beijing continue to deepen—and become more nuanced—each year. Everything indicates that in the twenty-first century there will be no more important bilateral relationship than that between China and the United States. There are both negative and positive aspects to the linkages between the two countries.

Security Issues: Taiwan and Beyond

Foremost on the negative side is the difference in perception on the part of each country concerning the status of Taiwan. The Taiwan Relations Act (TRA) of 1979 defines U.S. policy regarding Taiwan. The decision by the United States to establish diplomatic relations with the People's Republic of China (PRC) rests on the expectation, outlined in the TRA, that "the future of Taiwan will be determined by peaceful means" and that "any effort to determine the future of Taiwan by other than peaceful means . . . [will be] . . . of grave concern to the United States." The act also authorizes the U.S. government "to provide Taiwan with arms of a defensive character." In effect, the act serves as a guarantee of Taiwan's right to peaceful existence.

Although the TRA considers Taiwan's security "of grave concern to the United States," the act does not specify how Washington would react to a threat to the island's current status. For example, in March 1996 Democratic president Bill Clinton deployed two aircraft carrier battle groups off the coast of the island in response to ballistic missile tests by the PRC. In April 2001 Republican president George W. Bush stated that his administration would do "whatever it took to help Taiwan defend itself" if attacked by the mainland government.[3] These are but two brinkmanship actions by administrations from both political parties.

Relations between Beijing and Taiwan are highly unstable. The Beijing regime has maintained for decades that, at some point in time, Taiwan will revert to mainland sovereignty. For many in the United States and in Taiwan itself, however, the island's thriving democracy contrasts sharply with the authoritarian regime on the mainland, and these proponents insist that Taiwan must maintain its sovereignty. The two sides jostle back and forth, with the mainland sending sharp warnings while some on the island seek greater autonomy. In March 2005, for example, the Chinese legislature adopted an antisecession law. A year-and-a-half later Taiwan proposed to rewrite its constitution to replace the name Republic of China with Republic of Taiwan as a sign of increased independence.[4]

Both the United States and China are deeply concerned about any confrontation between the island and the mainland. China's overall goal is to maintain the status quo while keeping its options open for the future. For any current American government, this is an inherited policy with strong support from the Taiwan lobby in the United States and from a significant number of members of Congress. These tensions probably ensure that the current state of play will continue indefinitely, with all three parties alert to the potential for a rapid escalation if any one undertakes any precipitate action.

Taiwan is not the only concern to U.S. national security officials. In the 2006 Quadrennial Defense Review, China is judged to be the country with the "greatest potential to compete militarily with the United States."[5] The report elaborates by explaining that China is the world power most likely to "field disruptive military technologies that could . . . offset traditional U.S. military advantages."[6] From Beijing's perspective, U.S. strategic relationships in Asia are viewed with equal suspicion. A recent decision by Washington to negotiate a new security agreement with Tokyo—allowing the United States to base a nuclear-powered aircraft carrier and Patriot antiballistic missile batteries in Japan—is seen as provocative by Beijing. The American decision in July 2005 to share nuclear and space technology with India can also be interpreted as an effort to build a military counterpoise to China. Moreover, the United States is now involved in military training programs in two of China's neighbors, Vietnam and Mongolia.

Perhaps in reaction to these U.S. movements in Asia, Beijing supported an East Asian summit in December 2005. The meeting took place in Kuala

Lumpur, Malaysia, as an addition to an Association of Southeast Asian Nations (ASEAN) summit meeting.[7] The new concept is ASEAN-plus-three: the three additional members are China, Japan, and South Korea. The United States was not invited to participate or to observe. China's increased involvement in Asia can also be noted in China's role in the Shanghai Cooperation Organization and the six-party talks involving North Korea.[8] This approach reflects the oft-stated position of Chinese scholars that China seeks a peaceful rise to great-power status and that the PRC understands the possible downside of a more aggressive political or military strategy. Some analysts, however, view these regional moves, and particularly the expanded ASEAN-plus-three bloc, as threats to U.S. leadership in the Asia-Pacific Economic Cooperation Forum (APEC).[9]

Despite these important points of contention, it is North Korea's nuclear arms development that defines the need for China and the United States to work in tandem. The announcement in October 2006 that North Korea detonated a nuclear device heightened the need for collaboration. China is a critical lifeline for the regime in Pyongyang, supplying an estimated 90 percent of its petroleum and 40 percent of its food supply.[10] China's trade and investment with North Korea is estimated to be around $2 billion a year.[11] Their bilateral relationship is founded on the Sino–North Korea Friendship and Mutual Assistance Treaty of 1961. Until the nuclear test in 2006, Beijing refused to consider the use of sanctions against the North Korean regime. That position was driven by the fear of instability in North Korea: an influx of refugees, the collapse of a buffer-state regime, and, although a very different regime, the demise of an ideological colleague. As China's foreign policy has expanded, North Korea is viewed as part of its sphere of influence no matter how strained the bilateral relationship between the two communist states becomes.

Until the recent nuclear test by North Korea, the Chinese had opposed the U.S. position, which is defined as the demand for "complete, verifiable, irreversible dismantlement" (CVID) of nuclear weapons.[12] Beijing also criticized U.S. opposition to direct talks with Pyongyang. The substitute has been the six-party talks involving the United States, China, South Korea, Japan, Russia, and North Korea. With the unanimous approval of Resolution 1718 by the UN Security Council in October 2006, closer collaboration between Washington and Beijing is possible. The resolution puts in place sanctions that bar the sale or transfer of material that could be used to make nuclear, biological, and chemical weapons and ballistic missiles. These sanctions also forbid international travel and freeze overseas assets of anyone associated with North Korea's nuclear program.

These critical security issues provide an important justification for the high priority given to the China-U.S. relationship. Despite important differences on security priorities, there is a fundamental understanding of the sensitive policy issues that could suddenly intensify and create a crisis situation. That overarching objective—to remain alert and avert international crises—is the principal driver in relations between the two states and helps explain the relations of each with the countries in the Western Hemisphere.

China-U.S. Economic Ties

The Sino-U.S. economic relationship is also of critical importance. The numbers are staggering. Total trade between the two countries grew from $5 billion in 1980 to an estimated $343 billion in 2006, a growth rate unmatched by any other major U.S. trade partner.[13] For the United States, China is not only its fourth largest and fastest growing export market but also its second largest trading partner overall.[14] U.S. exports to China grew 20.5 percent between 2004 and 2005, compared to only an 8.4 percent increase to its second largest export market, Mexico.[15] One analysis suggests that this growth in Chinese consumption will continue, estimating that by 2014 China will be the world's second largest consumer market after the United States (China was seventh in 2004), with total household spending of approximately $3.7 trillion.[16] China's enormous infrastructure needs and an increasingly wealthy population will boost global demand for foreign capital, expertise, and consumer goods in the years ahead, and the United States stands to be a major beneficiary of these trends.

While the trade numbers are extraordinary, there is a downside to the relationship. Although China absorbs large amounts of U.S. imports, China exports an even larger, and growing, volume of goods to the United States. China is currently the second largest source of U.S. imports, which increased 18.2 percent from 2005 to 2006.[17] The large and growing U.S. trade deficit with China, up from $30 billion in 1994 to $232 billion in 2006, has created a major controversy in the United States.[18]

The U.S. trade deficit with China for the foreseeable future will be the most contentious issue between Washington and Beijing. Critics in the United States, both in Congress and in the private sector, argue that China uses unfair trade practices: an undervalued currency, a lack of intellectual property protection, dumping, and few labor and environmental standards. United States trade officials argue that the Chinese currency, the yuan, is undervalued by 15–40 percent, giving China's exporters an unfair advantage in the U.S. market.[19] Some in the United States claim that the undervalued currency threatens U.S. jobs and wages, but a recent study by the U.S. Bureau of Labor

Statistics shows that only about 2 percent of gross layoffs are due to a transfer of job opportunities outside the United States.[20]

The issue is further complicated by the accumulation of U.S. Treasury securities by the Chinese government. According to official figures, China's foreign-exchange reserves had surpassed $1.4 trillion by late 2007.[21] While the purchases fund the federal deficits of the United States and help keep U.S. interest rates relatively low, there is concern that China may control the economic future of the United States. Any move to transfer its holdings to other currencies would have an immediate, devastating impact on the U.S. economy. Others argue that China's financial interests are so intertwined with those of the United States that such a move is highly improbable if not unthinkable. The visit to Beijing by Secretary of the Treasury Henry M. Paulson in September 2006 was cordial, but it did little to achieve the U.S. administration's goals: Chinese currency realignment, restrictions on China's capital markets, resolution of trade disputes, and elimination of widespread piracy of U.S. software, movies, and pharmaceuticals. While Paulson and his Chinese counterparts agreed to a new strategic economic dialogue, it provided no concrete promises or results.

Efforts in the U.S. Congress to "punish" China for its recalcitrance to move on these policy questions are ongoing. For example, in 2005 Senators Charles Schumer (D-N.Y.) and Lindsey Graham (R-S.C.) introduced legislation to apply a 27.5 percent tariff on Chinese imports to the United States in an effort to force the government in Beijing to raise the value of its currency. Senators Charles Grassley (R-Iowa) and Max Baucus (D-Mont.) introduced a measure that would have forced the United States to veto any increase in International Monetary Fund (IMF) voting rights of a country with a "fundamentally misaligned" currency. Both measures were dropped after the Paulson visit to Beijing, but there is continuing unhappiness on Capitol Hill over the inability to win greater concessions from China.

The White House is keenly aware of the need to engage China on trade issues. In her first visit to Beijing as U.S. Trade Representative in August 2006, Susan Schwab urged China to play a greater role, commensurate with its new economic power, in reviving the cause of global trade liberalization, following the collapse of the Doha Round of the World Trade Organization (WTO) negotiations.[22] Schwab indicated that the United States would like to see new alliances formed between global trading powers to advance the stalled negotiations, including a more active role by China. To date, China has resisted taking a high profile in the Doha Round, arguing privately that concessions it made as part of its own entry into the WTO make it difficult to take a stand on a new round of market-opening measures.[23]

The 2006 annual meetings of the World Bank and the IMF in Singapore offer further insight into how the United States envisions China's responsibility in multilateral organizations. Despite the attempts of Senators Grassley and Baucus to the contrary, the United States was a strong supporter of increasing IMF quotas for China as well as for South Korea, Turkey, and Mexico. This reform process has been driven by the need to adapt IMF rules to reflect significant shifts in global economic power, particularly the rise of Asian and other rapidly developing countries. Clearly, the decision reflects the inexorable growth of the Chinese economy and the need to provide a greater role in the decisionmaking process for Beijing.

Sino-U.S. Energy and Environment Cooperation

An often overlooked area of importance in the bilateral relationship is the need for cooperation in the energy field. David M. Lampton argues that "the energy-related fates of China and America are intertwined in key areas—oil dependence, global warming, and air pollution."[24] Both countries are major petroleum consumers, and both are contributing to increasing demand. There is growing automobile ownership on the mainland due to a rapidly expanding, energy-consuming middle class. The challenge for both nations is to manage rising demand by cooperating in the development of new transportation, industrial, and construction technologies.

China's air pollution—sulfur dioxide, nitrogen oxides, particulates, ozone, and heavy metals—directly affects the United States. Up to one-third of the air pollution in the western U.S. states comes from China, as does one-fifth of the mercury in the Great Lakes. In addition, the United States is the world leader in pollution from carbon dioxide emissions and China is second.[25] It is thus clear that China and the United States need to work together in improving energy and environmental policy.

The Sino-U.S. Relationship in Perspective

Although China's economic clout and status should not be exaggerated, the fact that it has become an important global player calls for careful attention on the part of Washington in its strategic policy planning. As some analysts point out, because China's future and internal stability are far from certain, "further integrating China into the global community offers the best hope of shaping China's interests and conduct in accordance with international norms on security, trade and finance, human rights, and encouraging collaboration to confront the challenges both countries face."[26] Policymakers in the United States have encouraged China to become a responsible stakeholder in the international system, so that the management of differences between the two countries can be negotiated in a more stable framework of shared political, economic, and security interests.[27]

There is no doubt that the U.S.-China bilateral relationship is a top priority for both countries. A Chinese commentator put it this way: "The United States is a global leader in economics, education, culture, technology, and science. China, therefore, must maintain a close relationship with the United States if its modernization efforts are to succeed. Indeed, a cooperative partnership with Washington is of primary importance to Beijing, where economic prosperity and social stability are now top concerns."[28] These issues bind China and the United States in an ongoing dialogue and provide the framework for considering China's expanding role in the Western Hemisphere as well as the implications of that role for the future of U.S.–Latin American relations.

The United States and Latin America

Another key linkage in the newly emerging Sino, U.S., Latin American triangle is the relationship between the United States and Latin America.[29] There is no question that the United States remains a crucial market for the region's exports. U.S. foreign direct investment remains highly significant, and most Fortune 500 companies participate in the Latin American marketplace.[30] Moreover, the Organization of American States (OAS) and the Inter-American Development Bank (IADB), both organizations in which the United States is the largest contributor, remain important players in the Western Hemisphere.

But there has been a sense that relations are changing. Some Latin American governments blame the United States for the failures of the economic reform process instituted in the 1990s. Known as the Washington consensus, these market-oriented reforms were intended to make the region more competitive and to address critical issues such as unemployment, skewed income distribution, and lack of property rights. There is a general agreement that the program failed.

Beginning with the election of Hugo Chávez in Venezuela in 1998, political leaders have criticized both the philosophy and implementation of the Washington consensus. They argue not only that it failed to achieve its goals but also that it may actually have made the social and economic condition of many of the region's citizens worse. The rhetoric in some countries has become increasingly and jarringly antimarket and antiglobalization. In fact, the World Bank and the IMF, two institutions in which the United States is the major decisionmaker, are accused of adopting Washington consensus policies to benefit U.S. economic and financial interests.

The war in Iraq, U.S. military action in Afghanistan, the crisis in Lebanon, and related controversies are very unpopular in the region. In particular, the administration of President George W. Bush is widely viewed with antipathy. Expectations are low that the next U.S. administration will significantly improve U.S.–Latin American relations. Two important policy areas illustrate the troubled nature of the U.S.–Latin American relationship: U.S. immigration policy and trade policy. Both are considered critical to the region's security and development, and on both issues the United States has been found wanting.

Immigration Policy and the Failure to Reform

Immigration policy is of particular importance for Mexico and the countries of Central America and the Caribbean, but it has come to symbolize the indifference in the United States to the fate of millions of Latin American citizens. What is most striking about the failure of immigration reform is that it was originally a priority of the Bush administration. In his State of the Union address on January 20, 2004, President Bush proposed a guest worker program. This was primarily in response to homeland security concerns about illegal immigration and possible links to the war on terror as well as to pressure from both sides of the political spectrum.

Conservatives on the right expressed concern about uncontrolled flows of illegal immigrants into the country, who, they argue, often take jobs away from American citizens, cause a rise in community crime, and use scarce public resources for health and education. On the liberal left, the call to protect the civil rights of immigrants, both documented and undocumented, has grown. However, the need to protect the basic rights of anyone residing and working in the United States has been overtaken by the fear of open borders and the war on terror. The obvious contribution to the U.S. economy and to their home economies by immigrants is too often ignored. It has been argued that immigrants are crucial to the American economy because they do the jobs that even poor Americans will not. Furthermore, the billions of dollars they send home help maintain economic stability in their home countries.

The debate over immigration reform has deeply divided the United States. Public opinion polls show a hardening attitude toward immigrants, even legal ones. In three polls in mid-2006, nearly half of the respondents said immigration hurts the United States by taking jobs, burdening public services, or threatening "customs and values."[31] This indicates that immigration, once thought to be a foreign policy issue, is now driven by domestic political concerns.

In sum, a critical issue for many of the countries in the Western Hemisphere has been stalemated by U.S. domestic and partisan political concerns, and legislators are increasingly fearful of taking any action lest they suffer the electoral consequences. The prospects for effective legislation in the near future are poor, as is the likelihood that the necessary congressional leadership will emerge to make significant progress. In addition, the outgoing, lame-duck Republican president has limited suasion on Capitol Hill, especially when Democrats control both houses of Congress.

Regional Trade Policy

Another issue of critical importance to Latin America is access to the overly protected internal market of the United States (as well as that of the EU). On this issue, as with immigration, the United States and Latin America find themselves on opposite sides of the debate. The Free Trade Area of the Americas (FTAA), first proposed by President Bill Clinton at the 1994 Miami Summit of the Americas, has been recently described as "moribund."[32] The Clinton White House lost momentum for the FTAA when Congress refused to extend fast-track authority for the president. Fast-track authority allows the White House to submit a trade bill for an up or down vote without amendments. When President George W. Bush took office in 2000, he promised to restart what he called a "stalled" trade agenda. Congress granted the White House fast-track authority under a new name, trade promotion authority, or TPA, and supported the president in approving bilateral pacts with Jordan, Singapore, Morocco, and Australia.

But the broader, hemisphere-wide negotiations slowed and then stopped. Brazil, the cochair with the United States in the original effort to finish an FTAA agreement by January 2005, often led South American resistance to Washington in what was seen in the United States as a clear win. The task was complicated further by the election of Hugo Chávez in 1998, who declared the FTAA to be part of a U.S. strategy to exercise undue control over trade policy in the Americas, claiming it was part of an imperialist scheme. The FTAA also became an issue in the controversy surrounding the completion of the WTO Doha Round trade negotiations.

When it realized the FTAA talks were stalled, the White House opted for a second-best strategy: subregional or bilateral agreements. Chile was the first country in the region to sign a bilateral treaty with the United States. Santiago was pessimistic about the prospects for Mercosur (the common market of South America of which it is an associate member) and increasingly put off by the fiery anti-American rhetoric of Venezuela and the obstructionist tactics of Brazil and others, so it seized an opportunity to conclude an agreement with the United States.

The U.S. Trade Representative (USTR) office then pursued an agreement with the Dominican Republic and the countries of Central America. But when the draft legislation was submitted to Congress, anti–free trade sentiment in the United States was on the rise. Individual members of the House felt that important business and trade groups in their districts would be impacted negatively. The debate was heated, and the White House achieved victory by only two votes in the House in 2005 (the Senate had passed the bill by 54 to 45 votes earlier). But this difficult victory required significant high-profile lobbying: Vice President Dick Cheney spent most of the final day in the House soliciting votes. The administration was forced to horse trade with individual members of Congress, granting relief and concessions for special interests like the sugar and textile industries, in exchange for votes.

Subsequently, the United States negotiated bilateral agreements with Colombia and Peru; initiated talks with Panama; and encouraged interest from Uruguay in a framework trade agreement with the United States. But free trade sentiment remains low on Capitol Hill. Many members of Congress argue that free trade agreements often ignore lower labor and environmental standards in the smaller, developing countries, and job loss in the United States is a constant concern. Given the Democratic Party leadership's refusal to support President Bush on trade issues in November 2006, pending bilateral agreements with Latin American countries appear defeated. The FTAA will not move forward in the near future, if ever.

A parallel issue is the status of the Doha Round. That too appears to have lost momentum. As with the FTAA, the most contentious issue is agricultural subsidies in the developed world. Efforts over the last few years have failed to find a compromise, and each side blames the other for the failure. Frustrated with the lack of progress, the international business community has called on political leaders to find a compromise. Recently, the Transatlantic Business Dialogue (TABD) declared it "unacceptable" that differences over agriculture, representing less than 3 percent of transatlantic GDP, were dictating progress on increased market access for goods and services that compose the majority of world trade.[33] In essence, the TABD was far more sympathetic to the developing world than to the industrial countries.

One important event in the Doha process was the creation of the Group of Twenty (G-20) developing nations.[34] As Monica Hirst explains in chapter 5, the developing nations G-20 was established in August 2003 during the final stages of preparation for the Fifth Ministerial Conference of the WTO held in Cancún, Mexico. The focus was, and continues to be, fair agricultural policies on the part of the industrial countries. Although the Cancún meeting ended in failure, the G-20 has continued to be an important political force, lobbying for fairer trade rules. The G-20 has held frequent ministerial meetings and a series of technical exchanges. The latest meeting was held in

Rio de Janeiro in September 2006 with the significant participation of key trade officials from the United States, the EU, and the WTO. The Rio meeting called for a return to the negotiating table, but prospects for a breakthrough remain slim.

In early 2007 the Bush administration proposed serious reforms to current U.S. agricultural policies in a new farm bill submitted to Congress. The Bush initiative, deemed "the most reform-minded farm bill in decades," proposed to reduce farm subsidies by $10 billion over the next five years and eliminate payments to wealthy farmers.[35] The White House is concerned that without a substantial reduction in subsidies—especially for the key crops of cotton, corn, wheat, rice, and soybeans—the agriculture-exporting countries, particularly in the Americas, will "pick apart U.S. farm policies piece by piece" in the WTO dispute panel process in Geneva.[36] Brazil has already successfully done so in the case of cotton, winning a landmark decision against the United States. At the close of 2007, however, significant reform in U.S. farm policy seemed unlikely. In June of that year the House Agriculture Committee of the U.S. Congress rejected the White House reform proposals and chose to retain farm subsidies. The Senate version of the farm bill passed in November 2007 also left subsidies largely unchanged. Despite threats of a veto by the Bush administration, the prospects for significant reform in the foreseeable future are dim.[37]

Even with a U.S. initiative, progress would require reciprocal concessions by the EU to reduce its farm tariffs further and by the G-20 states to make deeper industrial tariff reductions. Given the internal dynamics of the EU, this appears unlikely. From the perspective of the Latin American countries and the G-20, the outlook is pessimistic. Rigidities in the industrial countries are driven by domestic constituent concerns of elected lawmakers. There is also deep-rooted resistance in Latin America to meeting the demands of the industrial countries for concessions on such key issues as intellectual property rights. While all of the participants in both the FTAA and the Doha talks trumpet the benefits of free trade, there is no appetite for concessions and compromise.

On the other hand, it is well understood in Latin American capitals that China plays a critical role in overall trade strategy. Its purchases of commodities and raw materials from the region drive trade surpluses year after year. For many observers, current prosperity in South America, at least, is in large degree due to the China trade dynamic. As Hirst explains in chapter 5, China has also made it clear on a number of occasions that it is a sympathetic member of the G-20. There are legitimate reasons for China to support Brazil, India, Argentina, South Africa, and the other members in terms of trade issues. But the importance of diplomatic and political support from Beijing is not yet recognized and appreciated in the region.

Latin America and the New Left

A final consideration in U.S.–Latin American relations is the emergence of what some have called the wrong left, as opposed to the right left. As Jorge Casteñada wrote:

> The leftist leaders who have arisen from a populist, nationalist past with few ideological underpinnings—Chávez with his military background, Kirchner with his Peronist roots, Morales with his coca-leaf growers' militancy and agitprop, López Obrador with his origins in the PRI— have proved much less responsive to modernizing influences. For them, rhetoric is more important than substance, and the fact of power is more important than its responsible exercise. The despair of poor constituencies is a tool rather than a challenge, and taunting the United States trumps promoting their countries' real interests in the world.[38]

From the viewpoint of some analysts as well as government officials, the wrong left appears to have the upper hand, at least in terms of rhetoric. For others, the situation is more nuanced. Some leaders committed to social change and development are also fiscal conservatives, such as the presidents of Chile, Brazil, and Uruguay. But Hugo Chávez of Venezuela embodies an ideological threat in the Americas not seen since Fidel Castro came to power in 1959. The wrong left is indeed anti-American, antimarket, anti-FTAA, anti-Doha, and antiimperialist. But is it the future of the region? And is it predominantly against any U.S. presence in the Western Hemisphere, or does it speak for long excluded and marginalized sectors of society that have never benefited from any model of economic development?

The United States fares badly in this debate. With huge budget and trade deficits, there is little disposable wealth to address pressing social needs. Foreign aid is not popular in Congress or with the American people. Moreover, in the region, the wrong left views institutions such as the IMF, the World Bank, and the IADB with great suspicion and as stalking horses for the United States. For the pessimists, the arrival of China in the Americas is inexorably going to lead to a strengthening of the wrong left. China's Communist Party and its ideological stance loom large for those leery of Beijing's strategic interests in the region. For those more optimistic, the expansion of China's interests in Latin America is a logical development given the mainland's rapidly growing economy, the need for natural resources and commodities, and the complementarities of its economy with most of the region's.

The Changing Relations between China and Latin America and the U.S. Response

Most authors in this volume agree that China's strategic agenda with Latin America is driven primarily by economic interests, although China has also noticeably intensified its diplomatic engagement with the region. For Latin America, China offers several attractive opportunities. Economically, Latin America can benefit from trade diversification, foreign direct investment, low-cost imports, and growth in sectors that are complementary to China's trade with the region. Diplomatically, Latin America stands to gain a higher profile in the international system through the proposed South-South cooperation agenda, at a time when the traditional engagement of the United States in the region has diminished due to events elsewhere in the world.

In her chapter, Monica Hirst argues that China and Latin America share a regionalist approach that fosters economic cooperation and peaceful coexistence among states, motivated by an interest in offsetting U.S. influence. Latin America and China could work toward a strategic partnership based on political and economic complementarities. Furthermore, as Hirst notes, there is strong potential for greater collaboration in education, science and technology, and health. However, Xiang Lanxin warns that the economic strategy China is following in Latin America resembles more a North-South model in terms of concentrated investments in the energy and commodities sectors, a pattern similar to the one China has been following in Southeast Asia and Africa.

Although China's increasing involvement in Latin America opens new opportunities for trade and investment, the downside to the expanding relationship is that, in the long run, it may work primarily in China's favor.[39] To date there have been significant complaints that cheap Chinese manufactured goods are replacing those produced domestically, in part because the wage differential is substantial. Thus far the country that has suffered most from Chinese competition is Mexico, as Francisco González explains in chapter 7. To protect themselves, Latin American countries have increasingly imposed non-tariff barriers against Chinese exporters. In fact, the countries in the region have together brought more antidumping cases against China in the WTO than has the United States.[40]

But overall the evidence indicates significant complementarities. As Devlin explains, export similarity indexes suggest that Chinese and Latin American exports are significantly different and, therefore, do not compete directly in third markets, with some important exceptions (certain sectors in Mexico and the Caribbean countries have been hard-hit by Chinese competition). The observed decline in Latin American exports to third markets, they contend, is due more to domestic, supply-side conditions than to lower demand because of competition with China's growing exports.

In chapter 7, González describes the China–Latin America economic relationship as a function of competition for the U.S. market. He asserts that the so-called commodity lottery helps explain the general trends in the Sino–Latin American economic relationship. Natural-resource-exporting economies like Chile and Peru are among the most complementary vis-à-vis China and have thus experienced big windfalls. Countries with a mixed-export structure, like Brazil and Argentina, have experienced large gains in the commodities sector but significant losses in the manufacturing sector. Countries that rely on low-skilled, labor-intensive manufactured goods, in particular Mexico and Costa Rica, have suffered the worst effects of China's growing presence in the Western Hemisphere.

For the majority of governments in Latin America, the trade relationship with China has been a bonanza, producing much-needed trade surpluses. While total trade is relatively small for both parties, the trend line is growing sharply upward. However, as Latin America's terms of trade improve as a result of commodity and raw material exports to China, concern over the apparent correlation between Chinese business cycles and world commodity prices continues to grow.[41] Some have also raised the fear that the heavy emphasis on exporting raw materials and commodities, which is the historical role and comparative advantage of Latin America, will preclude countries from seeking to add value to their exports. Thus the region will be vulnerable to the natural resource curse, in which foreign exchange earnings are obtained by the production of raw materials and commodities instead of the development of alternative exports with greater value in world markets.

As Devlin and González argue, the issue of competitiveness is crucial to the future participation of Latin America in the global economy. The 2006–07 Global Competitiveness Report, prepared annually by the World Economic Forum (WEF), supports the argument that Latin America needs to catch up with other developing regions, in particular Southeast Asia. Each year the WEF ranks a number of countries (125 in 2006) on a set of key indexes, the most important of which is the global competitiveness index, or GCI. The GCI "provides a holistic overview of factors that are critical to driving productivity and competitiveness, and groups them into nine pillars: institutions, infrastructure, macroeconomy, health and primary education, higher education and training, market efficiency, technological readiness, business sophistication, and innovation."[42]

Chile, as usual, ranks the highest in Latin America, at 27th place. Brazil, the most important economy in the region, fell from 57th to 66th place due to a particularly poor position in the macroeconomic column. Mexico, the region's second highest ranked economy, remained stable with a rank of 58. However, a lack of sound and credible institutions remains a significant stumbling block in many Latin American countries, such as Venezuela (88), Ecuador (90), Honduras (93), Nicaragua (95), Bolivia (97), and Paraguay (106). Their low overall rankings, which place them among the worst performers, are due to the absence of the basic elements of good governance, including reasonably transparent and open institutions. All of these countries suffer from poorly defined property rights, a top-heavy bureaucracy, and inefficient government operations. In addition, they suffer from unstable business environments, making it difficult for the domestic business community to compete effectively either within the region or in the world.[43] The lesson is clear: Latin America and the Caribbean must recognize the unflattering contrast with China in terms of competitiveness and view it as a wake-up service, as Devlin argues, to improve on the institutional deficiencies discussed by the WEF.

In addressing these concerns, Devlin and González share the view that Latin American governments need to implement smarter industrial policies that promote more efficient private-public alliances, innovation investment, and assistance in overcoming market failures as trade diversification increases—in sum, policies geared toward increasing international competitiveness. Xiang Lanxin argues that Latin America has much to learn from the Asian model about striking the right balance between the role of the state and that of the market. Mexico and the Central American and Caribbean countries, González asserts, should also take further advantage of their proximity to the United States.

The growing number of agreements between the governments of Latin America and China is a trend that signals a likely increase in Chinese FDI in the region. One recent example are agreements between Brazil and China on satellite development, in which China provided 70 percent of the financing and technology and Brazil the remaining 30 percent.[44] The two countries have also concluded agreements to build steel mills in the north of Brazil to process iron ore into steel.

In addition, as explained in chapter 8 by Luisa Palacios, China has been active in Latin America's oil industry. With China's oil consumption projected to reach 14 percent of total world consumption by 2030 (Palacios notes that in 2006 China accounted for 9 percent of the world's crude consumption), and with Chinese domestic oil production declining, China's dependence on oil imports will inevitably increase. The Chinese are already becoming important oil producers in Peru and Ecuador, and they are beginning to invest in the energy sectors of Bolivia, Brazil, Colombia, and Venezuela.

Nonetheless, Devlin explains that, to date, information on Chinese FDI in the region is scant, while China remains a relatively modest overseas investor. According to Devlin, officially approved Chinese FDI in Latin America only reached $77 million in 2005, less than 1 percent of China's total FDI that year. Thus Latin America is, in relative terms, still a minor destination for Chinese FDI.[45]

The Taiwan issue also plays an important role in Sino–Latin American relations, as China campaigns to displace official recognition of Taiwan in favor of the one-China policy. As noted by Juan Gabriel Tokatlian in chapter 4, twelve of the twenty-four countries that currently recognize Taiwan are in Latin America—primarily Central America and the Caribbean—and they have been the focus of China's foreign aid programs, which have funded the construction of hospitals, schools, and roads in many of these countries.

China's Expansion into the Western Hemisphere in Context: A New Transpacific Triangle?

Thus far there is little or no evidence that China's growing presence in Latin America has other than diplomatic, trade, and investment goals. Beijing has been careful to downplay any connection with the wrong left. Relations with states such as Venezuela, Cuba, and Bolivia have been carefully correct and courteous. If there is any warmth in emerging relationships, it is with countries like Chile, which clearly belongs to the right left, and Brazil, which offers the richest variety of needed commodities and raw materials. In this sense, as Xiang Lanxin notes, China cannot avoid the geopolitical implications of its ties with Latin America, because the U.S. factor remains key in Sino–Latin American relations.

The United States needs to carefully balance the high-politics bilateral relationship and not let it be colored by concerns that China has nefarious goals in the Americas. As Jiang Shixue and Xiang Lanxin explain, the fourth generation of Chinese leaders is well aware of the skepticism in some U.S. circles about the new and expanding presence of China in the region. And they are aware that transparent relations best serve their longer-term interests in the Western Hemisphere. Other Asian analysts also stress the peaceful goals of China in the emerging global system. Zheng Bijian, for example, argues that China is not seeking international hegemony but, rather, is engaged in advocating "a new international political and economic order, one that can be achieved through incremental reforms and the democratization of international relations."[46]

Just as the arrival of China may provide an important opportunity for Latin America to rethink its need to increase its competitiveness in the global market, it may also serve to open a debate in U.S. policy circles about more imaginative policies regarding immigration, trade and investment, and other priorities of the region. There is only slight room for optimism in this regard, however. Ultimately, what is clear is that we do not need a debate about whether or not the United States has lost Latin America, particularly to China. As Tokatlian notes, "it would be counterproductive to return to an apocalyptic geopolitics approach based on an overblown fear of an alleged Chinese takeover of Latin America." Instead, the expanding role of China in Latin America should be viewed as a singular opportunity to strengthen all three relationships in the Sino, U.S., Latin American triangle.

Notes

1. For more on assessing China's power, see David M. Lampton, "The Faces of Chinese Power," *Foreign Affairs* 86, no. 1 (2007): 115–27.

2. For more on China's peaceful rise, see Zheng Bijian, "China's 'Peaceful Rise' to Great-Power Status," *Foreign Affairs* 84, no. 5 (2005): 18–24.

3. Christopher Bolkcom, Shirley A. Kan, and Amy F. Woolf, *U.S. Conventional Forces and Nuclear Deterrence: A China Case Study,* Report RL33607 (Washington: Congressional Research Service, 2006; www.fas.org/sgp/crs/natsec/RL33607.pdf [December 2007]).

4. Domestic Taiwanese politics were probably a significant factor in this move, as Taiwanese president Chen Shui-bian sought to deflect attention away from charges of corruption.

5. U.S. Department of Defense, *Quadrennial Defense Review Report, February 6, 2006,* p. 29.

6. Ibid.

7. ASEAN was established in 1967 with the objective of accelerating economic growth, social progress, and cultural development in the region, in addition to promoting regional peace and stability. The ten ASEAN member states are Brunei Darussalam, Cambodia, Indonesia, Laos, Malaysia, Myanmar, Philippines, Singapore, Thailand, and Vietnam.

8. Created in 2001, the Shanghai Cooperation Organization (SCO) is an intergovernmental group focused on mutual security and is composed of six countries: China, Russia, Kazakhstan, Kyrgyzstan, Tajikistan, and Uzbekistan.

9. APEC was established in 1989 with the goal of facilitating economic growth, cooperation, trade, and investment in the Asia-Pacific region. The forum's twenty-one members are Australia, Brunei Darussalam, Canada, Chile, People's Republic of China, Hong Kong, Indonesia, Japan, Republic of Korea, Malaysia, Mexico, New Zealand,

Papua New Guinea, Peru, Philippines, Russia, Singapore, Chinese Taipei, Thailand, United States, Vietnam.

10. Larry A. Niksch, *North Korea's Nuclear Weapons Program,* Report IB91141 (Washington: Congressional Research Service, 2006; www.au.af.mil/au/awc/awcgate/crs/ib91141.pdf [December 2007]).

11. "North Korea and Those Six-Party Talks," *Economist,* February 11, 2006, p. 62. All currency amounts are in U.S. dollars unless otherwise noted.

12. Niksch, *North Korea's Nuclear Weapons Program,* p. 5.

13. Craig K. Elwell, Marc Labonte, and Wayne M. Morrison, *Is China a Threat to the U.S. Economy?* Report RL33604 (Washington: Congressional Research Service, 2007; www.fas.org/sgp/crs/row/RL33604.pdf [December 2007]).

14. Ibid.

15. Ibid.

16. This study was conducted by Credit Suisse using 2004 U.S. dollars. Credit Suisse, *The Rise of the Chinese Consumer Revisited* (2006), quoted in ibid.

17. Elwell, Labonte, and Morrison, *Is China a Threat to the U.S. Economy?*

18. Ibid.

19. "Sen. Schumer, 34 Other Lawmakers File Petition Calling for Action against China's Unfair Currency Manipulation," press release, office of Senator Charles Schumer, April 20, 2005 (http://schumer.senate.gov/SchumerWebsite/pressroom/record.cfm?id=261020& [December 2007]).

20. Elwell, Labonte, and Morrison, *Is China a Threat to the U.S. Economy?*

21. "Monthly Foreign Exchange Reserves," State Administration of Foreign Exchange, Beijing (www.safe.gov.cn [December 2007]).

22. Richard McGregor, "U.S. Presses China to Take Doha Role," *Financial Times,* August 30, 2006, p. 6.

23. Ibid.

24. David M. Lampton, "Rapporteur's Summary," *U.S.-China Relations, Eighth Conference* (Washington: Aspen Institute, 2006), p. 1.

25. Ibid., p. 2.

26. Council on Foreign Relations, *U.S.-China Relations: An Affirmative Agenda, a Responsible Course* (Washington: Council on Foreign Relations, 2007), p. 97.

27. Robert B. Zoellick, deputy secretary of state, "Whither China? From Membership to Responsibility," remarks to the National Committee on U.S.-China Relations, New York, September 21, 2005.

28. Wang Jisi, "China's Search for Stability with America," *Foreign Affairs* 84, no. 5 (2005): 39–48, quotation on p. 39.

29. This section is based on "Estados Unidos y América Latina: estado actual de las relaciones," *Nueva Sociedad,* no. 26 (2006): 110–25.

30. U.S. direct investment on a historical cost basis was $353 billion in 2005. Bureau of Economic Analysis, "U.S. Direct Investment Abroad: Country Detail for Selected Items" (http://bea.gov/bea/di/usdctry/longctry.htm [December 2007]).

31. June Kronholz, "Immigration Stalemate: Congress' Failure to Resolve Issue Feeds Ire of Activists on Both Sides," *Wall Street Journal*, September 6, 2006 (Eastern edition), p. A6.

32. Guy de Jonquieres, "Do-It-Yourself Is the Best 'Plan B' for Free Trade," *Financial Times*, August 23, 2006, p. 15.

33. Stephanie Kirchgaessnerin, "Business Chiefs Call on Bush to Spur Doha Talks," *Financial Times*, August 21, 2006, p. 7.

34. This G-20 should not be confused with the Group of Twenty created in 1999 and composed of developing as well as industrialized nations.

35. Alexei Barrionuevo, "Bush Offers to Cut Farm Subsidies by $10 Billion," *International Herald Tribune*, February 1, 2007, p. 11.

36. Philippe de Pontet, "Eurasia Group Note—TRADE: G20 summit in Rio to call for resumption of Doha negotiation this year," September 8, 2006; e-mail newsletter.

37. Dan Morgan, "Bush Vows to Veto Senate's Farm Bill," *Washington Post*, November 6, 2007, p. A8.

38. Jorge Castañeda, "Latin America's Left Turn," *Foreign Affairs* 85, no. 3 (2006): 28–43, quotation on p. 38.

39. Thus far the trade component has been most important; China's commitment to foreign direct investment has been less apparent.

40. Argentina alone brought forty antidumping cases against China between 1995 and 2004; combined with Peru (seventeen) and Brazil (fifteen) during the same period, the total number of antidumping cases in the region exceeded those brought against China by the United States (fifty-seven) and by the European Union (fifty-two). Scott Kennedy, "China's Porous Protectionism: The Changing Political Economy of Trade Policy," *Political Science Quarterly* 120, no. 3 (2005): 407–32.

41. Daniel Lederman, Marcelo Olarreaga, and Eliana Rubiano, "Latin America's Trade Specialization and China and India's Growth," quoted in Daniel Lederman, Marcelo Olarreaga, and Guillermo Perry, "Latin America and the Caribbean's Response to the Growth of China and India: Overview of Research Findings and Policy Implications," paper prepared for World Bank and IMF annual meetings, Singapore, August 2006, p. 13.

42. Augusto Lopez-Claros, ed., *The Global Competitiveness Report, 2006–2007* (Geneva: World Economic Forum, 2006), p. xiv.

43. Ibid., p. xvi.

44. Lederman, Olarreaga, and Perry, "Latin America and the Caribbean's Response to the Growth of China and India," p. 4.

45. It should be noted that most Chinese FDI figures for Latin America obtained from the Chinese Ministry of Commerce include what is known as round-tripping—funneling funds from domestic offshore tax havens before channeling them back as FDI—which distorts outflow and inflow FDI data. Thus there is a wide variation in figures cited. Figures that claim that Latin America is one of the largest recipients of Chinese FDI include round-tripping in the countries that are the main beneficiaries

(offshore tax havens), such as the Cayman Islands, the Virgin Islands, and Bermuda. The oft-repeated promise by President Hu Jintao to increase Chinese investment in Latin America to $100 billion by 2010, which Jiang Shixue contends was a misunderstanding by the media, illustrates the challenge in reading actual figures and estimated future investment.

46. Bijian, "China's 'Peaceful Rise' to Great-Power Status," p. 18.

PART I

The Changing Landscape in Sino–Latin American Relations: Views from China and Latin America

JIANG SHIXUE

2

The Chinese Foreign Policy Perspective

Contact between China and Latin America can be traced back to the 1570s, when Sino–Latin American trade across the Pacific began to flourish. China exported silk, porcelain, and cotton yarn to Mexico and Peru in exchange for silver coins and other items. In the nineteenth century, peasants from southern China traveled to South America and the Caribbean as contract laborers to work in mines and plantations. Yet until recently, Latin America was a largely unfamiliar region for most people in China. Significant language, cultural, geographic, and political barriers, coupled with poor media coverage of the region, explains to some extent why contact between China and Latin America remained historically limited.

However, at the start of the twenty-first century, China has "rediscovered" Latin America. In an unprecedented display of attention by the Chinese government, President Hu Jintao and Vice President Zeng Qinghong each visited the region within a two-month period in late 2004 and early 2005. Two other high-profile visits took place a few months later.[1] These recent developments have not gone unnoticed.

China's foreign policy priorities evolved considerably during the second half of the twentieth century, and at the dawn of the twenty-first century, it is clear that rapid economic growth is bringing about a fundamental transformation in China's global role. It is in this context that this volume examines the emerging economic and geopolitical implications of China's growing presence in the Western Hemisphere. Foreign policy analysts outside China have begun to debate what China's growing presence in Latin America means not only for the region but also for the rest of the world—and in particular, for the United States. As Riordan Roett and Guadalupe Paz state in chapter 1—and

27

the other authors reiterate throughout this volume—the triangular nature of China's relations with the countries of the Western Hemisphere, where the United States is the hegemonic presence, offers a unique set of challenges and opportunities. China understands the sensitive character of its deepening ties with Latin America, a region traditionally perceived as the backyard of the United States, and in no way should China's growing presence be interpreted as a challenge to U.S. hegemony in the hemisphere.

To better understand the current state of Sino–Latin American affairs, it is important to review the recent historical evolution of China's relations with the region, which can be divided into two distinct periods: the cold war years and the post–cold war era. Within this historical framework, this chapter presents the Chinese foreign policy perspective on why diplomatic and economic ties between China and Latin America are expanding and concludes with a brief assessment of the implications for Sino-U.S. relations. The chapter is divided into three sections. The first section provides an overview of China's foreign relations during the cold war period. The second section offers an overview of China's changing foreign policy priorities in the post–cold war era, including China's ongoing efforts to promote South-South relations, and analyzes the current trends in Sino–Latin American affairs. The third section concludes with a brief analysis of the main reasons that deepening ties between the two regions ought not be viewed as a potential threat to U.S. interests.

The Cold War

When the People's Republic of China (PRC) was founded in 1949, one of the most urgent tasks for the new Chinese leadership was to break the economic embargo instituted against China by the Western powers. China placed great emphasis on people-to-people contact with other countries, primarily through the Chinese People's Association for Friendship with Foreign Countries (CPAFFC).[2] Nonetheless, for more than a decade after the PRC was established, China was unable to make any diplomatic breakthroughs in Latin America, to some extent as a result of U.S. pressure on its southern neighbors to avoid ties with communist countries.

In January 1950, before the UN Security Council vote on the Soviet proposal to replace Taiwan's seat in the United Nations with the newly founded PRC, the United States lobbied strongly against the proposal. After learning of Ecuador's intent to sever relations with Taiwan, the U.S. government pressured the Ecuadorian representative to the United Nations, Homero Viteri-Lafronte, to change his country's position. The following month, fearing that other countries in the region would consider cutting ties with Taiwan, the Truman administration issued a letter to the Latin American embassies in Washington urging them to follow a common policy under the aegis of the United States.[3]

The Cuban revolution in 1959 offered a valuable opportunity for China to take a new look at Latin America, with the realization that revolution in the backyard of the United States was not only possible but had become a reality. As a result, the Institute of Latin American Studies (ILAS), a national research organization dedicated to studying the region, was established in China in 1961. Cuba was the first Latin American country to recognize the PRC.[4] In September 1960 Chinese premier Zhou Enlai told Castro that "China would furnish all the necessary assistance to the Cuban people fighting for freedom."[5] In April 1961, when U.S. president John F. Kennedy approved the Bay of Pigs invasion by Cuban exiles, the Chinese government issued a strongly worded statement denouncing the event. Public marches took place throughout China in support of the Cuban people, who were viewed as standing up against U.S. imperialism.

Throughout the 1960s China expressed support for other Latin American countries that confronted the United States. For example, when riots broke out in Panama in January 1964 over a flag incident with U.S. citizens in the Panama Canal Zone, which resulted in more than twenty deaths, Chairman Mao Zedong issued an angry statement announcing that China stood by the Panamanian people and fully supported their just struggle.[6] When the United States intervened with the use of force during an internal political crisis in the Dominican Republic in April 1965, Chairman Mao made a similar statement denouncing the U.S. action.

During the height of the cold war in the 1960s and 1970s, China considered Latin America and other developing regions the battleground of the United States and the Soviet Union in their competition for hegemony. China also believed that a third world war was quite possible, given the accumulation of weapons of mass destruction by both superpowers. One of China's primary objectives thus became to unite with other developing countries in an effort to prevent such a war. China received wide support from Latin America for reentry into the United Nations in 1971. China, in turn, consistently voiced its support for a new world order as advocated by Latin America. On the occasion of a banquet in honor of visiting Mexican president Luis Echeverría on April 20, 1972, Chinese premier Zhou Enlai stated: "Latin America is emerging on the world stage with a new face. . . . The Chinese government and the Chinese people firmly support the just struggle of the Latin American people and believe that a united Latin America, through its struggle, will win a greater victory over the expansionary influence of imperialism [in the form of] new and old colonialism."[7]

During the disastrous years of the Cultural Revolution (1966–76), which curtailed China's political, economic, diplomatic, and social development, China still managed to make modest progress in certain areas of its foreign affairs. For example, China established diplomatic relations with Chile on December 15, 1970, making Chile the first South American country to recognize China. Also, after U.S. president Richard Nixon made his historic visit to China in February 1972, many Latin American countries began to change their attitudes toward China and expressed interest in developing relations.

In February 1974 Mao Zedong put forth the well-known three worlds theory when he stated to a visiting foreign leader that the United States and the Soviet Union were the first world; in the middle was the second world, which included Japan, Europe, Australia, and Canada; and the remaining countries comprised the third world.[8] In the following years, China's foreign policy rhetoric came to be dominated by the notion that China, itself a member of the third world, would join forces with fellow developing countries to engage the members of the second world in the quest to counter the imperialist tendencies of the first world countries, in particular the Soviet Union.

After the third plenary session of the Communist Party of China's Eleventh National Congress in 1978, China implemented important changes in its domestic and foreign policy strategies under the leadership of Deng Xiaoping. The rationale behind China's 1978 reform process was twofold. On the domestic side, the goal was to allow market forces to play a more prominent role in the economy by reducing the scope of government intervention. On the international front, economic liberalization was expected to attract more foreign capital, promote technology transfers, and stimulate growth in labor-intensive export sectors. During this period of reform, Deng played a central role in promoting a better understanding of the international landscape. During a meeting with Brazilian president João Figueiredo in Beijing in May 1984, Deng identified peace and development as the two most pressing world challenges, categorizing them as the East-West problem (peace) and the North-South problem (development). As it turns out, these concepts would outlive the cold war.

The Post–Cold War Era

China embarked on a process of economic liberalization more than a decade before the collapse of the Berlin Wall, and positive results were already evident by 1989.[9] As market forces began to play an increasingly important role in China's economic development, and as the country integrated into the global economy, the living standards of the Chinese people began to rise. China clearly understood that its economic liberalization program depended on a peaceful and stable international environment in the post–cold war era, in turn recognizing the need to adjust its foreign policy toward that end.

The key to sound foreign policy in any country is a clear and rational understanding of the current international situation. From China's perspective, the post–cold war era was likely to exhibit four central trends. First, peace and development—not revolution and war—would increasingly become the norm.[10] Second, with the collapse of the Soviet Union, the bipolar international world order would be replaced by a multipolar one, with China acting as one of five poles.[11] Third, hegemonic tendencies would continue among the most powerful nations, in particular the United States. This largely explains why today the world has one superpower—the United States—and a small group of other strong nations. And fourth, China and other developing countries would seek to unite in the struggle against an unjust world order in which the rules of the game are determined by the developed nations.

The cold war ended shortly after the domestic political unrest in China's Tiananmen Square in May and June of 1989. The Tiananmen Square incident triggered an international campaign of sanctions against China led by the United States. Confronted with such a critical situation, particularly in the face of political uncertainty in the Soviet bloc, Deng Xiaoping proposed the "guiding principle of twenty-four characters," which is based on six central recommendations:[12]

—Observe world events with a calm mind

—Stand firmly

—Confront difficulties with confidence

—Keep a low profile

—Never assume a leadership role

—Take action

This principle, presented in many of Deng's speeches in the late 1980s and early 1990s, symbolized his thinking on China's foreign policy priorities in the context of a changing world order.[13]

The downfall of socialism in the Soviet Union and Eastern Europe in 1989 and 1990, concomitant with the emerging challenges and uncertainties of the post–cold war era, shocked the Chinese public and generated an atmosphere of great concern about China's future. Deng urged the Communist Party of China (CPC), the government, and the people to remain calm until the implications of the changing global landscape became clear, including the manner in which the West would exert pressure on China. At the same time, he reminded the Chinese people that the environment of transition also created new opportunities for China to advance its economic reform agenda. In the early stages of political change in the Soviet bloc, Deng promoted staying the socialist course in China while continuing to move forward with economic reform. On the world stage, Deng insisted that China should keep a low profile and refrain from assuming any leadership roles in the developing world, although international events could at times require taking action.

A Low Profile versus Action

Since its formulation in the early 1990s, Deng's guiding principle has become the foundation of China's foreign policy. However, a consensus has never been reached on the balance between keeping a low profile and taking action. Some people believe that although China has made remarkable economic strides, it is still a developing country and, therefore, has a long way to go before it can wield significant influence internationally. Advocates of a low international profile argue that the Chinese government should focus on domestic problems and limit its involvement in global affairs. Advocates of a higher international profile argue that China is well positioned (through its size and its market size, its history, its permanent membership in the United Nations, and its nuclear capability) to voice the concerns of developing nations and to demonstrate resistance to the hegemonic tendencies of the United States and other Western countries. Despite the schism between the two camps, and with neither side able to gain the upper hand, China has managed to make impressive progress in its foreign policy since 1989. Several examples illustrate this point:

—China has established strategic partnerships with multiple countries, partnerships that have enabled China to develop bilateral relationships that yield more consistent and mutually beneficial results.[14]

—China now takes a more active part in regional cooperation with Asia-Pacific countries, ASEAN members, and Central Asian nations.[15]

—China regained full sovereignty over Hong Kong in 1997 and Macau in 1999.

—China now sends out peacekeeping missions to many parts of the world.

—China has established diplomatic relations with more than forty countries, including Israel in January 1992, Korea in August 1992, South Africa in January 1998, and Costa Rica in June 2007.[16]

—China joined the World Trade Organization in 2001, after fifteen years of negotiations and bargaining.

—China is in a position to advocate its own sovereignty and that of other developing countries in the United Nations and other international forums.

These diplomatic achievements, widely recognized by the global community, have inexorably raised China's international profile. As a result, most countries, including the United States, have begun paying closer attention to China. Voicing the view of the United States, Deputy Secretary of State Robert Zoellick stated the following during a bilateral dialogue in 2005: "As it becomes a major global player, we are now encouraging China to become a 'responsible stakeholder' that will work with the United States and others to sustain, adapt, and advance the peaceful international system that has enabled its success."[17] Although a generally positive statement, Zoellick's remarks underscore the fact that China's higher international profile does not come without some complications. For those in China who support a more active international role for their country, the labels of *major global player* and *responsible stakeholder* are reasons for pride because they represent, in their view, a status of international importance, affording China stronger bargaining power vis-à-vis the United States and other Western countries. However, for those who argue that the "guiding principle of twenty-four characters" calls for a lower international profile, such labels represent a clear drawback. Still others warn that China should not fall victim to bullying by the United States in the international arena.[18]

International Harmony

In today's China, Confucianism remains a strong social influence, and harmony is considered a quintessential element of civilization. It is generally believed in China that without harmony, political stability and economic growth are impossible to achieve and maintain. In 2006 the CPC released a communiqué stating that "social harmony is the intrinsic nature of the socialism with Chinese characteristics and an important guarantee of the country's prosperity, the nation's rejuvenation, and the people's happiness."[19]

These general principles also have resonance in China's foreign policy discourse. In September 2005, during the United Nations summit celebrating the organization's sixtieth anniversary, President Hu Jintao made a statement on world harmony. Pointing out that the new century has ushered in bright prospects for progress, Hu went on to say that "in the critical historical period of coexistence of opportunities and challenges, all countries must unite in the effort to build a truly harmonious world with long-lasting peace and common prosperity."[20] President Hu also proposed four measures that would stimulate world harmony:

—Creating a new security concept of mutual trust, mutual benefit, equality, and collaboration, and establishing a fair and effective collective security mechanism

—Respecting each country's right to choose its own social system and development strategy according to its own national conditions

—Safeguarding UN authority through reasonable and necessary reform, increasing the organization's efficiency, and strengthening its capacity to cope with new threats and challenges

—Implementing tangible UN measures to meet successfully the millennium development goals, accelerating the development process of developing nations, and truly making the twenty-first century "the century of development for everyone"[21]

At the end of his speech, Hu stressed that in the long history of human progress the fate of mankind has never been as interdependent as it is today, concluding that common goals and challenges provide an opportunity for greater unity and harmony.[22]

Economic and Political Relations with Latin America

Although economic liberalization since the Deng modernization period has yielded impressive results, the process has inevitably encountered problems along the way. Frictions have grown between China and countries that employ antidumping regulations and other measures to restrict Chinese exports. China views the United States as a country that uses its economic leverage to exert political pressure on China, which is one reason that China seeks to diversify its economic relationships. Latin America, with a population of more than 500 million and an economy of nearly $3 trillion, is an attractive market for Chinese products.[23]

China also faces a shortage of natural resources, due in large part to its enormous population and rapid economic growth. The timber industry provides a good example of the extent of China's natural resource problem. China's forest area is 1.2 million square kilometers, and timber resources amount to approximately 10 billion cubic meters. These two absolute numbers are huge in comparison with other countries, yet China's forest area is a mere 0.10 hectares per capita, and timber resources are less than 10 cubic meters per capita, while the world average per capita is 1.07 forest hectares and 83 cubic meters of timber resources.[24] According to a report published in 2006, China's coal, oil, and gas reserves in per capita terms are only 70, 11, and 4 percent, respectively, of the world average.[25] There is no question that China must drastically improve its efficiency in natural resource consumption while looking for new reliable supply sources abroad.

The 1990s witnessed parallel economic liberalization programs in China and Latin America as well as stronger economic ties between the two regions. Since then, Chinese investment in Latin America and bilateral trade has been growing significantly, as illustrated by Robert Devlin in chapter 6. Latin America's significance for China, of course, also extends beyond the economic realm. Latin America is a potential partner in China's ongoing quest to establish a just and harmonious world order. As Monica Hirst explains in chapter 5, multilateral organizations such as the United Nations provide a forum in which China and Latin America can join forces and express shared views on a number of international issues in the context of South-South collaboration.

On the political and diplomatic fronts, China's presence in Latin America has been growing steadily. Since 1990 ministerial delegations from China and the Rio Group have held talks on at least fifteen occasions.[26] Since 1997 five high-level meetings between China and Mercosur (the common market of the South) have been held. On May 26, 2004, the Organization of American States (OAS) accepted China as a permanent observer.[27] China has also gained observer status in the UN Economic Commission for Latin America and the Caribbean (ECLAC), the Latin American Integration Association (ALADI), the Inter-American Development Bank (IADB), and the Latin American Parliament (Parlatino).

The Communist Party of China and Party-to-Party Diplomacy

As a socialist country under the leadership of the Communist Party, China has always placed great emphasis on developing party-to-party relations with other nations, primarily to enhance state-to-state relations. In Latin America, more than ninety political parties of varied ideological persuasions have established relations with the CPC.[28] These relationships are promoted primarily through exchange visits and seminars. As fellow members of the developing world, the CPC and its Latin American counterparts exchange views on strategies to improve governance, the management of party affairs, political modernization, and socioeconomic development.

China also attributes great importance to its relations with the legislative bodies of those countries where party-to-party relations are strong, knowing that political parties must compete for representation. The CPC also maintains relations with the four major multilateral organizations for political parties in Latin America: the Socialist International Committee for Latin America and the Caribbean, the São Paulo Forum, the Christian Democrat Organization of America, and the Permanent Conference of Latin American Political Parties.

The CPC's relations with political parties throughout Latin America have resulted in a greater awareness of the current realities and have contributed to the establishment of diplomatic ties in some countries. Good working relationships between the CPC and the major political parties in Bolivia,

Nicaragua, and Uruguay played an important role in establishing diplomatic relations with those countries in the 1980s.[29] Today the CPC has ties with more than twenty political parties in ten of the twelve countries that maintain diplomatic relations with Taiwan. Since 2001 the CPC has sent delegations to nine of those countries in an effort to advance China's diplomatic interests.

Other Issues

China's strong stance regarding Taiwan, China's relations with Caribbean nations, and China's people-to-people exchanges with Latin America are also part of China's growing relations with Latin America.

Regarding Taiwan, China stands firm on its position that its independence cannot be tolerated, a point of friction with countries such as the United States. In this context, Latin America plays a major role in China's campaign to convince other countries to withdraw diplomatic recognition of Taiwan as part of its high-priority goal of achieving peaceful reunification.[30] China maintains that, as a part of its national territory, Taiwan has no right of representation as an independent entity in international forums, nor can it establish diplomatic ties or enter into relations of an official nature with foreign countries.[31]

Despite vigorous efforts to win the support of other countries, including those in Latin America with whom it maintains diplomatic ties, Taiwan has repeatedly failed to win a seat in the United Nations. China also criticizes Taiwan's dollar diplomacy tactics to maintain its ties with the twelve Latin American countries that do not support the one-China policy. For more on this debate, see chapter 4.

Regarding the Caribbean, in recent years China has been paying closer attention to the these nations. As part of a strategy to increase its influence in the region, China joined the Caribbean Development Bank in 1998 as a nonregional member. Initially taking a 5.77 percent capital stake, China contributed $1 million in 2002 to establish a technical cooperation fund.[32] In early 2003 State Councilor Wu Yi visited eight Caribbean countries, marking the first time a Chinese leader visited all the countries that have established diplomatic relations with China since the 1970s.[33] More than ten agreements in the fields of agriculture, energy, and technology transfer were signed during Wu's visits.

During the Seventh China International Forum for Investment and Trade (CIFIT) in September 2003 in Xiamen, Fujian Province, one full day was dedicated to the Caribbean. Some forty public and private sector representatives from the eight Caribbean nations that Wu visited took part. In late 2004 the Chinese government proposed the China-Caribbean Economic and Trade

Cooperation Forum, a ministerial-level organization that would convene every three to four years in China or a Caribbean country to promote stronger economic and trade ties. The first meeting was held in February 2005 in Jamaica and was attended by China's Vice President Zeng Qinghong.[34]

Although trade between China and the Caribbean nations has been steadily growing, totals are still relatively low. Countries recognizing China's market economy status are poised to benefit the most from the potential trade with China.[35] China's largest trade partners in the region are Cuba, Jamaica, Antigua and Barbuda, the Bahamas, and Trinidad and Tobago. The main exports from China include machinery, electronics, textiles, light industrial products, and pharmaceuticals. China imports primarily raw materials from the Caribbean. China has also listed several Caribbean nations as tourist destinations, which will spur growth in the region's tourism industry.[36]

Although several Caribbean countries established diplomatic relations with China in the 1970s, the issue of Taiwan remains a sticking point for China's policy in the region. Of the countries that maintain diplomatic relations with Taiwan—the Dominican Republic, Haiti, Saint Kitts and Nevis, Saint Lucia, and Saint Vincent and the Grenadines—the PRC's diplomatic efforts are concentrated on the two largest, the Dominican Republic and Haiti. One of the most important steps to improve relations was China's deployment of 125 antiriot police to Haiti in 2004 as part of a UN peacekeeping mission.[37] The following year, Cai Wu, vice minister of the Department of International Liaison of the Chinese Communist Party's Central Committee, led a high-level delegation to Haiti and the Dominican Republic as part of the party-to-party foreign policy strategy employed by China in countries with which it holds no formal diplomatic ties. Although China's overall trade levels with those two Caribbean countries remain low, commercial relations have been on the rise since the 1990s.

Among the other areas of Sino–Latin American cooperation are people-to-people exchanges. Sister city relationships have been established between fifty-seven Chinese and Latin American cities in at least fifteen Latin American countries, including Panama, a country that has no diplomatic ties with the PRC.[38] Chinese tourism in Latin America, as well as cultural and friendship delegations to the region, have also increased significantly.

In science and technology, the most notable example of cooperation was the joint launch of two satellites by China and Brazil (for more on this subject, see chapter 5, by Monica Hirst). Although this is considered one of the greatest success stories of South-South technological cooperation, cooperation also extends to agriculture, forestry, fisheries, animal husbandry, medicine, earthquake prediction, manufacturing, information technology, biology, geology, and aerospace.

Conclusion: China's Ties with Latin America and Their Implications for Sino-U.S. Relations

In 2004 Chinese president Hu Jintao presented three goals for Sino–Latin American relations:

—Strengthening strategic ties and enhancing mutual political trust

—Taking practical and creative steps to tap the potential for economic cooperation

—Attaching greater importance to cultural exchanges to deepen mutual understanding[39]

Latin American leaders have expressed similar hopes that relations with China would be further strengthened. For example, before a trip to China in 2004, President Néstor Kirchner stressed the importance that Argentina placed on its relations not only with the United States and Europe but also with China, stating that Argentina can learn from China's experience.

Although Sino–Latin American relations have been developing rapidly and smoothly in recent years, a few problem areas are evident. The physical distance between China and Latin America is the most obvious and difficult obstacle to surmount, as it takes several weeks to sail across the Pacific and more than twenty hours to fly from one hemisphere to the other.

Growing concern in Latin America about China's rise in today's global arena is attributed by the latter primarily to a knowledge gap about China's foreign policy and economic priorities. The fact that some business sectors in Latin America are affected by relatively cheap goods from China explains to some degree the characterization of China as a "threat" to the region. However, if there is growing evidence of Latin America's lagging competitiveness in certain sectors at the international level, should this evidence not serve as a wake-up service for the region, as Devlin explains it chapter 6? China's economic liberalization has made the country wealthier, and with a population of 1.3 billion, it offers an enormous market to the world, including Latin America. Therefore, China's rise should be viewed as an opportunity, not a threat.

Many Latin American countries have resorted to antidumping measures to limit the inflow of Chinese exports. Mexico was the first Latin American country to levy a high tax against China in the early 1990s, charging an antidumping tariff of more than 1,100 percent on Chinese shoes and other products, in effect banning these products from the Mexican market. Mexico also disappointed China as the last country in the world, even behind the United States and Europe, to back China's entry into the WTO.

Misunderstandings in other areas have also occasionally led to tensions between China and its counterparts in Latin America. In November 2004, during President Hu Jintao's visit to several countries in the region, some Latin American newspapers inaccurately reported that China would invest $100 billion in the region in the next ten years. During an address to the Brazilian Congress on November 12, 2004, Hu mentioned the figure of $100 billion in reference to bilateral trade flows, stating that China and Latin America should aim to increase bilateral trade to that level by 2010.[40] In the same speech, President Hu also expressed his hopes that efforts would be made to speed up progress in foreign investment, with the target of doubling the current value of Chinese investment in the region, also by the year 2010. Hu's statement was misinterpreted to mean that a sharp increase was forthcoming, inevitably resulting in disappointment when investments did not come pouring in.

Taiwan is, of course, one issue that will continue to be of great importance in China's diplomatic relations. To settle the Taiwan question and achieve national reunification is a sacrosanct mission of the Chinese government, with "peaceful reunification" and "one country, two systems" as the guiding policy.[41]

China's growing ties with Latin America also have implications for Sino–U.S. relations, as China's presence in the region continues to cause concern in the United States. At a hearing of the Western Hemisphere Subcommittee of the House International Relations Committee on April 6, 2005, Representative Dan Burton stated:

> The traditional goals of U.S. policy in Latin America have always included promoting political stability, promoting democracy, increasing access to markets, and preventing the rise of hegemonic power. Until we know the definitive answer to this question of whether China will play by the rules of fair trade and engage responsibly on transnational issues, I believe we should be cautious and view the rise of Chinese power as something to be counterbalanced or contained, and perhaps go so far as to consider China's actions in Latin America as the movement of a hegemonic power into our hemisphere.[42]

Mistakenly interpreting the strengthening of Sino–Latin American relations as a danger to the United States, Burton went on to state,

> I believe China's rising economic, political, and military influence in the Western Hemisphere poses serious challenges to the United States in the years ahead. And if we are not careful, Beijing's influence could easily unravel the region's hard-won, U.S.-backed reforms to fight against corruption, human rights abuses, increase government transparency,

and combat intellectual property violations, and the democracies that we see as fledgling democracies could be in real jeopardy.[43]

The news media in the United Sates also present a jaundiced view of China's interest in Latin America. For instance, the *Wall Street Journal* reported that "the rise of China in the region could complicate U.S. efforts to control illegal immigration, weapons shipments, the drug trade and money laundering because China is cooperating with Latin countries that are not especially friendly toward those efforts. Some of these nations may try to use the Chinese alternative to challenge U.S. hegemony."[44] Such hyperbole is inaccurate and unnecessary. Latin America has remained on the path of economic liberalization for the better part of the last two decades, and the region hopes to attract increased foreign investment to stimulate growth. China is one of many economic players seeking partnership and cooperation with Latin America.

China is well aware of the fact that the United States considers Latin America its backyard, and China has no intention of challenging U.S. hegemony in the region. China and Latin America have been pursuing similar parallel paths of economic liberalization, and in the context of globalization, there is a clear opportunity for South-South cooperation. Both China and Latin America would benefit from working together toward regional peace and development in Asia and Latin America, an outcome that can only be considered favorable for the United States.

Notes

1. In November 2004 Chinese president Hu Jintao paid official visits to Brazil, Argentina, Chile, and Cuba; and in January and February 2005 Chinese vice president Zeng Qinghong visited Mexico, Peru, Venezuela, Trinidad and Tobago, and Jamaica. In May 2005 Jia Qinglin, chairman of the National Committee of the Chinese People's Political Consultative Conference (CPPCC), visited Mexico, Cuba, Colombia, and Uruguay; and in September 2005 Chinese president Hu Jintao visited Mexico as part of his tour to North America and the United Nations, making this his second trip to Latin America in less than one year.

2. The CPAFFC, founded in May 1954, was initially called the Chinese People's Association for Cultural Exchanges with Foreign Countries.

3. The letter, published in U.S. State Department, *Foreign Relations of the United States,* in 1950, is cited in Tao Wenzhao, "Meiguo, laiyi yu zhongguo zai lianheguo de daibiaoquan" [The United States, Trygve Lie, and China's representation in the UN], *Meiguo yanjiu* [American Studies Journal] 10, no. 4 (1996): 30–46.

4. It is reported that at a rally held in Havana on September 2, 1960, Castro told the audience: "The Revolutionary Government of Cuba would like to ask the Cuban people if you would like Cuba to establish diplomatic relations with the People's Republic of China." The crowd, raising its hands, cried, "Yes, yes!" Then, walking toward the head of the New China News Agency stationed in Havana, Castro said, "Here is the Chinese representative. From now on, I declare that Cuba cut its relations with the puppet regime of Chiang Kai-shek (in Taiwan)." For a more detailed account of the scene, see Wang Taiping, ed., X*in zhongguo waijiao 50 nian* [50 years of the new China's foreign diplomacy] (Beijing: Beijing chubanshe [Beijing Publishing House], 1999), pp. 1636–37.

5. Cited in Zhang Guang, *Zhongguo de waijiao zhengce* [China's foreign policies] (Beijing: Shijie zhishi chubanshe [World Affairs Press], 1995), p. 91.

6. Ibid.

7. Wang, *Xin zhongguo waijiao 50 nian*, p. 1660.

8. "Chairman Mao Zedong's Theory on the Division of the Three Worlds and the Strategy of Forming an Alliance against an Opponent," Ministry of Foreign Affairs of the PRC, November 17, 2000 (www.mfa.gov.cn/eng/ziliao/3602/3604/t18008.htm [December 2007]).

9. This section is based on previous research by the author, "China's Foreign Policy in the Post–Cold War Era" (http://blog.china.com.cn/sp1/jiangshixue/094402 39378.shtml [December 2007]).

10. In an article published in 1924, Soviet leader Joseph Stalin considered war and revolution to be the defining characteristics of the age. This ideology had great influence on China's diplomacy until the end of the 1970s.

11. The other four poles were thought to be the United States, Russia, Europe, and Japan.

12. These six recommendations are represented by twenty-four Chinese written characters, which explains the name of the principle.

13. For more on China's foreign policy principles, see Liu Huaqiu, vice minister of foreign affairs, "Zhongguo jiang yiongyuan zhixing dudi zhizhu de waijiao zhengce" [China will always pursue a peaceful foreign policy of independence and self-determination], article published in the Communist Party of China Central Committee's *Qiushi Magazine,* December 1, 1997, pp. 2–9 (English translation, www. nti.org/db/china/engdocs/liuqiu.htm [December 2007]). An earlier summary version can be found at the web portal of China's embassy in the United States, titled "Liu Huaqiu on China's Foreign Policy," August 16, 2004 (www.china-embassy.org/eng/ zmgx/zgwjzc/t35078.htm [December 2007]).

14. China currently has more than twenty "strategic partnerships" with other countries and organizations around the world.

15. The Shanghai Cooperation Organization, whose members include China, Russia, and four Central Asian nations, is the first international organization based in China and also the first such organization named after a Chinese city.

16. To date China has established diplomatic relations with 169 countries.

17. Deputy Secretary Robert Zoellick's statement at the conclusion of the Second U.S.-China Senior Dialogue, December 8, 2005 (www.state.gov/r/pa/prs/ps/2005/57822.htm [December 2007]).

18. It is telling that during a visit to the United States in April 2006, when President George W. Bush used the term *stakeholder,* President Hu Jintao reiterated that China and the United States are more than international "stakeholders," they are also "constructive partners."

19. Communist Party of China, communiqué of the Sixth Plenum of the 16th CPC Central Committee, October 11, 2006 (http://english.gov.cn/2006-10/11/content_410436.htm [December 2007]).

20. Hu Jintao, speech delivered at a plenary session during the summit on the sixtieth anniversary of the establishment of the United Nations, September 16, 2005 (www.fmprc.gov.cn/eng/wjdt/zyjh/t212614.htm [December 2007]).

21. Ibid.

22. Ibid.

23. All currency amounts are in U.S. dollars unless otherwise noted.

24. Guo Yuanzheng, "Lizuo kechixu fanzhan, jiakuai kaituo lamei ziyuan shichang" [Opening the natural resources market at a quicker pace, on the basis of sustainable development], *Ladingmeizhou yanjiu* [Latin American Studies Journal], no. 1 (1999): 18.

25. Cui Minxuan, ed., *2006 Zhongguo nengyuan fazhan baogao* [2006 development report of China's energy] (Beijing: Sheke wenxian chubanshe [China Documentation Press of Social Sciences], 2006).

26. For more on the Rio Group, see chapter 5 by Monica Hirst.

27. The resolution was sponsored by Argentina, Bolivia, Brazil, Chile, Colombia, Mexico, Peru, Uruguay, and Venezuela. On behalf of the organization, Ambassador Miguel Ruiz Cabañas stated that China's observer status would promote closer ties between that country and the members of the OAS. Cited in "OAS Accepts China as Permanent Observer," *People's Daily,* May 27, 2004 (http://english.peopledaily.com.cn/200405/27/eng20040527_144506.html [December 2007]).

28. See Dai Binggou, "New Characteristics of the Communist Party of China's International Work since Its Fifteenth National Congress" (www.idcpc.org.cn/english/article/20021011.htm [December 2007]).

29. When Nicaragua established diplomatic ties with Taiwan in November 1990, the PRC terminated relations with the Central American nation.

30. As of mid-2007, twenty-four countries maintain diplomatic relations with Taiwan, twelve of them in Latin America (see chapter 4 by Juan Tokatlian for a complete list). The PRC's position on those countries that maintain diplomatic relations with Taiwan is that they ignore UN resolutions regarding the status of Taiwan, belittle themselves by keeping ties with a province of a sovereign nation, and offend the Chinese people.

31. Nevertheless, considering the needs of Taiwan's economic development and the practical interests of Taiwan compatriots, the Chinese government has not objected to nongovernmental economic or cultural exchanges between Taiwan and foreign countries.

32. Caribbean Development Bank (CDB), "CDB and China Establish Technical Cooperation Fund," *CDB News* 21, no. 1 (2003): 3.

33. These countries are Suriname, Guyana, Trinidad and Tobago, Barbados, Saint Lucia, Antigua and Barbuda, the Bahamas, and Jamaica. Wu Yi was then also member of the Political Bureau of the Chinese Communist Party's Central Committee.

34. For the full text of Zeng's speech at the opening ceremony of the China-Caribbean Economic and Trade Cooperation Forum, see "Working Together to Write a New Chapter in the History of China-Caribbean Mutually Beneficial Cooperation," February 2, 2005 (http://jm.chineseembassy.org/eng/zt/zqhfzxfy/speech_zeng/t211544 .htm [December 2007]).

35. To date, thirteen Latin American countries, including Antigua and Barbuda, Guyana, Saint Lucia, Dominica, Suriname, Trinidad and Tobago, and Jamaica in the Caribbean, have granted China market economy status.

36. These countries are Antigua and Barbuda, Barbados, the Bahamas, Grenada, Guyana, Saint Lucia, Dominica, Suriname, Trinidad and Tobago, and Jamaica.

37. "China Sends Riot Police to Haiti," *China Daily,* October 17, 2004 (www.china daily.com.cn/english/doc/2004-10/17/content_383085.htm [December 2007])

38. Li Xiaolin, vice president of the Chinese People's Association for Friendship with Foreign Countries, cited in Li Jianmin, "China Seeks to Make Friends with All the World" (www.chinese-embassy.org.uk/eng/zt/Features/t214558.htm [September 2007]).

39. President Hu Jintao, "Joining Hands to Enhance Friendship between China and Latin America," speech at the Brazilian Parliament, November 12, 2004 (www. fmprc.gov.cn/ce/cede/det/jj/t170469.htm [September 2007]); Xinhua, "President Hu Expounds Proposal for Ties with L. America," *People's Daily Online,* November 14, 2004 (http://english.peopledaily.com.cn/200411/13/eng20041113 _163814.html [September 2007]).

40. Ibid.

41. Taiwan Affairs Office of the State Council and Information Office of the State Council, "White Papers on Taiwan Issue: The Taiwan Question and Reunification of China," Beijing, August 31, 1993.

42. Chairman Dan Burton, "Opening Statement," hearing, China's Influence in the Western Hemisphere, Subcommittee on the Western Hemisphere, Committee on International Relations, U.S. House of Representatives, April 6, 2005 (http://inter nationalrelations.house.gov/archives/109/bur040605.pdf [September 2007]).

43. Ibid.

44. Mary Anastasia O'Grady, "The Middle Kingdom in Latin America," *Wall Street Journal,* September 3, 2004, p. 11.

XIANG LANXIN

3 | An Alternative Chinese View

China's success in expanding its influence in Latin America is changing the geopolitical dynamics of the Western Hemisphere. To mitigate the resulting reactions of alarm and preoccupation about the potential long-term impact of China's expansion into the region, the Chinese launched a diplomatic offensive to convince other nations that what China is experiencing is a so-called peaceful rise. Furthermore, China claims that its presence in Latin America is not driven by ideological factors, nor is it intended to affect third parties, in particular the United States. This peaceful offensive seems to have a more positive reception in Latin America, whereas in Washington there is a growing suspicion that China has a well-thought-out design or grand strategy to undermine the traditional U.S. dominance in the region.

In reality, however, China has yet to define the nature of its relationship with Latin America. For many years Latin America was far from a major concern in Chinese foreign policy, and today there is still a significant gap between the two regions in understanding each other. Most Chinese experts on Latin American affairs speak English rather than Spanish or Portuguese, and cultural exchanges remain miniscule. Nonetheless, as Jiang Shixue outlines in chapter 2, the ties between the two continents have been growing considerably in the last years. China's policymakers often apply to Latin America a term similar to *manifest destiny*—the Chinese saying "Close neighbors are more important than distant relatives"—not because the region belongs in either category but because China views Latin America as a distant neighbor, with whom the prospects of closer ties seem to be expanding despite the challenges of physical distance.

According to Chinese policy analysts, the nascent special relationship between China and Latin America is being built on three pillars. First, China and Latin America share a common sense of colonial and semicolonial (in Chinese terminology) roots. Foreign domination, poverty, and the struggle for independence are the common threads of their modern histories. Second, as developing regions, China and Latin America face similar economic challenges. They learn from each other's successes and failures with particular interest and a strong sense of shared experiences. Third, as explained by Francisco González in chapter 7, their economies are considered to be, by and large, more complementary than competitive. China has an insatiable appetite for the energy, agricultural, and mineral resources that so heavily dominate Latin America's exports. Furthermore, most Latin American countries, afflicted by decades of debt and currency crises, have benefited less and less from foreign direct investment since the 1997 Asian financial crisis. China, with over $1.4 trillion in reserve assets in late 2007, is well positioned to be a major influence in Latin America.[1] On the downside, some Latin American manufacturing sectors are hard hit by China's global competitiveness in consumer products, even if the region is less affected than Europe, Africa, the United States, or Japan.

With the rapid strengthening of Sino–Latin American relations since the late 1990s, Chinese leaders and analysts have emphasized that China's policy priorities in the Western Hemisphere are compatible with a universal pattern of economic globalization and that other traditional concerns, especially the geopolitical dimension, have become less relevant. This is the official Chinese government view, presented in chapter 2 by Jiang Shixue. In an effort to provide a broader analysis of the forces behind China's growing interest in Latin America, this chapter disputes the claim that China is following solely a "going global" strategy and argues instead that old concerns—geopolitical factors in particular—are still the primary drivers of Chinese policy toward Latin America, albeit in a new context.

China's Changing Perceptions of Latin America

Since the founding of the People's Republic of China (PRC) in 1949, China's perception of Latin America has had three distinct dimensions: geopolitical, developmental, and economic. Throughout the cold war period the geopolitical dimension towered above all other policy objectives, while economic interaction between the two regions remained limited. Since the 1970s Latin America has been viewed as an alternative development model for China, and after the 1980s Latin America became a more important factor in China's own economic development.

From a historical perspective, however, it is clear that China's foreign policy toward Latin America has been primarily driven by a one-dimensional concern: global geopolitics. China has never accepted the Yalta Treaty's postwar power reconfiguration, nor has China ever felt comfortable with the accompanying Bretton Woods system of a liberal international economic order dominated by the United States and embodied in the International Monetary Fund (IMF) and the World Bank. For decades, China has been an antisystem power, in sharp contrast to the many states subscribing to the Yalta and Bretton Woods agreements. In this context, China's policies toward Latin America during the cold war, as alluded to in chapter 2, inevitably carried a distinctly anti-American element.

Foreign Policy Priorities under Mao

One of Mao's original contributions to Chinese foreign policy ideology was the perception of the world in terms of fundamental and inexorable contradictions. The first was the contradiction between two opposing camps, socialism and capitalism. The second stressed the contradiction between the proletariat and the bourgeoisie within capitalist countries. The third contradiction was between oppressed nations and imperialist states. Thus, applying Mao's logic, Sino–Latin American policy was based on the idea that the United States and the Soviet Union would always contend over spheres of influence from Europe to Latin America, Asia, and Africa. It was also believed that the best chance to undermine the influence of the two superpowers lay in revolutionary or national liberation movements in vast areas of the developing world.

During the cold war, however, Latin America was more a cluster of client states than rebels in the existing international system. Most Latin American political elites were vehemently anticommunist and considered part of the U.S. sphere of influence, so Latin America remained a difficult region for Mao's global revolutionary scheme to penetrate. Therefore, lacking local power bases and real influence, China did not pay much attention to the region in the 1950s and 1960s. The Cuban Revolution's challenge to the Monroe Doctrine did not catch Mao's eye until 1964, when the Chinese leader launched an international studies project in three top universities: Beijing University, Renmin (People's) University, and Fudan University. The prestigious Beijing University was assigned the task of studying national liberation movements with a special emphasis on Latin America. Renmin University, once a leading party school, was assigned the task of studying international communist movements. These were the two most popular fields at the time. Fudan University, based in Shanghai, was directed to focus on the more daring topic of the modern capitalist world.

From the start, Latin American studies in China were directly linked to Mao's political ideology and the policy objective of undermining U.S. supremacy in the world. Aside from the translation of a limited number of works on Latin American history—usually by Marxist authors—little attention was paid to politics, economics, and the internal social dynamics of the continent. Spanish language training never acquired sufficient funding to make a noticeable impact and thus attracted relatively few students.

Ironically, the Nixon-Kissinger diplomatic opening with China in the early 1970s jump-started a process in which Beijing gradually abandoned the cause of exporting revolution, but it also allowed further neglect of Latin America. As part of the American cold war containment strategy, the move toward normalization of Sino-U.S. relations prematurely promoted China to the position of the third most important world power, though without real economic or military strength. By manipulating the so-called China card, the United States created a grand Washington-Beijing-Moscow strategic triangle. This encouraged Mao to briefly return to the traditional Chinese "Middle Kingdom" complex. With China at the center of world politics once again, Mao fancied that he could become the natural leader of the third world in the struggle against the first world and the two superpowers at its helm, especially the Soviet Union.[2]

On balance, Mao's Latin American policy made little progress. First, Fidel Castro was forced to make a strategic choice between Moscow and Beijing when the Sino-Soviet relationship turned sour, which eventually resulted in a major border clash between the two powers in the late 1960s. At that juncture, Castro decided to distance himself from Mao. From the mid-1960s on, China could no longer count on Castro's support on the international stage. Second, military juntas in Latin America were, more often than not, pro-American, right-wing regimes. The only promising socialist state, Salvador Allende's Chile, was eliminated by Beijing's ad hoc strategic partner of the 1970s, the United States. In the Chilean case, China could do little, given its policy priority of undercutting Soviet influence at the global level. Overall, Latin American internal affairs often seemed to take a wrong turn at the wrong time for China: Castro's revolutionary role in the Western Hemisphere was undermined by the Sino-Soviet schism, and Allende's revolution occurred at the moment of the Sino–U.S. rapprochement. The same pattern of ill timing in Sino–Latin American affairs continued for some time after Mao's death in 1976.

Evolving Perceptions in the Post-Mao Era

As explained in chapter 2, when Deng Xiaoping returned to power in the late 1970s he shifted China's top priority to economic development, at the same time that Latin America's economies took a turn toward steady growth for most of the decade. This parallel period of economic development prompted China to begin paying closer attention to Latin America's experience and to study the region's development theories. However, just as China began to appreciate the success stories of its distant neighbors, Latin America suffered a drastic economic downturn, pulling the entire region into a severe debt crisis.

During the so-called lost decade of the 1980s, when Latin America's economic development stalled, the Chinese economy began to take off, despite the political setback caused by the Tiananmen crisis in 1989. At that time, just as China shelved the political reform agenda after 1989, Latin America embarked on widespread democratization. The fact that political democratization seemed to stem from economic liberalization caught the Chinese policy elite by surprise, particularly in light of China's continuing admiration for the perceived political and economic successes of Chile's Augusto Pinochet. In the mid-1990s the need for new thinking about the Western Hemisphere was placed on the policy agenda for the first time. Even so, it was not until the end of the 1990s that the Chinese government began to pay closer attention to Latin America's internal dynamics, while reexamining China's own vital national interests.

A pioneer in this new thinking was the late Li Shenzhi, a famous liberal intellectual and former vice president of the Chinese Academy of Social Sciences (CASS) who was also an important policy adviser to China's leadership in the 1980s. Li, who is considered one of the first Chinese intellectuals to take the concept of globalization seriously, argued that Christopher Columbus's discovery of America should be accepted as the first wave of globalization, an idea that was taboo during Mao's era and too Eurocentric to be accepted in China even after Mao's death. Under Li's direction, the Chinese published the translation of *The Cambridge History of Latin America*, which exposed Chinese scholars to non-Marxist historical perspectives for the first time.

More important, the policy elites represented by Li were drawn to Latin American affairs for internal political reasons. As advocates of political reform, they paid particular attention to the sudden failures of many established Latin American political parties with an authoritarian past. For example, Li attributed the defeat of Mexico's long-ruling Institutional Revolutionary Party (PRI), the failure of Indonesia's Suharto, and the downfall of the Taiwan Nationalist Party—three events that took place almost simultaneously—to the effects of globalization, concomitant with the growing popular desire for democracy. He argued that the intrinsic social transformation that resulted from democratic electoral processes should not be dismissed, as it had been in the past.

After the extraordinarily unpopular Tiananmen crisis, the political liberalization trends across the globe served as a wake-up call for Beijing's political elite. Because China's leadership was, and still is, obsessed with the relationship between political stability and the social shock resulting from economic modernization, Li believed that the Pinochet political model—an orderly transition of power from authoritarianism to democracy—had an enlightening effect on China. This intellectual insight established, for the first time in China's history, a link between the internal politics of a Latin American country and the political future of the Communist Party of China (CPC), breaking away from the days when the region was viewed merely as a potential partner in anti-American campaigns. Because China's leadership always gives policy priority to international issues that may have a direct impact on domestic stability, it is at this juncture that Latin America began to draw the attention of the country's top leadership.[3]

A Key Foreign Policy Dilemma: The U.S. Factor

Official rhetoric aside, there is no doubt that Beijing's decision at the end of the twentieth century to intensify its engagement with Latin America was largely motivated by the pressing issue of energy security (for more on this issue, see chapter 8 by Luisa Palacios). The unusually frequent visits by top leaders during the first decade of the twenty-first century helped solidify ties with the major countries in the region. Yet an important foreign policy dilemma arises from China's new interest in Latin America: simply put, relations with the United States. This is the main reason that it would be misleading to argue that geopolitical concerns are not a major factor in Sino–Latin American relations.

It is ironic that, at the turn of the nineteenth century, U.S. policymakers looked to China, a weak and divided country at the time, as a new El Dorado for trade and investment, yet at the start of the twenty-first century the situation seems to be reversed. The U.S. Open Door policy was a conscious and integrated effort to solve economic problems at home by expanding eastward into the Chinese market, while the colonization of the Philippines was aimed at creating a springboard to penetrate China. Washington has recently begun to show concern about China's expansion into Latin America as well as China's widespread penetration into the U.S. domestic consumer market. Many members of the policy elite in Washington believe China now poses a direct threat to the guiding principle of U.S.–Latin American relations first proclaimed in the 1820s in the Monroe Doctrine. Nonetheless, the U.S. government has thus far found little reason to be truly alarmed about China's presence in Latin America. Roger Noriega, former assistant secretary of state for Western Hemisphere affairs, could say only that "China's growing presence in the region reflects its growing engagement throughout the world. It does not necessarily constitute a threat to U.S. interests."[4] The neoconservative argument, however, stresses the opposite view: that China has successfully employed its own version of an open door policy to strike back at the United States.

But the geopolitical reality is more complicated. As China was developing the market foundation for its monumental economic takeoff during the 1990s, Latin America's political left turn once again came at the wrong time. From the start, China's economic reform relied heavily on foreign direct investment from the West, in particular from the United States and Japan. Thus, because China needed to drastically reduce geopolitical tensions with the United States, deepening relations with anti-U.S. regimes in Latin America posed too great a risk, although China could not ignore the native, popular roots of these emerging movements.

As of the end of the 1980s the U.S. factor began to disappear from Beijing's official language when issuing policy statements relating to Latin America. Deng Xiaoping initiated this trend by announcing in November 1988 that "Chinese policy toward Latin America is to establish and nurture good relations with Latin American countries and set an example for the world to see how a model of South-South cooperation can succeed."[5] In an earlier speech, Deng had declared, "People often say that the twenty-first century will be a Pacific Century . . . but I think it could also be a Latin American Century."[6]

Yet behind these lofty words was a concern that China's growing ties with Latin America would alienate the United States. According to the most common interpretation of Deng's well-known "guiding principle of twenty-four characters" (see chapter 2 for details), Beijing should play a passive role in global geopolitics and instead seize the opportunity of a prolonged period of relative global stability to promote economic development. But after Deng's death in 1997, China's new generation of political leaders faced a different situation. For the first time, China's enormous and growing energy demand reached geopolitical levels, becoming much more than just a development issue. The concept of "energy politics" did not enter Chinese policy discourse until the late 1990s, when the leading state-owned oil companies, including Sinopec, were compelled to set up geopolitics research centers.

In the meantime, popular Latin American leaders with social backgrounds generally sympathetic to Maoist ideology have begun thinking about China as a successful model of defiance against U.S. power and as a useful vehicle in their efforts to break the yoke of the Monroe Doctrine. In this regard, Beijing faces a dilemma in its effort to penetrate Latin America, as it coincides with an upsurge of homegrown anti-Americanism. In the past Latin American Maoist guerrilla groups rarely received any support from the CPC; in fact, native political movements in Latin America have been largely absent from Beijing's radar screen since the days when Mao promoted the national liberation doctrine around the globe. Although China had always been sympathetic to such movements to counterbalance U.S. power, today it is more mindful of the triangular nature of China's relations with Western Hemisphere countries and increasingly cautious about Washington's stance.

Traditionally, Chinese officials dealt only with political elites in the Western Hemisphere, and even party-to-party contacts were limited to established left-wing organizations such as the Socialist International in Latin America.[7] In general, the Chinese Communist Central Committee had little knowledge about Latin American popular parties led by people like Luiz Inácio Lula da Silva in Brazil, Hugo Chávez in Venezuela, and Evo Morales in Bolivia. As recently as 2001 Li Shenzhi seemed to know little about the rise of Chávez, while he still believed that Augusto Pinochet's government was a model for political transition from authoritarianism to democracy. The only problem, Li argued, was that "Old Pi"—the sobriquet for Pinochet employed by the PRC's policy elite—was not as smart as another contemporary authoritarian patriarch, Singapore's Lee Kuan Yew, about the use of political coercion.[8]

China's rapid emergence in the last decades cannot hide its knowledge deficit about recent political events and current trends in Latin America. Of all the democratic governments in the Western Hemisphere, only the United States failed to condemn the attempted coup against Venezuela's Hugo Chávez in 2002, prompting wide speculation that the U.S. government was behind it. But Washington, whose actions undermined the credibility of the United States in the hemisphere, was not the only government to misjudge the situation. The Chinese government also hesitated to condemn the coup, exposing its habitual inability to read correctly the region's political barometers. Ultimately, the PRC was able to save face with the Chávez administration by signing new oil deals and endorsing Venezuela's (unsuccessful) bid for the UN Security Council seat in 2006.

On the whole, Beijing has failed to find a way out of its geopolitical dilemma in the Western Hemisphere. Chinese leaders have a penchant for finding overarching concepts and catchphrases to describe China today—for instance, advocating a "peaceful rise" (*heping jueqi*) policy in a coordinated attempt to convince the outside world that China wants to help build a "harmonious world" (*hexie shijie*)—but such rhetoric has proved insufficient to assuage fears about China's global emergence. Although China has established several so-called strategic partnerships throughout the region—with Brazil, Mexico, and Venezuela, among others—it should be noted that the Chinese definition of *strategic* is relatively narrow and refers primarily to economic and energy interests. Clearly, the current regime's main concern in the Western Hemisphere is to avoid any geopolitical consequences resulting from its expansion into Latin America. Beijing is attempting to confront this foreign policy dilemma through a nonideological approach, hoping that it will complement the current economic development ("going global") strategy.[9]

The Geopolitics of Development

The development paths followed by Latin America and China since the 1970s could not be more different. Although Latin America served as a positive model for China in the 1970s, since the 1980s the region has been plagued by policy mistakes with dire consequences. According to an influential report released in 2004 by experts in the Chinese intelligence community, Latin America's import substitution industrialization (ISI) model was inadequate, as it erroneously stressed government intervention at the expense of market development—that is, big government, small market.[10] More important, foreign borrowing became the engine of growth.

It was only after the debt crisis that Latin American countries began to adopt neoliberal economic policies. However, as is widely believed today, the so-called Washington consensus failed to address key issues in institutional and social development. The neoliberal model prescribed the opposite of the ISI model—that is, a small government, big market approach—in effect moving away from an inward-looking economic model to an outward-looking, export-led growth model. Although these changes helped Latin America break the vicious cycle of debt crises, it also brought about severe consequences by neglecting the government's role in the social arena. Excessive market liberalization in turn led to economic stagnation after 1998. The overall result is that the income gap is widening, social unrest is on the rise, and economic risk is growing. It is thus often argued that Latin America has much to learn from the Asian model about striking a delicate balance between the role of the market and the role of the state. With the benefit of hindsight and considering the successes of the Asian economic development model, China today is in a position to draw useful lessons from the Latin American experience since the 1990s.

With regard to current trends, China is particularly interested in three areas: the idea of Latin American regional integration, the idea of a hemispheric free trade area, and the idea of a South American oil cartel. To China's leadership, the Latin American regional integration momentum is both promising and puzzling. These various integration schemes indicate that there is geopolitical fluidity in the region, but so far Beijing has been unable to devise a strategic plan to confront the potential challenges posed by such regional arrangements.

In general, regional integration schemes draw enormous attention in China. There is great concern, for example, that the proposed Free Trade Area of the Americas (FTAA) will have a profound trade diversion effect that will damage China's commercial activity in the Western Hemisphere. However, Chinese analysts seem optimistic, arguing that as long as two conditions are met, Chinese trade is unlikely to suffer severe setbacks. First, China must maintain its export volume with North America—and the United States in particular—even if it means increasing surpluses in China's favor. And second, if the Chinese do invest more in manufacturing sectors in Latin America, the local advantage must help maintain the competitiveness of its products. Chinese direct investment in Latin America to date is still concentrated in shares of energy, minerals, and related local companies. Investment in joint ventures and Chinese-owned companies in trade and manufacturing sectors remain small: some 380 firms with $3 billion as of 2005, half of which is invested in Venezuela.[11]

Nonetheless, it is still quite possible that the FTAA could prove to be a significant challenge. On the one hand, China could face strong competition from Central and South American producers of consumer goods as a result of the agreement as well as constant pressure from the United States to redress trade imbalances and raise the value of its currency. On the other hand, even if the FTAA allowed the U.S. market to absorb more low-technology products from Latin America, resulting in a reduced U.S. trade deficit vis-à-vis China, the volume of exports from the PRC to the United States will be negatively affected. Either way, China would stand to lose.[12]

The proposed FTAA—comprising some thirty countries, many of which can compete with China on specific products—could create such a level of competitiveness in almost every sector that the trade diversion effect could have serious consequences for the PRC's economic ties with the region. Eventually, physical distance and inadequate trade and business travel routes could turn into the Achilles' heel of China's seemingly invulnerable economic rise.

Moreover, North American products would enjoy easy penetration into Latin American markets, with a local advantage unobtainable by any outside trading partners. Fortunately for China, the FTAA has yet to materialize, providing considerable breathing space for some years to come. But the challenges posed by such a project cannot be dismissed, should it regain momentum in the future.

The trade shock resulting from the 1994 North American Free Trade Agreement (NAFTA)—signed by the United States, Mexico, and Canada—is still fresh in the memory of China's policymakers. Chinese textile products had a dominant position in the U.S. market until the NAFTA treaty granted Mexico important tariff benefits on goods entering the United States. By 1998 Mexico's textile exports surpassed China's, and they remain higher today. According to a 2006 study conducted by the Organization for Economic Cooperation and Development (OECD), Mexico is the top competitor for Chinese textiles in Latin America, and, at the global level, it is more competitive than Hungary and just behind the Czech Republic vis-à-vis China.[13]

In sum, however, the current geopolitical atmosphere in the Western Hemisphere seems more conducive to Chinese economic expansion than restrictive. What Chinese policymakers truly wish to see, and some Latin American leaders are also determined to pursue, is the revival of the Latin American integration project started by Simón Bolívar at the beginning of the nineteenth century. Hugo Chávez of Venezuela sees himself as the standard-bearer of a modern version of this concept, as he attempts to take on Bolívar's mantle to restart this centuries-old dream. In China, Chávez's so-called Bolivarian Revolution has begun to draw attention, particularly as a potential vehicle for countries in Latin America to move away from the Monroe Doctrine concept. Should the Bolivarian regional integration proposal gain traction, the first logical priority would be to reduce the region's dependence on the North American market. Hence China's attractiveness as an alternative market and partner.

The Geopolitics of Energy and Resources

Although official Chinese government rhetoric seeks to promote the idea of South-South cooperation in its dealings with Latin America, the PRC's trade pattern with the region in fact resembles a North-South model, with trade and investment heavily tilted toward energy and natural resources. At the end of the twentieth century Latin America was an ideal region for Chinese expansion. In this regard, two factors are crucially important. First, Latin America's economic conditions were most receptive to Chinese economic penetration. After twenty years of neoliberal policy proposals by the IMF and the World Bank, Latin Americans remain afflicted by poverty and indebtedness. At the same time, foreign direct investment has taken a downward spiral in Latin America, leaving the region in urgent need of financial support. China's arrival is thus timely. Second, since the failure of the ISI model and the growing wariness toward outside tutelage in economic policymaking, Latin American leaders have begun paying closer attention to the Chinese model of export-led growth. With a lack of alternatives from the United States and other regions, the Chinese model is increasingly attractive and inspiring.

Infrastructure investment is another area that has received little attention from Washington. The lion's share of funds flowing from the United States to Latin America today is targeted toward fighting drug production and trafficking. President Hu Jintao's controversial statement in 2004 about a $100 billion ten-year investment plan for Latin America included a particular focus on infrastructure improvement.[14] Such an offer could hardly be refused, and although it has yet to materialize, Latin American leaders increasingly see China not only as a key commercial partner but also as a potential source of much-needed infrastructure investment.

This begs the question of why the Chinese are willing to make such an offer, which brings geopolitics back to front and center. There is no shortage of speculation, ranging from an alleged desire by China to create a global anti-American coalition to the idea that China's corrupt elite are simply looking to meet their money laundering needs. But most observers would agree that energy and resource security is the primary motive for China's interest in infrastructure development in the region. Latin America's rich oil and mineral reserves, coupled with vast agricultural resources, are becoming a critical source to satisfy China's growing appetite for those commodities.

The fact remains that Chinese trade and investment in the region cannot escape the stigma of a neocolonial pattern, especially given China's very narrow commodity needs. The historical precedent of success in this framework is, ironically, not the United States, but Great Britain. From the sixteenth to the early twentieth century, Britain invested heavily in South America to extract primary materials and agricultural goods to sustain its enormous industrial manufacturing capacity. Today 75 percent of Brazil's total exports to China is limited to five primary and agricultural products. Likewise, the most important Argentine export to China is soy beans, and Chile and Peru rely on exports of one product to China, copper. Whether this trade pattern is sustainable and for how long remains a key question.

Conclusion

China's strategy to skirt around the geopolitical implications of its recent incursion into Latin America, although considered by and large benign within Latin America, seems rather ineffective thus far when considering the U.S. stance. The U.S. side of the Sino–Latin American–U.S. triangle, though strategically absent for the most part in China's public discourse, remains of critical importance. It is without a doubt (as explained in chapter 1 and chapter 4) an asymmetrical triangle. However, the United States has yet to demonstrate a belief that China's presence in Latin America presents a real threat to U.S. influence. According to the Chinese scholar Zhu Hongbo, the U.S. government banks on the notion that shared democratic and security values with most of its Latin American neighbors will guarantee U.S. primacy in the region.[15] If that is the case, China can easily move forward with its nonideological foreign policy offensive in the Western Hemisphere.

However, there are three main reasons why this conclusion seems overly optimistic. First, China cannot avoid the geopolitical implications of its economic ties with Latin America. Venezuela is a case in point. Considered by many part of an ongoing anti-American campaign, President Hugo Chávez has actively lobbied for a leftist regional bloc to build a network of oil refineries in Latin America that would provide a stable oil supply to the region and generate new earnings for social and development spending.[16] Naturally, from the U.S. perspective, any indication that China wishes to make an arrangement with an emerging Latin American oil cartel would be interpreted as a direct strategic challenge to U.S. vital energy interests. Chávez is known to purposely resort to such tactics, however unfeasible they may be, to alienate the United States, which continually complicates the geopolitical landscape for countries like China. For example, in reference to China's dealings with developing countries such as Venezuela, writers like Noam Chomsky have argued that Latin America and East Asia are declaring their independence from the United States simultaneously and with a certain degree of coordination.[17]

Second, the Taiwan issue remains an important factor. As Jiang Shixue and Juan Gabriel Tokatlian point out in chapters 2 and 4, of the twenty-four countries that still maintain diplomatic ties with Taipei as of late 2007, twelve are in Latin America. It is quite likely that any alienation between China and the United States over Sino–Latin American relations would undermine China's efforts to persuade those countries to support the one-China policy. Under certain circumstances, the U.S. government would not hesitate to exert pressure on its Latin American neighbors and to provide sufficient incentives to undercut Beijing's diplomatic efforts regarding the Taiwan issue.

Third, China's use of coded language—such as the concept of its "peaceful rise"—in its discourse about its Latin American strategy only leads to speculation about veiled geopolitical interests in the region and, as a result, about possible violations of the Monroe Doctrine. Clearly, the Monroe Doctrine is a moribund concept in the context of a democratic Latin America, with or without China's presence. But China cannot prevent U.S. policymakers from using such rhetoric to caution against the potential "dangers" of China's active presence in Latin America, whether convincing reasons exist or not.

In sum, Beijing's nonideological approach fails to convince the United States that its intentions in the Western Hemisphere are nothing but benign. Given the importance of Sino-U.S. relations and the geopolitical implications of this reality, there is an urgent need for both Beijing and Washington to openly recognize the triangular nature of Sino–Latin American relations and to engage in dialogue about trilateral strategic interests.

China today is very much in the Victorian England phase, although it will not admit it. Along with heavy investment, China aims to further penetrate Latin American markets with manufactured goods, to the dismay of many local producers. Within a very short time China has shown its capacity and acumen to become one of the leading investors and trade partners in Latin America. Willingly or not, China is performing the traditional roles played by the United States in trade and the Europeans in investment. This is potentially a ground-shifting change in the geopolitics of the Western Hemisphere, and by assuming this new role China must also bear the geopolitical consequences and responsibilities that come with it. It would be difficult to imagine that China can escape the kinds of problems faced by those two other actors when exerting their influence in Latin America, but one can argue that China does offer a unique opportunity for the region to experiment with a new model of international relations. Latin America seems ready to diversify its trade patterns and to elevate its international status. Having already transitioned from a transatlantic model with Europe to a transcontinental model with the United States, is it unreasonable to speculate that a new transpacific model may be on the horizon? This is the question that will likely frame the challenges and opportunities ahead for Sino–Latin American–U.S. relations.

Notes

1. "Monthly Foreign Exchange Reserves," State Administration of Foreign Exchange, Beijing (www.safe.gov.cn [December 2007]). All currency amounts are in U.S. dollars, unless otherwise noted.

2. See chapter 2, by Jiang Shixue, for an overview of Mao's Three Worlds theory. According to this theory, promulgated in 1974, Latin America was to be one of the junior partners in the global antihegemony campaign led by China and the third world.

3. For a more detailed discussion on this point, see Xiang Lanxin, "Why Washington Can't Speak Chinese," *Washington Post*, Outlook, April 16, 2005, p. B3.

4. Roger Noriega, *Testimony before the House Subcommittee for the Western Hemisphere*, April 6, 2005.

5. *People's Daily*, Beijing, November 8, 1988, p. 1.

6. *People's Daily*, Beijing, May 16, 1988, p. 1.

7. The Socialist International is a worldwide organization of social democratic, socialist, and labor parties (www.socialistinternational.org).

8. *World Knowledge* [Shijie Zhishi magazine] 6 (2003): 25–36.

9. For a detailed critique of this approach, see Xiang Lanxin, "Never Say 'Rise,' Careful about 'Harmonious,'" *United Morning News*, Singapore, May 17, 2006.

10. "A Study on Chinese Latin American Policy," *Contemporary International Relations* 4 (2004): 19.

11. Xie Kang, "The Present Status and Prospects of Chinese Trade and Investment in Latin America," *Journal of World Economy* 11 (2005): 13–19.

12. See an earlier and interesting study by Wang Xiaode, "Trade Liberalization in the Americas and Its Impact of Trade Diversion on Chinese Exports," *Journal of Latin American Studies* 6, no. 4 (2002): 28–36.

13. See Jorge Blázquez-Lidoy, Javier Rodríguez, and Javier Santiso, "Angel or Devil? China's Trade Impact on Latin American Emerging Markets," in *The Visible Hand of China in Latin America,* edited by Javier Santiso (Paris: OECD, Center for Development, 2007).

14. Muazzam Gill, "Outside View: China's Growing Global Clout," United Press International, December 9, 2004.

15. Zhu Hongbo, "Recent Development of Sino-Latin American Relations and the U.S. Policy towards Latin America," *Journal of Latin American Studies* 28, no. 4 (2006): 60–65.

16. Leslie Mazoch, "Chávez Pledges Oil, Financing to Allies in Latin America," *Associated Press Financial Wire*, April 30, 2007, p. 12.

17. Noam Chomsky, "Latin America and Asia Are at Last Breaking Free of Washington's Grip," *Guardian*, March 15, 2006, op. ed.

JUAN GABRIEL TOKATLIAN

4

A View from Latin America

At the start of the twenty-first century, political, economic, and security relations between Latin America, the People's Republic of China (PRC), and the United States have been marked by uncertainty about the future, increasing complexity, and, as Xiang Lanxin argues in chapter 3, the return of geopolitics. In this scenario the policies of a dominant superpower inevitably intersect with those of an ascendant power whose presence is growing in a peripheral region. Furthermore, current Sino–Latin American–U.S. dynamics are unfolding in a historic, political, and social context that could potentially lead to either conflict or cooperation or a combination of both. Although the China-U.S. relationship is of paramount importance to political and economic actors in Beijing and Washington, there is an increasing need to factor in the triangular dimension that involves Latin America. This chapter seeks to explain and interpret the geopolitical aspects of the Sino–Latin American–U.S. triangle from the perspective of Latin America's regional interests.

The main debates in the United States as to whether China constitutes a threat or an opportunity, whether Beijing is a revisionist or a conservative power, or whether its expansive aims beyond Asia are benevolent or malevolent are valuable and significant, but they often reflect only the perspective of the United States.[1] From Latin America, however, China's growing presence in the region is perceived less as a negative event and more as a promising trend. As chapters 2 and 3 explain, China's presence in Latin America from the 1950s to the 1970s was marginal, focused primarily on cultural diplomacy, driven by ideological motives, and based on revolutionary rhetoric. This diplomatic strategy relied on the dividends of destabilization, was accompanied by anti-U.S. slogans, and was geared toward strengthening pro-Chinese (and anti-Soviet) political parties and movements.[2] China's international behavior during that period was that of a revisionist actor who sought to change the rules of the game through aggressive means.

In contrast, Beijing's approach to the region today involves active economic diplomacy characterized by pragmatism, conciliation, and stability. As noted in the previous chapters of this volume, China's goal and main challenge is to deepen its relations with the countries of Latin America without irritating Washington. Overall, China's expanding interest in the region appears to be moderate, nonconfrontational, and in favor of the status quo.[3] Diplomatically, China has proceeded in a judicious fashion, which explains in part why regional forces have not emerged to veto a policy of prudent and consistent engagement toward China.[4] At the present time, nothing indicates that Latin America would ever accept a paternalistic, externally induced security dilemma with China, and the region has no reason to feel insecure vis-à-vis Beijing in response to certain ideologically driven pressure groups in Washington.

This chapter is based on the premise that it would be counterproductive to return to an apocalyptic geopolitics approach based on an overblown fear of an alleged Chinese takeover of Latin America.[5] In its overview of contemporary relations between Latin America, China, and the United States, the chapter examines the specific initiatives undertaken by Beijing vis-à-vis the Western Hemisphere and weighs the geopolitical effects for Latin America. From this analysis, the chapter then draws some conclusions that serve to explain the Sino–Latin American–U.S. triangular relationship.

A Conceptual Framework

Defining the frame of reference used to evaluate the geopolitics of the Latin America, China, and U.S. triangle is a key first step when assessing the region's recent developments. In so doing, six elements stand out. First, relations between Latin America, China, and the United States are characterized by an asymmetrical dynamic. This reflects a profound disparity of power, which gives rise to "systemic differences in interests and perceptions."[6] Applying and expanding on Brantly Womack's analysis of asymmetry among states in international relations, it is possible to distinguish two simultaneous and separate types of power relationships in the Chinese–Latin American–U.S. triangle: one between the United States and China and another between the United States and Latin America. In the Sino-U.S. relationship, China has been able to reduce the power gap between the two states. In the U.S.–Latin American relationship, on the other hand, the power gap is expanding. In a hierarchical configuration, the United States operates as a global power, China as a regional power, and Latin America as a subordinate region.[7]

As a result of this structural condition, Washington tends to have somewhat simplistic perceptions about China and Latin America, albeit rather contrasting ones. With regard to China's growing economic, military, and symbolic attributes such as "soft power," the United States has clearly overreacted.[8] In Latin America, inattention has been the predominant characteristic of U.S. engagement. The resulting dynamics are recurrent anxiety from the most powerful and an endemic sense of annoyance from the weakest.[9] The greatest challenge is thus the management of this asymmetry: finding a way to "neutralize possible areas of conflict . . . and . . . control the escalation of misunderstanding."[10]

Second, the nature of the Sino–Latin American–U.S. relationship must be defined. The most salient characteristic of this relationship is that it does not constitute a strategic triangle. According to Lowell Dittmer, a triangular relationship is strategic only when: "(a) it circumscribes the possible relationships among three rational, autonomous actors, (b) the bilateral relationship among any two of these actors is contingent on their relationship with the third, and (c) each actor actively seeks to engage one or the other or both to forestall its defection or hostile collusion and advance its own interests."[11]

While the United States and China constitute two unitary and independent actors, Latin America is a mosaic of countries whose international conduct has different degrees of autonomy. The bilateral ties of each pair in this triangle are not closely intertwined, nor are they equally vital for the three parties. The reciprocal significance of Washington-Beijing relations is, for each, greater than their respective relationships with Latin America. In addition, the U.S. impact on the external and internal politics of Latin America is much more important than China's. Latin America is not as high a priority for China when compared to other more developed countries or those in its regional sphere.[12] Furthermore, the history of this triangle has not had significant impact on the international balance of power, nor does it appear likely to in the near future. This uneven trilateral relationship does not produce automatic frictions. Though in any triangle there are competing elements, especially between its strongest vertexes, a nonstrategic triangle implies that it is easier to identify areas for tripartite cooperation. In this context, cooperation is a result of choice as well as circumstance.[13]

Third, it is important to clarify the prevailing strategies among the members of the triangle. The United States continues to reaffirm its primacy by showing little tolerance for the rise of any peer competitor. China is an ascendant nation that aims to increase its internal and regional power as well as to secure its future as an influential global actor. Latin American countries are following, by and large, a strategy of diversification, though alignment with and away from the United States fluctuates regularly. The main goal of the countries in Latin America is to foster development and increase international autonomy, consistent with the view that domestic prosperity and national security are more likely to prevail in an international system with a wider distribution and diffusion of power.

The intersection between these strategies does not necessarily lead to reduced conflict or greater cooperation among the three parties. The main obstacles to stronger, more benign tripartite ties could come from the United States, given its policy of primacy.[14] One way to elude potential conflict—which would most likely surface in Latin America, as it is the weakest vertex of the asymmetric trilateral relationship—is to seek a balanced understanding of intentions. When analyzing the potential rise of a peer competitor, it is usual to underscore the importance of evaluating the attributes of power and the underlying motivations of the emerging competitors. Nonetheless, as Eric Nordingler argues, "security policies are thus to be matched up with capabilities rather than intentions."[15] In this regard, there are three possible approaches to the question of intentions: one may be a believer, an agnostic, or an atheist. In other words, one can argue that intentions are highly significant and have a decisive impact (believer); one can accept that intentions may have a relative impact but that most important is what countries actually do as well as the consistency between what they do and what they say (agnostic); or one can believe that intentions have no weight whatsoever (atheist). This chapter takes an agnostic position with respect to intentions.

Fourth, in this triangle, geography matters. Latin America is located in the same hemisphere as the world's leading superpower. Latin America has traditionally been a secure region for the United States. During the cold war the region was of limited importance to Washington, and in the post–cold war era, even more so, particularly after the terrorist attacks of September 11, 2001.[16] In the hemispheric context, the United States has clearly reaffirmed its hegemony, which is increasingly consolidated and with no challengers on the horizon. Regardless of the relevance of the Monroe Doctrine, no other principle contests it.

To understand why Europe could not dispute U.S. hegemony in Latin America historically, understanding the European dynamic is essential. As explained by Christopher Layne:

The distribution of power in Europe differed markedly from that in the Western Hemisphere. Bids for European hegemony failed, because the distribution of power in Europe was multipolar: other great powers could—and did—coalesce to muster sufficient countervailing power to defeat aspiring hegemons. The United States, on the other hand, succeeded in attaining regional hegemony because when its expansion gathered steam in the late nineteenth and early twentieth centuries, it was expanding into a power vacuum. No great powers—either regional or extra-regional—were capable of opposing—much less stopping—U.S. hegemonic expansion in the Western Hemisphere.[17]

By analogy, if one considers that "Eastern Eurasia today contains four countries that might plausibly be described as great powers (India, Japan, China, and Russia), as well as several medium powers, most of them wealthy and technologically advanced," then it is very unlikely that China will have the capacity and the will to seriously rival the United States in the Americas.[18] China is a regional power, but it is not the hegemonic actor of eastern Eurasia, where the distribution of power is increasingly multipolar. China is not a world power, and it cannot easily become one by challenging the United States via Latin America, whether through soft power or aggressive action.[19] Geography is another crucial factor when gauging China's potential to penetrate a periphery as distant as Latin America.

Fifth, Latin America's current situation warrants careful consideration. Two specific trends cut across the hemisphere: deinstitutionalization and fragmentation. Both appear to be intensifying at the outset of the twenty-first century, and they are the backdrop of the present crises in the region. Deinstitutionalization (a process that unfolded over three decades) and fragmentation could lead to accelerated processes of social polarization, political implosion, and territorial partition.

During the 1970s Latin America experienced a lost decade in political terms. The expansion of authoritarian governments in the region (with scant islands of limited democracy) was characterized by abuse of power, disrespect for the rule of law, human rights violations, the elimination of a political generation just coming of age, the weakening of the political parties, and the devaluation of public ethics. All of these factors led to an enormous deterioration of institutions. The 1980s was a lost decade in economic terms: low growth, high indebtedness, enormous volatility, a rapid expansion of informal labor markets, poor technological capacity, and a sharp decline in quality of life. In the 1990s Latin America experienced another lost decade in social terms: inequality widened, class and ethnic conflict increased, poverty and extreme poverty indexes remained high, citizen violence flared, unemployment grew, education was neglected, and health services deteriorated.

Fragmentation occurred in the political, economic, and diplomatic processes. In addition, the concept of "Latin America" is becoming increasingly diluted. Today it seems more relevant to speak of a North America that extends from Canada to Panama (including the Caribbean) and centers on the United States in terms of trade, investment, and immigration, and of a South America that extends from Colombia to Argentina as a distinct geopolitical unit. After 9/11 the greater Caribbean Basin, which includes the Caribbean islands, Panama, Central America, and Mexico, has become part of the U.S. defense perimeter, and it is included in the U.S. notion of homeland security. Within South America, two subregions can be identified: the Andean countries and the Southern Cone. The first grouping is experiencing profound domestic turbulence, and two countries in particular are causing concern abroad: Colombia and Venezuela.[20] The critical issue for the region is to ensure that future ties with China do not lead to further deinstitutionalization and fragmentation.

Sixth, values matter. Latin America shares (and contributes to) the democratic values of the West. In addition, the last authoritarian wave of the 1970s led to a reassessment of democracy in terms of the importance of defending human rights, respect for pluralism, and the rule of law. Despite clear limitations and inherent internal contradictions, the countries of the region have continued moving forward with democratization. In this regard, China's internal political model is not especially attractive for Latin America.

However, the PRC's external diplomatic model is more seductive: multipolarism (as opposed to unipolarism), multilateralism (as opposed to unilateralism), noninterference (as opposed to interventionism), soft power (as opposed to hard power), pragmatism (as opposed to ideologization), collaboration (as opposed to domination), and persuasion (as opposed to coercion); are all attractive notions in Latin America. These policies coincide with certain Latin American traditions and aspirations and have become more captivating by virtue of recent developments in U.S. foreign policy.[21]

In sum, one of the greatest challenges for Latin America with regard to the region's triangular relationship with China and the United States is to preserve and deepen democratic values internally and to take advantage, diplomatically, of those opportunities created by the ascendant weight of China in international politics. The security issues constitute an interesting indicator of the delicate balance that will ultimately determine which model better serves the national interests of Latin America in the long run.

An Empirical Approach to the Geopolitics of Sino–Latin American–U.S. Relations

One way to analyze the geopolitical issues arising from the new Sino–Latin American–U.S. triangle is to draw a distinction between sensitive and substantive security issues. Sensitive issues affect the security of individual states and are linked to the foreign policy and defense agendas of Beijing and Washington. Substantive security issues have a dual component: they affect primarily the countries of Latin America and they have an interconnected effect on the security of the region's societies.[22] The following discussion examines both types of security issues with the aim of providing a better understanding of where they fall on a continuum between conflict and cooperation.

Sensitive Security Issues: China

As Xiang Lanxin highlights in chapter 3, two critical geopolitical issues stand out in Beijing's relationship with Latin America: Taiwan and energy security. The importance of the Taiwan question is well known. Half of the twenty-four countries that recognize the Taipei government are in Latin America. The distribution is as follows: twelve in Latin America and the Caribbean (Belize, Dominican Republic, El Salvador, Guatemala, Haiti, Honduras, Nicaragua, Panama, Paraguay, Saint Kitts and Nevis, Saint Lucia, and Saint Vincent and the Grenadines); five in Africa (Burkina Faso, Gambia, Malawi, São Tomé and Príncipe, and Swaziland); six in the Pacific (Kiribati, Marshall Islands, Nauru, Palau, Solomon Islands, and Tuvalu); and one in Europe (the Vatican). The fact that a majority of countries that recognize Taiwan are in the Americas in large part reflects the sphere of influence of the United States.

The realities for Central America, the Caribbean, and South America with respect to the Taiwan question are different. In the Caribbean islands a sort of checkbook diplomacy can be observed, whereby Taiwanese dollars compete with Chinese renminbis for diplomatic recognition. Little will change in this region of tiny island countries due to their urgent need for resources, the political volatility of successive administrations, and persistent U.S. influence. In Central America the context also seems unfavorable for China because Taipei's efforts have been more vigorous and sophisticated—although Beijing successfully lured Costa Rica to switch diplomatic recognition from Taiwan to the PRC in mid-2007. Taiwan has thus far negotiated free trade agreements with Panama in 2003, Guatemala in 2005, Nicaragua in 2006, and El Salvador and Honduras in 2007 and seeks to sign one with the Dominican Republic.[23] All of these countries except Panama already have free trade agreements with the United States.[24] Moreover, the nations of Central America and Mexico are the most affected by the scale of the Chinese maquiladoras and by China's growing exports to the United States. Such circumstances make it difficult for Beijing to compete for diplomatic recognition, a policy priority that will require time, patience, discretion, and money.

Paraguay, the only South American country to maintain relations with Taiwan, has received intensive diplomatic attention in recent years from high-level Taiwanese officials, including heads of state. While bilateral trade is limited, more than 20 percent of Paraguay's debt is with Taiwanese banks. Most likely, only a major shift in government control combined with indirect diplomatic efforts by the Mercosur governments would lead Asunción to modify its position against the one-China policy.[25] On the whole, the Taiwan issue in Latin America is a legacy of the cold war associated with the projection of U.S. influence in the Pacific. As is true for European countries, in Latin America there are no specific political, economic, or ideological reasons to worry about Taiwan in terms of regional security.[26]

On the subject of energy, China's growing and massive need for hydrocarbons and minerals may be its main source of vulnerability. Thus, as explained in more detail by Luisa Palacios in chapter 8, Beijing has been actively engaged in energy diplomacy for some time and became increasingly active in Latin America at the start of the twenty-first century. Several considerations are relevant when examining China's new regional interest in energy. First, volatility in the Middle East combined with growing uncertainty in oil-rich neighboring countries such as Russia have led China to seek investment opportunities in other regions, in particular Africa and Latin America. Second, Beijing has sought to diversify its energy sources and to "disassociate energy security initiatives from other security matters."[27] Third, China has been forced to seek energy sources where it can rather than where it wants to, with little concern for the political and environmental consequences of related exploration and drilling operations.[28] Fourth, China is not the only growing economy in search of energy sources—India's growing energy demand has also spurred worldwide demand for hydrocarbons. Fifth, China's expanding energy ties do not appear to have anti-U.S. connotations. Accordingly, "the argument that China is trying to use its growing power from expanding overseas energy investment to drive U.S. influence out of certain parts of the world . . . is both speculative and dangerous."[29]

The geopolitical significance of energy in the triangular relationship between Latin America, China, and the United States becomes troublesome to a large extent because of the dynamics between Latin America and the United States rather than because of China's international strategy. Neither Latin America in general nor South America in particular has been able to articulate a solid, sustainable, and coordinated energy policy that provides the region a fluid, reliable, and secure energy supply. The Chinese presence may create the illusion of good business in some countries, but it cannot hide the absence of coherent and strategic national and regional energy policies. The United States also lacks sensible, secure, and efficient energy policies. Washington may speculate that China has unfathomable objectives in Latin America, but it cannot ignore its own mixed record on energy conservation and the development of energy sources other than oil.

For Latin America, avoiding a possible energy rivalry between the United States and China in the region is critical, especially when international conflicts on oil and gas are on the rise and instability plagues the region. Latin America could fall victim to unwanted consequences from a reactivated energy cold war. Such a scenario can be avoided if all three parties adopt consistent, cooperative policies.[30]

Sensitive Security Issues: United States

In addition to the issues of Taiwan and energy resources, the United States has a number of security concerns relating to China's growing presence in Latin America. These include China's military projection in the region, the Panama Canal, and the specific country cases of Colombia, Cuba, and Venezuela. The military question is potentially the most sensitive. U.S. officials, academics, and journalists have expressed increasing uneasiness over China's presence in the region. For example, U.S. Southern Command (SOUTHCOM) commander, General Bantz J. Craddock, stated the following during a congressional hearing on March 9, 2005:

> An increasing presence of the People's Republic of China in the region is an emerging dynamic that must not be ignored. . . . The PRC's 2004 Defense Strategy White Paper departs from the past and promotes a power-projection military. . . . In 2004, national level defense officials from the PRC made 20 visits to Latin American and Caribbean nations, while Ministers and Chiefs of Defense from nine countries in our AOR [area of responsibility] visited the PRC.[31]

Similarly, in a 2006 essay, June Teufel Dreyer of the University of Miami asserted, without specifying numbers, that "senior Latin American officers who used to travel to the United States for training are now going to China instead."[32] Bill Gertz wrote in the *Washington Times*, again with no specific figures, that "China is stepping up military training in Latin America."[33] And Kelly Hearn, in the same newspaper, stated that China is "eyeing the region as a market for its growing arms industry."[34]

The empirical evidence, however, indicates that it is the United States that has considerably increased its military projection in Latin America. From 1997 to 2000, when General Charles Wilhelm headed the U.S. Southern Command, and from August 2002 to July 2004, when General James Hill held that post, these commanders made more visits to the region than any high-level civilian official of the U.S. government.[35] The Southern Command in Miami has had more employees working on Latin America than the combined Washington employees of the Departments of State, Agriculture, Commerce, Treasury, and Defense.[36]

Increased deployment by the Southern Command in the Caribbean and Latin America can be observed at bases such as Guantánamo Bay in Cuba, Fort Buchanan in Puerto Rico, and Soto Cano in Honduras.[37] SOUTHCOM has established forward operating locations (now called cooperative security locations) in Manta in Ecuador, Reina Beatrix in Aruba, Hato Rey in Curaçao, and Comalapa in El Salvador.[38] It operates an extensive radar network (three fixed radars in Peru and three fixed radars in Colombia, plus eleven mobile and secret ones operating in six Andean and Caribbean countries) for antidrug operations.[39] After a brief dip in the late 1990s, the number of Latin American and Caribbean military personnel who receive training in the United States has been on the rise. From 2001 to 2004 the United States trained 68,807 soldiers from Latin America and the Caribbean, and 2001–03 military sales to the region by private U.S. companies were $3.5 billion.[40]

There are still more initiatives providing military resources to Latin America and the Caribbean, and others that offer professional exchanges and educational programs. These initiatives, excluding antinarcotics assistance and other Department of Justice programs, focus on a host of subjects: antiterrorism assistance, counterterrorism fellowships, programs at the Center for Hemispheric Defense Studies, deployment for training, drawdowns, direct military sales, enhanced international peacekeeping capabilities, excess defense articles, foreign military financing, foreign military interaction, foreign military sales, humanitarian assistance, Inter-American Air Forces Academy programs, international military education and training, joint combined exchange training and other special forces training, naval small craft instruction and technical training school, service academies, Spanish Helicopter Institute for Security Cooperation programs, and Western Hemisphere Institute for Security Cooperation programs (formerly known as the School of the Americas).[41]

The available data show that the military projection of the United States in Latin America is growing and that China's military rapprochement with the region is insignificant.[42] While some U.S. "hawks" obsess over a hypothetical and massive sale of Chinese weaponry to Latin America, it was Russia, not China, that agreed to sell (for $3 billion) armaments (helicopters, airplanes, rifles) to Venezuela in 2005 and 2006.[43] The United States has sold airplanes and missiles to Chile as well as helicopters and torpedoes to Peru. Saudi Arabia has sold airplanes to Brazil. Several European countries, including Spain, France, Italy, the Netherlands, and Germany, have sold patrol cars and airplanes to Venezuela, tanks and artillery to Colombia, submarines, tanks, and ships to Argentina, frigates to Peru—and the list goes on.[44] A conservative assessment of these lists would conclude that there is an arms race going on in the region.

Security concerns surrounding the Panama Canal are based on the fact that two of the four ports situated on the Caribbean and the Pacific are controlled, by way of concession (for twenty-five years starting in 1997), by the Chinese (Hong Kong-based) company Hutchison Whampoa, which has close ties to the Chinese government and armed forces. The worry is that the company's state-private link could be manipulated by the PRC to interrupt shipping in the Canal Zone, which would in turn thwart international trade and harm U.S. security interests.

This apprehension seems exaggerated for several reasons. First, when the United States agreed on the canal transfer to Panama, it was by then strategically obsolete.[45] Second, the Torrijos-Carter treaties, along with the 1978 DeConcini amendment, gave the United States the right to defend the neutrality of the canal in the face of any threat, even after its transfer to Panama.[46] If the canal is threatened, the United States can deploy security forces on the isthmus without prior consultation with Panama. Third, while Hutchison Whampoa manages the ports of Balboa and Cristóbal, one of the terminals of the port of Colón is controlled by the U.S. company Stevedoring Services of America; the other is operated by the Taiwanese company Evergreen Marine Corp. Panama's strategy has been to try to strike a balance in the concessions of the main ports.

Fourth, Hutchison Whampoa is a large international corporation with port operations in fifty-four countries (among them, the Port of Felixtowe, the largest in the United Kingdom, and the container port of Duisburg in Germany, the largest inland port in the world), with a turnover of $31 billion in 2005.[47] What motivation could this firm possibly have to interrupt the lucrative movement of goods in the Panama Canal and risk its multimillion-dollar revenues along with its reputation for efficiency? And fifth, in large measure, Hutchison Whampoa appears to have less to do with ideology than with business. According to Alberto Alemán Zubieta, administrator of the Panama Canal Authority, the problem is not Chinese influence in the Canal Zone but the fact that the influential and powerful U.S. corporation Bechtel, whose bid was much lower than Hutchison Whampoa's, lost the original concession.[48] In 2003 conservative Republican Richard Perle was involved in a scandal directly related to the Chinese company. Perle, at the time a member of the Defense Policy Advisory Board, was hired by the telecommunications firm Global Crossing (then in bankruptcy)—which paid him $125,000 and promised an additional $600,000 once the deal was closed—to get Defense Department approval of the sale of the company to Hutchison Whampoa. He was ultimately forced to step down from that position when this deal received public attention.[49]

In sum, nothing indicates that Beijing has sought or is seeking to provoke Washington by means of aggressive action in the Panama Canal or that Panama is willing to tolerate or promote threats against the United States, with whom it is currently discussing the possibility of a bilateral free trade agreement.[50] It would be useful for Panama, China, and the United States to work on effective port security mechanisms in the Canal Zone to prevent terrorist attacks and guarantee trade flows through the canal.

To understand the nature of the very limited relations between Beijing and Bogotá, one must first consider the general framework of U.S.-Colombian ties. The core of Washington's policy toward Bogotá is summarized in Plan Colombia.[51] It calls for a more punitive antinarcotics policy and a more head-on counterinsurgency in Colombia. As the 1990s drew to a close, Washington saw Bogotá as facing two simultaneous and intertwined threats that, if not answered militarily, could lead to the collapse of the Colombian state. On the one hand was the intractable drug problem. Although Colombia received approximately $1.4 billion in aid from the United States from 1989 to 1999, drug trafficking did not decline. Even worse, the political insurgency continued to grow stronger economically, territorially, and militarily. From 1995 to 1998 the Colombian army suffered the worst casualties of the protracted armed conflict.

With the terrorist attacks of September 11, 2001, and the response of the George W. Bush administration, the "war on terrorism" component became more prominent. According to Andrew Feickert, "U.S. military operations in Afghanistan, Africa, the Philippines, and Colombia are part of the U.S.-initiated global war on terrorism."[52] Undeniably, Colombia has one of the largest deployments of U.S. special operations forces. After 9/11 the fruitless dialogue between the Pastrana administration and the Fuerzas Armadas Revolucionarias de Colombia (FARC)—which lasted from January 1999 to February 2002—was lost in the rush of events, and the Colombian conflict was internationalized through the massive indirect intervention of the United States.

Between 2000 and 2006 Washington disbursed nearly $4.7 billion, dispatched over 800 members of the military and over 600 private security contractors, and turned Colombia into the fifth largest recipient of such aid in the world (after Iraq, Afghanistan, Israel, and Egypt).[53] Washington's "war on drugs" and "war on terrorism" policies were to be waged essentially by the Colombians themselves in the front lines, accompanied by a U.S. rearguard to shore up the Colombian government, preventing more U.S. casualties in new theaters of combat operations. Since its inception, Plan Colombia has yielded meager and ambivalent results. Nonetheless, nothing appears to change the course of U.S. assumptions and tactics employed thus far.

In this context, China's rapprochement with Colombia has been cautious, indicating that Beijing understands the significance of Bogotá for Washington today.[54] China is also judicious when dealing with governments engaged in conflict with armed groups labeled as terrorist organizations. Domestic difficulties with groups who demand growing autonomy and have taken to violence to advance their claims, such as the Uyghur Muslim minority in the province of Xinjiang, coupled with the problems of immediate neighbors beset by terrorist movements, have prompted Beijing to express its commitment to fighting terrorism and its understanding of the plight of other nations that suffer from this phenomenon. In the case of Colombia, President Álvaro Uribe expressed gratitude during his visit to China in 2005 for the support that President Hu Jintao had provided in Colombia's struggle against terrorism and drug trafficking.[55] In addition, China must take into account Colombia's neighbors in terms of its own interests with those nations while also assessing their stance on the Colombia-U.S. relationship: Venezuela, for example, is more important for China than Colombia, due in large part to its energy resources. Whether by resignation or by conviction, most South American countries are inclined to accept Plan Colombia and the resulting military presence of the United States in Colombia.

Two other crucial cases for U.S. security concerns in the region are Cuba and Venezuela. Cuba's ties with Beijing are long-standing and have grown stronger in the post–cold war era following the implosion of the Soviet Union, to a great extent because of the island's urgent material needs and China's need for minerals and hydrocarbons. In recent years, Chinese investment has focused on nickel and oil. However, China is not alone—other countries have also increased their investment in Cuba. For example, Canada's Sherritt International Corporation has penetrated the nickel market, while investors from Norway (Norsk Hydro), India (ONGC Videsh), and Spain (Repsol/YPF) manage offshore oil exploration operations. Washington's obstinate decision to maintain an unsuccessful embargo for more than four decades has kept U.S. companies from reaping the benefits of new economic openings in Cuba since the 1990s.

While some consider socialism to be the main common factor between China and Cuba, this ideological dimension appears not to have much weight in contemporary bilateral relations, at least as expressed by the official Chinese side.[56] As Manfred Wilhelmy von Wolf and Augusto Soto note, "One must avoid understanding the People's Republic of China exclusively in light of the official ideology. Since the reforms introduced by Deng [Xiaoping], the practical import of ideological orientations is less and less relevant for the actors involved, and, hence, the relativity of a political system that considers itself communist."[57]

From the Cuban standpoint, China is very significant: in 2005 the PRC became Cuba's second most important trading partner (after Venezuela). Moreover, the mere existence of a stronger and more assertive China gives Havana more room to maneuver internationally. Practical considerations on both sides have fostered a relationship that does not—and probably never will—carry the intensity, depth, and fundamental importance of Cuban-Soviet relations during the cold war.[58]

Since the deterioration of Fidel Castro's health, various scenarios on Cuba's future suggest a gradual political transition. This process will not necessarily be as turbulent as it might have been in the early 1990s, when the disappearance of the Soviet Union led to Cuba's economic collapse and Havana's diplomatic eclipse. Cuba's economic and political cataclysm in the 1990s resulted in a dramatic decline in social conditions; this situation, in turn, led to increased speculation that the Miami exile community and the Washington hard-liners might act to further destabilize Cuba. Today Venezuela's economic and energy assistance has replaced the Soviet cold war role in Cuba, while the tourism industry has managed to generate a slight improvement in living conditions for certain segments of the population. In terms of internal security, the unity of the Cuban armed forces appears to be genuine, Florida has lost influence in U.S. policy toward Cuba, and Washington can't risk another international fiasco like those experienced in the Middle East, the Persian Gulf, and the Korean Peninsula.

Beyond the inevitable end of the Castro regime, the important issue is that the possibility of a gradual and bloodless transition to a more plural structure is feasible, which could lead toward greater democratization. Some analysts anticipate that "China will almost certainly be a major influence on Cuba's immediate post-Fidel reforms."[59] It is clear that some Cuban leaders feel a certain admiration for the Chinese economic model, and commercial and investment ties, which are becoming increasingly important, may facilitate more fluid political relations. Washington must understand that a prudent and positive role for Beijing in Cuban matters does not constitute inappropriate meddling in its "backyard" but rather a potential contribution toward the goal of achieving a peaceful transition.

Venezuela is possibly a more delicate case in the context of Sino–Latin American–U.S. relations. Most observers and decisionmakers in the United States share concerns about the expanded ties between Beijing and Caracas. Chinese investment in the Venezuelan energy sector, as well as bilateral trade, continues to grow. Caracas wishes to increase oil exports to China, and President Hugo Chávez visited China four times between 1999 and 2006. The diplomatic agreements made between the two countries during this period span a variety of areas: energy, mining, agriculture, taxation. Military contact between Venezuela and China is incipient and could be stepped up after Washington's decision in May 2006 to prohibit arms sales to Caracas.[60]

Beijing's closer ties with Caracas have thus far not yielded adverse effects on U.S. commercial interests in Venezuela. The June 2006 report by the U.S. Government Accountability Office on the possible impact of a disruption in oil exports or refining does not mention China's appetite for Venezuelan oil and current investment policies as a threat to U.S. energy interests in Venezuela.[61] At the same time, according to analysts, bankers are reaping large profits under the current regime in Venezuela, and bilateral trade, which increased significantly since 2005, has benefited the U.S. manufactured goods export sector.[62]

Both Sino-Venezuelan relations and U.S.-Venezuelan relations are marked by a combination of pragmatic and ideological elements. From Beijing's perspective, as William Ratliff notes, pragmatism dominates its ties with Caracas; that is to say, there is little if any ideological common ground between the Chinese leadership and Venezuela's government.[63] China does not seem interested in a high-profile relationship with Venezuela should it have a detrimental impact on Sino-U.S. ties. Caracas is also pragmatic with regard to its interest in greater interaction with Beijing, despite President Chávez's rhetoric invoking Mao and his teachings, rhetoric that is hardly heard in today's China.

As to Venezuelan-U.S. relations, Chávez initially remained pragmatic in his dealings with the U.S. private sector but stepped up his nationalist policies and anti-U.S. ideological rhetoric in recent years. Chávez's decision to nationalize the oil sector led to significant losses in 2007 for U.S. oil companies such as ConocoPhillips and ExxonMobil, which refused to accept the minority ownership terms offered by the Venezuelan government. Chávez continues to sustain his domestic agenda while playing an increasingly radical political role internationally. Ultimately, it is the U.S. government that faces the greatest dilemma, having made its ideological posturing vis-à-vis the rest of the world its raison d'être, particularly in the wake of 9/11.

Current tensions between Washington and Caracas occur in a regional framework that differs from the past. From the end of World War II to date, Latin America has undergone several self-proclaimed revolutionary experiences, in some cases resulting in drastic changes in political institutions, economic foundations, and social structures.[64] Of these revolutionary experiences, three failed to expand beyond national borders due to a series of internal and external factors: the Peronist Revolution, the Cuban Revolution, and the Sandinista Revolution. In all three cases, dissolution, containment, and rollback halted potentially drastic change in Latin America.

The Peronist Revolution was unable to project itself abroad because it succumbed internally. Successive coups in Argentina weakened the Peronist movement in political and electoral terms, and over time Peronismo gradually lost its spirit of radical transformation and became a docile movement, divided between neopopulist conservatism and moderate reformism.

The Cuban Revolution, more ambitious in its goal to have an international scope, never took hold beyond its own borders as a result of the containment strategy adopted by the United States in the 1960s. Outside pressure, more than internal will, limited Cuba's capacity for revolutionary projection. In fact Washington, with the help of most Latin American countries, succeeded in diplomatically encircling Fidel Castro's regime. After a failed attempt to eliminate the regime militarily through invasion, the U.S.-led economic blockade hindered Cuba's economic development, and Cuba's aspiration to foster revolutionary movements in Latin America and other regions had diminished even before the collapse of the Soviet Union, its main source of economic support.

The Sandinista Revolution, which from the start had minimal prospects of spreading to the rest of the region, was not sustainable due to combined pressures. Through a low-intensity war, the United States succeeded in halting and then reversing the revolutionary movement in Nicaragua. In this case, domestic politics played a role, as the internal opposition, known as the contras, received support from Washington. Within a short time the revolution was rolled back, the Nicaraguan establishment regained power, and Sandinismo became much less radical.

Chávez's Bolivarian Revolution, with clear expansionary ambitions, has yet to produce any real changes in Latin America outside of Venezuela's borders, with the exception of helping sustain Cuba's Castro regime.[65] As the option of dissolution faded after Venezuela's failed coup attempt in 2002,

Washington might opt to attempt a strategy that combines containment and rollback, but how and with whom such a strategy could be carried out is unclear. Venezuela, unlike Nicaragua and Cuba, is economically significant at the global level because of its energy resources. This means that no regional government—not even the Colombia of reelected Álvaro Uribe or the Peru of President Alan García—wants a policy of diplomatic encirclement, much less one of military hostility, by supporting anti-Chávez forces or any anti-Venezuela scheme. In general, Latin American governments have established nonideological relationships with Caracas, seeking access to its foreign exchange, its markets, and its energy resources. While the United States may see radical populism as the new communism, most of the nations in the area consider poverty, inequality, and corruption the real enemies.

In this context, the United States is more isolated than Venezuela; it does not find any takers for a coercive diplomacy against Venezuela. Chávez, meanwhile, continues to reinforce his regional influence with active energy diplomacy. This leads to a worrisome corollary: while Chávez seeks more international influence without being deferential to the immense power of the United States, the U.S. administration shows signs of increased exasperation and possibly aggressive inclinations. Furthermore, as Washington becomes more frustrated, Caracas assumes a haughtier tone. In this scenario, a future collision between the United States and Venezuela becomes more likely. A new concerted diplomacy—with a decisive role for Washington, the active participation of the leading countries of Latin America, and a supplemental role for China—could help avert a crisis between the United States and Venezuela.

Substantive Security Issues: Latin America

The Latin American countries are well aware of the importance of the sensitive security issues that China and the United States face with respect to the region. But there are wide-ranging problems that impact the day-to-day lives of the people of Latin America. In this regard, several of China's policies on substantive security issues are essential for the region. These substantive security issues include weak states and insecurity in terms of human rights violations, destruction of infrastructure, and institutional collapse; the illicit drug trade; organized crime; small arms trade and violence; the environment; and corruption.

Haiti is the archetype of what the United States calls a failed state and what China calls an area of instability.[66] The case of Haiti has garnered diplomatic agreement among Latin America, the United States, and China, and nine Latin American countries plus the United States and China have deployed forces in Haiti as part of the United Nations mission.[67] However, the problems inherent in weak states cannot be overcome through humanitarian missions. Getting back on track with the debate on economic development as applied to the specific cases of such weak states is crucial. If China continues to claim that it shares the concerns of the periphery, it should take up anew the cause of development, which faded somewhat in the post–cold war context and almost completely evaporated in the aftermath of 9/11.

Regarding the question of illicit drugs, while the Chinese economy is not dominated by drug trafficking (though the influence of drug trafficking is enormous in the economies of the cities of Macau, Fujian, and Dalian), several factors make China vulnerable.[68] These include the increase in internal drug consumption (not only of opiates but also of marijuana, ecstasy, and amphetamines); the boom in heroin production in Central Asia (displacing, in part, Southeast Asia); the use of China as a transit route; the expansion of the Chinese gangs in partnership with gangs from Colombia, Australia, and Burma, among others; and rising domestic crime tied to the drug business. If China becomes part of the demand for narcotics—as has been the case for the United States, which then spread to Europe and Russia—then the difficulties that Latin America already faces is this area will likely be exacerbated.

Recent years have witnessed a proliferation of links among criminal groups of various national origins, including the transnational deployment of criminal networks and strategic alliances in the management of illegal businesses. Chinese mafias (such as Fuk Ching, Flying Dragons, and Tai Chen) have been detected in the triborder area of Argentina, Brazil, and Paraguay associated with several forms of contraband.[69] In other parts of Latin America, such as Mexico and Central America, Chinese criminal groups have used the area as a springboard for human trafficking to the United States.[70] In the case of South America, the issue is more complex and delicate because Washington believes extreme Islamic terrorist sleeper cells are located there. Although there are no concrete indications of terrorist activity there, since 2006 the three triborder countries, at Brazil's initiative, have shared a regional intelligence center for monitoring criminal activities in the area, a program that was well received by the United States. China should join the initiative by providing relevant information; not only would it be in its interest to do so, but also it would foster closer ties between Beijing and Asunción, which could further the PRC's one-China policy objectives.

On the issue of small arms and violence, the World Health Organization states that the number of homicides perpetrated with small arms in Latin America ranges between 73,000 and 90,000 a year, three times the world average.[71] According to the same data, violence has become the leading cause of death for people between the ages of fifteen and forty-four. Furthermore, the small arms industry covers a $4 billion legal market and an illegal market of approximately $1 billion.[72] While the United States is the leading exporter of small arms and has shown little inclination to reduce its exports, China's export figures are not made available to the public, nor does China wish to take part in the international codes and regimes that govern small arms sales.[73] Washington's and Beijing's stances are lethal for Latin America, as the region suffers the tragic consequences of this lucrative business.

A fifth substantive security issue is the environment. Based on its own internal experience, China does not identify environmental issues as a significant component of its international agenda. Examples such as the Chinese-owned Shougang Hierro Peru mine and the deaths of local miners due to unsafe conditions are telling in terms of China's scant sensitivity to environmental considerations.[74] Although it is possible that a new generation of Chinese leaders will show more interest in this matter, the political leaders in Latin America must also strengthen their own environmental controls over foreign investment in general and Chinese investments in particular.[75] China's formidable appetite for energy resources, with the often negative consequences of their extraction methods, is a serious problem for Latin America in terms of environmental costs.

Finally, corruption continues to be a major issue in Latin America. Although not apparently a security problem, the consequences of corruption in terms of insecurity and lack of citizen protection are enormous. Corruption undermines the operation of the judicial apparatus, weakens the development of democracy, compromises the efficiency of civilian institutions, corrodes the security forces, deepens social inequality, further ingrains patron-client political behavior, and offers extraordinary power to established groups. Corruption is also rampant in China, a confluence with serious consequences for Latin America in terms of both Chinese investment in Latin America and Latin American investment in China.[76]

These security issues, which unquestionably affect the geopolitical dynamics of the Sino–Latin America–U.S. triangle, call for action in several areas. The conditions necessary to address these issues in Latin America and China include the following: effective prevention rather than indiscriminate repression, active collaboration rather than individually turning inward, firm public policies rather than states coopted by privileged interests, internal and external social consensus rather than aggressive imposition from outside, and genuine political will rather than opportunistic leadership.

Conclusion

This chapter examines the geopolitical factors that shape the asymmetrical triangle formed by China, Latin America, and the United States. Overall, Washington seems excessively wary of China's presence in Latin America while simultaneously neglecting its southern neighbors. Furthermore, the United States has shown little interest in Latin America's perspective on China's growing presence in the Western Hemisphere.[77] Fortunately, however, the Sino–Latin American–U.S. triangular relationship has not engendered major tensions or unmanageable challenges. Thus top officials in Washington as well as in Beijing and Latin America have ample opportunity to pursue more comprehensive trilateral cooperation initiatives, particularly as it becomes increasingly clear that China's closer ties with Latin America have not come at the expense of U.S. security and economic interests in the region.

China remains on an ascendant course and will continue on that path for the foreseeable future. Washington's erratic and equivocal policy stance toward Latin America is likely to continue as well. Therefore, Beijing's strategy toward the region combines both necessity and opportunity. There is no indication that China's intention is to challenge the United States in the Western Hemisphere; in fact, as explained in chapters 2 and 3, the Chinese government has actively sought to convince the United States and the rest of the world that its intentions are benign, thus the self-portrayal of a peaceful rise. China's behavior in Latin America at the outset of the twenty-first century has been far from that of a revisionist power.[78] Beijing's strategy has been to proceed cautiously and diligently, curtailing the likelihood that the region will develop or adopt a policy aimed at rolling back China's presence. Limitations on China's penetration into Latin America will likely come from internal political, social, and economic conditions in China rather than from external barriers imposed on the PRC by the region. It would be an unfortunate mistake if Washington pursued a geopolitical strategy that would force Latin America to choose between the United States and China. The last thing the region needs is a new zero-sum game—history has shown that in such scenarios the losses usually outweigh the gains and that fragmentation tends to win over integration.

As this chapter illustrates, the Sino–Latin American–U.S. triangular relationship is characterized by a complex and unique division of interests. For the United States the threats and challenges coming from the wider Caribbean Basin (Mexico, Central America, the Caribbean islands, Colombia, and Venezuela) are considered the most important with regard to its national security. For China, Taiwan's future and securing energy resources are the central security questions pertaining to the region. Therefore, it will be necessary to pay close attention to events and initiatives in those areas.

Two central conclusions can be drawn from the analysis dividing the geopolitical dynamics of the triangle into sensitive and substantive security issues. First, the sensitive issues of most concern to China and the United States, which could have a negative impact on their bilateral relations, are not necessarily conducive to conflict. Some issues may require mutual accommodation (such as the Taiwan issue and energy security), while others may require subtle mechanisms of consultation (the cases of Cuba and Venezuela, for example). And there are other areas neither problematic (such as the case of Colombia and the issue of the Panama Canal) nor real (for example, China's military presence in the region). Obviously, Latin America cannot play a passive role in these matters, as there are clear interests at stake in the countries of the region. Latin America should, at the very least, pursue ad hoc forms of trilateral dialogue and monitoring.

Second, the substantive issues of most concern to Latin America, if they are to be resolved, require cooperative approaches. Such cooperation could involve all three parties, without individual costs and with shared benefits. Latin America should take the lead and propose specific ideas, alternatives, and policies to best ensure the security of the region's citizens. Addressing these substantive issues also reinforces the importance of preserving and deepening democracy in Latin America. China may offer some attractive foreign policy ideas, but its domestic policy is considered by most to be far from desirable.

In conclusion, China, Latin America, and the United States are well positioned to devise a viable, nonconfrontational, geopolitical strategy to manage the asymmetrical triangle. There is no doubt that such an approach would best satisfy Latin America's needs and ensure a more stable future in the context of the triangular relationship.

Notes

1. On the issue of China as a threat or an opportunity, see Denny Roy, "The 'China Threat' Issue: Major Arguments," *Asian Survey* 36, no. 8 (1996): 758–71; Peter Van Ness, "The Impasse in U.S. Policy Toward China," *China Journal* 38 (July 1997): 139–50; and Robert R. Ross, "Assessing the China Threat," *National Interest*, no. 81 (Fall 2005): 81–87. On the issue of China as a revisionist or conservative power and its intentions beyond Asia, see John J. Mearsheimer, "China's Unpeaceful Rise," *Current History* 105, no. 690 (April 2006): 160–62; Michael D. Swaine and Ashley J. Tellis,

Interpreting China's Grand Strategy: Past, Present, and Future (Santa Monica: Rand, 2000); Guoli Liu, ed., *Chinese Foreign Policy in Transition* (New York: Aldine de Gruyter, 2004); Yong Deng and Fei-ling Wang, eds., *China Rising: Power and Motivation in Chinese Foreign Policy* (New York: Rowman and Littlefield, 2005); Avery Goldstein, *Rising to the Challenge: China's Grand Strategy and International Security* (Stanford University Press, 2005); and David Shambaugh, ed., *Power Shift: China and Asia's New Dynamics* (University of California Press, 2005). One should also note that the United States is viewed and analyzed by China with a certain degree of suspicion. See, for example, Phillip C. Saunders, "China's America Watchers: Changing Attitudes toward the United States," *China Quarterly,* no. 161 (March 2000): 41–65; and Rosalie Chen, "China Perceives America: Perspectives of International Relations Experts," *Journal of Contemporary China* 12, no. 35 (May 2003): 285–97.

2. On Chinese–Latin American relations from the 1950s to the early 1970s, see Cecil Johnson, *Communist China and Latin America, 1959–1967* (Columbia University Press, 1970); Marisela Connelly and Romer Cornejo Bustamante, *China-América Latina: Génesis y desarrollo de sus relaciones* (El Colegio de México, 1992); Robert L. Worden, "China's Balancing Act: Cancun, the Third World, Latin America," *Asian Survey* 23, no. 5 (1983): 619–36; Frank Mora, "The People's Republic of China and Latin America: From Indifference to Engagement," *Asian Affairs: An American Review* 24 (March 1997): 35–58; and Xu Schicheng, "Las diferentes etapas de las relaciones sino-latinoamericanas," *Nueva Sociedad,* no. 203 (May–June 2006): 102–13.

3. It should be noted that the adoption of a pro–status quo type of conduct by China does not mean that there are not areas of competition between Beijing and Washington or that the Chinese strategy toward Latin America does not contain elements that give rise to specific divergences between the region and Beijing. Similarly, to say that China does not behave at present like a revisionist power is not tantamount to asserting that Beijing is fully satisfied (the Taiwan question is a clear example of that) or secure (due mainly to its persistent internal weaknesses). What seems clear is that it would be very costly for China to engage in defiant and risky conduct regionally and internationally. Accordingly, it is fundamental for Latin America that China continues to be integrated into the international system, to strengthen its ties of positive interdependence with the region, and to contribute to global peace and security. On more recent Chinese–Latin American relations, see Stephanie Reiss, "La diplomacia del dragón. La diplomacia de China Popular con respecto a América Latina desde 1989," *Desarrollo y Cooperación,* no. 1 (2001): 26–29; François Lafargue, "China's Strategies in Latin America," *Military Review* 86, no. 3 (2006): 80–84; Jorge I. Dominguez, "China's Relations with Latin America: Shared Gains, Asymmetric Hopes," working paper (Washington: Inter-American Dialogue, 2006); Florencia Jubany and Daniel Poon, "Recent Chinese Engagement in Latin America and the Caribbean: A Canadian Perspective," research report (Ottawa: FOCAL, 2006); Guillermo R. Delamer and others, "Chinese Interests in Latin America," in *Latin American Security Challenges,* edited by Paul D. Taylor (Newport: Naval War College, 2004); June Teufel Dreyer, "From China with Love: P.R.C. Overtures in Latin America," *Brown*

Journal of World Affairs 12, no. 2 (2006): 85–102; Martín Pérez Le-Fort, "China y América Latina: Estrategias bajo una hegemonía transitoria," *Nueva Sociedad*, no. 203 (May–June 2006): 89–101; Zhang Xinsheng, "Los cambios de Latinoamérica y las relaciones entre China y Latinoamérica," *Foreign Affairs en Español* 6, no. 2 (2006; www. foreignaffairs-esp.org/20060401faenespessay060222/zhang-xinsheng/los-cambios-de-latinoamerica-y-las-relaciones-entre-china-y-latinoamerica.html [December 2007]); and Sergio Cesarín and Carlos Moneta, eds., *China y América Latina: Nuevos enfoques sobre cooperación y desarrollo. ¿Una segunda ruta de la seda?* (Buenos Aires: INTAL, 2005).

4. As Tsebelis argues, "In order to change policies a certain number of individual or collective actors have to agree to a proposed change. I call such actors veto players." George Tsebelis, *Veto Players: How Political Institutions Work* (Princeton University Press, 2002), p. 2. It should be mentioned that in the white papers on defense in the South American countries, and on the web pages of the ministries of defense of Latin America, China is not identified as a threat to the national security of the various countries of the region. In addition, according to a survey done by the BBC in 2004, public opinion in Latin America considered China's influence in the world to be positive. See "22-Nation Poll Shows China Viewed Positively by Most Countries Including Its Asian Neighbors" (www.globescan.com/news_archives/bbcpoll3.html [December 2007]). Even more interesting is the fact that another survey done in Mexico in 2004 found that "surprisingly, Mexicans are more likely to have favorable feelings toward China than toward Brazil." See Guadalupe González, Susan Minushkin, and Robert Y. Shapiro, eds., *Global Views 2004: Mexican Public Opinion and Foreign Policy* (Mexico City: CIDE, 2004), p. 31. At the same time, the deterioration of the U.S. image in Latin America is alarming. See Lisa Haugaard, *Tarnished Image: Latin America Perceives the United States* (Washington: Latin America Working Group, 2006). This is different from what is happening in the United States, where in a temporary compromise among the different pro- and anti-China actors (business lobby/defense lobby, hard-liners/soft-liners, neoconservatives/liberals, adversarial internationalists/conciliatory globalists), Washington combines a strategy of engagement and hedging.

5. Hepple uses the image of an apocalyptic geopolitics when analyzing the U.S. perception of the projection of the Soviet Union in Latin America during the cold war. See Leslie W. Hepple, "South American Heartland: The Charcas, Latin American Geopolitics and Global Strategies," *Geographical Journal* 170, no. 4 (2004): 359–67.

6. Brantly Womack, *China and Vietnam: The Politics of Asymmetry* (Cambridge University Press, 2006), p. 17.

7. China has not so much emerged as a new power as it has simply reappeared on the international stage with renewed power and influence. It has had historical moments when it weighed heavily on the world scene, but it has also experienced lengthy periods of turning inward, derived from internal and external factors. Gradually overcoming this subordinate condition requires a major effort on the part of a country that has been dominated, a sustained and consistent effort that demands that it minimize external restrictions and maximize internal strengths. For weaker actors

to offset the imbalance in international power, certain internal conditions must be in place: resource mobilization, political will, strategic clarity, and institutional capacity.

8. On Chinese soft power, see Bates Gill and Yanzhong Huang, "Source and Limits of Chinese Soft Power," *Survival* 48, no. 2 (2006): 17–36; and Joshua Kurlantzick, *China's Charm: Implications of Chinese Soft Power,* Policy Brief 47 (Washington: Carnegie Endowment, 2006). On the U.S. overreaction to Chinese power, see Emma V. Broomfield, "Perceptions of Danger: The China Threat Theory," *Journal of Contemporary China* 12, no. 35 (May 2003): 265–84; and Chengxin Pan, "The 'China Threat' in American Self-Imagination: The Discursive Construction of Other as Power Politics," *Alternatives: Global, Local, Political* 29, no. 3 (2004): 305–31.

9. What I have called the frustrated superpower syndrome has emerged in U.S.–Latin American relations. The syndrome can be observed in this familiar pattern: a group of countries or a region is deemed irrelevant by a major power because it is considered safe or nonthreatening. The region may also be considered unimportant due to cultural bias or because of its negligible material significance. Thus the area receives only intermittent attention. In Latin America's case, Washington does not perceive the region in a categorically negative way; it is not viewed as an enemy but as a dependent counterpart. The bureaucratic politics around low-value areas are largely a rerun of past scenarios. Occasionally, the hope of a breakthrough raises expectations that the region will somehow be transformed. But disappointment ensues. Time and again, the same time-tested, largely ineffective strategy is employed and the outcome is identical: no major achievements, no great transformation. Then frustration sets in. In the end, the superpower really has no intention of rethinking its relations with that region. A new cycle begins and a larger frustration looms just over the horizon. Juan Gabriel Tokatlian, "America Should Look More Often in Its Own Backyard," *Financial Times*, March 9, 2006, p. 13.

10. Womack, *China and Vietnam*, p. 89.

11. Lowell Dittmer, "The Sino-Japanese-Russian Triangle," *Journal of Chinese Political Science* 10, no. 1 (2005): 1–21, quotation on p. 1.

12. Nor is it feasible to conceive of this triangular relationship as resulting in an arrangement of Sino-U.S. codomination with respect to Latin America. It is unlikely that Washington would accept such a decisive role for China in the region, that Beijing would have the capacity and the interest to project itself so actively in the area, or that the leading Latin American countries would renounce their respective aspirations for autonomy and accept a passive role in the face of the establishment of a Sino-U.S. axis to manage Latin America's most important affairs.

13. As Stein notes, "Nations choose to cooperate when it is in their interest to do so, and it is the concatenation of forces of circumstance that shapes international affairs." Arthur A. Stein, *Why Nations Cooperate: Circumstance and Choice in International Relations* (Cornell University Press, 1990), p. 207.

14. Primacy, by definition, entails designing and implementing an aggressive foreign and defense policy. The logic of preserving supremacy at any cost leads one to be tempted to use force recurrently and vehemently. This can lead, in turn, to an arbitrary

use of military might, ignoring the conditions of legitimacy and legality required in international relations when one has recourse to military action. In addition, the policy of primacy entails huge defense budgets for years, which may generate an unexpected imbalance in civilian-military relations. Finally, the absolute preeminence of a single power is not inevitably the guarantee of less instability and insecurity in the global system nor an assurance of less vulnerability for the most powerful actor. For more on the U.S. policy of primacy, see Barry R. Posen and Andrew L. Ross, "Competing Visions for U.S. Grand Strategy," *International Security* 23, no. 3 (1996–97): 5–53; and Stephen M. Walt, *Taming American Power: The Global Response to U.S. Primacy* (New York: W. W. Norton, 2005).

15. Eric A. Nordingler, *Isolationism Reconfigured: American Foreign Policy for a New Century* (Princeton University Press, 1995), p. 37. See also Thomas S. Szayna and others, *The Emergence of Peer Competitors: A Framework for Analysis* (Santa Monica: Rand, 2001).

16. Nonetheless, from a Latin American point of view, and taking as a point of reference the international system as a whole, one cannot deny that the region is of relative importance. This recognition is based on the concrete fact that Latin America is a genuine environmental power in terms of biodiversity; it has major energy, water, and natural resource reserves; it has a dual projection, toward the Atlantic and the Pacific; it is mostly democratic; it has been advancing significantly in the protection and defense of human rights; the proliferation of weapons of mass destruction is absent; it has made key contributions to international law in terms of peaceful coexistence among nations; it has in general a moderate diplomatic profile; it has not been fertile ground for fratricidal wars; and it is culturally rich and developed. In short, Latin America, despite the enormous social, economic, and political difficulties it faces, contributes decisively to international peace and security.

17. Christopher Layne, *The Peace of Illusions: American Grand Strategy from 1940 to the Present* (Cornell University Press, 2006), p. 22.

18. Quotation in C. Dale Walton, "Beyond China: The Geopolitics of Eastern Eurasia," *Comparative Strategy* 21, no. 3 (2002): 203–12, quotation on p. 208.

19. In this context—at least based on the region's historical experience—Erikson's assertion that China could become "a conventional regional rival to the United States in the Western Hemisphere" seems exaggerated. Daniel P. Erikson, "A Dragon in the Andes? China, Venezuela, and U.S. Energy Security," *Military Review* 86, no. 4 (2006): 83–89, quotation on p. 89. This does not mean that all of Beijing's policies toward Latin America are benign, merely that it is not advisable to magnify the scope of the supposed Chinese challenge in the Americas. The fear on the part of the United States of China's presence in Latin America is more a reflection of recurrent fears and omnipotent impulses than of a moderate, lucid, and practical consideration.

20. For more on the U.S. defense perimeter, see John A. Cope, "A Prescription for Protecting the Southern Approach," *Joint Force Quarterly*, Inside Issue 42 (2006): 17–21.

21. At the same time U.S. foreign policy in recent years has had increasingly negative reception abroad. For an analysis on mounting anti-U.S. sentiment internationally,

see Julia E. Sweig, *Friendly Fire: Losing Friends and Making Enemies in the Anti-American Century* (New York: Public Affairs, 2006).

22. One sensitive and substantial security issue is nonproliferation of nuclear power for military purposes. This issue does not appear to have an explicit place in the tripartite agenda between Latin America, China, and the United States. However, it would be essential for the three parties to make a joint commitment to keeping Latin America and the Caribbean a nuclear-free zone.

23. See www.bilaterals.org (September 2007).

24. Four of the countries of the area—El Salvador, Honduras, Nicaragua, and the Dominican Republic—accompanied militarily (Costa Rica, in Central America, and Colombia, in South America, did so politically) the "coalition of the willing" organized by the United States to invade Iraq in 2003. One will have to note in the future whether that military experience, together with the close economic ties that would stem from the free trade agreement between the United States and Central America plus the Dominican Republic (CAFTA), lead to changes in the direction of a more intense and intimate relationship on security issues. On this possibility, see Michael J. Dempsey and Geoffrey D. Keillor, "Latin American Coalition Support: Lessons Learned in Iraq," *Military Review* 86, no. 2 (2006): 71–75.

25. See "Presidente taiwanés visita Paraguay," (http://news.bbc.co.uk/hi/spanish/misc/newsid_4979000/4979448.stm [December 2007]). On recent U.S.-Paraguayan military relations, see Juan Gabriel Tokatlian, "Internacional la presencia militar de Estados Unidos en Paraguay: ¿Un giro geopolítico decisivo?" *Debate*, no. 132 (December 2005; www.udesa.edu.ar/files/ img/Humanidades/230905toka.htm [December 2007]).

26. W. Bruce Weinrod, "U.S. and European Approaches to China," *Mediterranean Quarterly* 17, no. 2 (2006): 17–21.

27. T. S. Gopi Rethinaraj, "China's Energy and Regional Security Perspectives," *Defense & Security Analysis* 19, no. 4 (2003): 377–388, quotation on p. 387.

28. The usual criticism in some circles in the United States to the effect that China has no scruples about associating with "pariah" countries that produce hydrocarbons is correct but not so unusual. For each "indecorous" partner of China in the Middle East, Asia, Africa, or Latin America in relation to oil, one can identify one (or more) "unpresentable" partners of the United States in that same business. Indeed, unfortunately, the history of oil and gas operations in developing countries and how they have been run by developed countries is a very bloody and predatory history in which the value of democracy has traditionally been marginal and rhetorical.

29. Bo Kong, *An Anatomy of China's Energy Insecurity and Its Strategies* (Washington: Pacific Northwest National Laboratory/U.S. Department of Energy, 2005), p. 62. See also Chietigj Bajpaee, "Chinese Energy Strategy in Latin America," China brief (Washington: Jamestown Foundation, 2005); Charles E. Ziegler, "The Energy Factor in China's Foreign Policy," *Journal of Chinese Political Science* 11, no. 1 (2006): 1–23; and Wenran Jiang, "China and India Come to Latin America for Energy," in *Energy Cooperation in the Western Hemisphere: Benefits and Impediments,* edited by Sidney Weintraub, Annette Hester, and Veronica R. Prado (Washington: CSIS, 2007).

30. The experiences of the Middle East and Central Asia are eloquent: the combination of oil diplomacy and realpolitik in contexts of domestic institutional fragility and fierce social struggle has been and is lethal for both regions. Any policies formulated should include—and not exclude—complex cases such as Venezuela.

31. General Bantz J. Craddock, United States Army Commander, United States Southern Command, posture statement before the 109th Congress, House Armed Services Committee, March 9, 2005 (www.ciponline.org/colombia/050309crad.pdf [December 2007]).

32. Dreyer, "From China with Love," p. 91.

33. Bill Gertz, "Chinese Military Trains in West; Fills the Hole Left by U.S. Limits," *Washington Times*, March 15, 2006, p. 1.

34. Kelly Hearn, "China's 'Peaceful' Invasion: Latin America Attractive as Market for Arms Sales," *Washington Times*, November 20, 2005, p. 1.

35. On Wilhelm's visits to the region, see Brian Loveman, "Introduction: U.S. Regional Security Policies in the Post–Cold War Era," in *Strategy for Empire: U.S. Regional Security Policy in the Post–Cold War Era*, edited by Brian Loveman (Lanham, Md.: Scholarly Resources Books, 2004). On Hill's visits to the region, see Adam Isacson, Joy Olson, and Lisa Haugaard, *Blurring the Lines: Trends in U.S. Military Programs with Latin America* (Washington: LAWGEF/CIP/WOLA, 2004).

36. Dana Priest, *The Mission: Waging War and Keeping Peace with America's Military* (New York: W. W. Norton, 2003).

37. The number of U.S. bases abroad climbed from 702 in 2003 to 770 in 2005. Department of Defense, *Base Structure Report* (Washington: U.S. Government Printing Office, 2005).

38. The cooperative security locations are thought to have been developed mostly in Africa and Latin America; they are intended to become "focal points for combined training with host nations and other allies and partners, and they will have the capacity to expand and contract on the basis of operational needs." Ryan Henry, "Transforming the U.S. Global Defense Posture," in *Reposturing the Force: U.S. Overseas Presence in the Twenty-first Century*, edited by Carnes Lord (Newport, Va.: Naval War College Press, 2006), p. 47.

39. Center for International Policy, *Just the Facts: A Civilian's Guide to U.S. Defense and Security Assistance to Latin America and the Caribbean* (Washington, 2006; http://ciponline.org/facts/ [December 2007]).

40. All currency amounts are in U.S. dollars unless otherwise noted. See Isacson, Olson, and Haugaard, *Blurring the Lines;* and Center for International Policy, "DCS: Direct Commercial Sales," in *Just the Facts.*

41. Center for International Policy, "U.S. Security Assistance to the Western Hemisphere, by Program," in *Just the Facts.* Regarding excess defense articles: under section 516 of the Foreign Assistance Act of 1961 (P.L. 87-195, or FAA), as amended, the U.S. government has the authority to transfer surplus military equipment to foreign security forces. Defense articles no longer needed by the U.S. armed forces and eligible for transfer range from rations and uniforms to used vehicles, cargo aircraft, and ships.

According to the State Department, excess defense articles (EDA) "are transferred in an 'as is, where is' condition to the recipient . . . with the recipient responsible for any required refurbishment and repair of the items as well as any associated transportation costs."

42. In fact, the interest, influence, and impact of the Southern Command in the region—especially in contrast to the civilian apparatus of the State Department—is such that one can speak of the U.S. Southern Command as a proconsul of the United States for the area.

43. M. K. Bhadrakumar, "Venezuela, Russia: Comrades in Arms," *Asia Times Online,* August 2, 2006 (www.atimes.com/atimes/Central_Asia/HH02Ag01.html [December 2007); and Jeremy Wolland, "Venezuela, Russia Sign Weapons Deal," *Arms Control Today* (www.armscontrol.org/act/2006_09/venrussia.asp [December 2007]).

44. Fabián Calle, "Armamentismo en Sudamérica: ¿Salto tecnológico o desequilibrio?" *DEF Magazine,* no. 8 (April 2006; www.defdigital.com.ar/2006/08-numero/nota _tapa.htm [December 2007]).

45. Alfred Schandlbauer, "The Declining Strategic Relevance of the Panama Canal," monograph (Inter-American Defense College, 2004).

46. The amendment states that "the United States has the responsibility to assure that the Panama Canal will remain open and secure to ships of all nations. The correct interpretation of this principle is that each of the two countries shall, in accordance with their respective constitutional processes, defend the Canal against any threat to the regime of neutrality, and consequently shall have the right to act against any aggression or threat directed against the Canal or against the peaceful transit of vessels through the Canal." Mark P. Sullivan, "Panama: Political and Economic Conditions and U.S. Relations" (Washington: Congressional Research Service, 2006; http:// fpc.state.gov/documents/organization/77706.pdf [December 2007]).

47. On the Chinese company, see www.hutchison-whampoa.com (December 2007).

48. Demetrio Olaciregui, "Nuevo valor estratégico del Canal," *Artículos de Opinión, Plan Maestro, Autoridad del Canal de Panamá,* October 28, 2005 (www.pancanal.com/ esp/plan/opiniones/2005/10/28/pr55.html [December 2007]).

49. Ari Berman, "Payments for Perle," *Nation,* August 18, 2003 (www.thenation. com/doc/20030818/berman [December 2007]).

50. J. F. Hornbeck, "The Proposed U.S.-Panama Free Trade Agreement" (Washington: Congressional Research Service, 2007; http://fpc.state.gov/documents/ organization/89921.pdf [December 2007]).

51. A relatively positive balance of Plan Colombia can be found in Connie Veillette, "Plan Colombia: A Progress Report" (Washington: Congressional Research Service, 2005; www.fas.org/sgp/crs/row/RL32774.pdf [December 2007]).

52. Andrew Feickert, "U.S. Military Operations in the Global War on Terrorism: Afghanistan, Africa, the Philippines, and Colombia" (Washington: Congressional Research Service, 2005; www.fas.org/man/crs/RL32758.pdf [December 2007]); and Andrew Feickert, "U.S. Special Operations Forces (SOF): Background and Issues for

Congress" (Washington: Congressional Research Service, 2004; www.globalsecurity. org/military/library/report/crs/rs21048-3.pdf [December 2007]).

53. The figures on U.S. assistance to Colombia (83 percent of which is police and military aid) are available at the Center for International Policy, "U.S. Aid to Colombia since 1997: Summary Tables" (www.ciponline.org/colombia/aidtable.htm [December 2007]).

54. As indicated by Jubany and Poon, "China has not pursued relations with Colombia aggressively, suggesting attentiveness to the strong security and aid ties linking Colombia and Washington." Jubany and Poon, "Recent Chinese Engagement in Latin America and the Caribbean," p. 28.

55. Office of the Presidency of Colombia, "China y Colombia relanzan relaciones diplomáticas y comerciales," Casa de Nariño Presidencia de la República de Colombia, September 8, 2006 (www.presidencia.gov.co/sne/2005/abril/06/05062005.htm [December 2007]).

56. Jiang Shixue, "Cuba's Economic Reforms in Chinese Perspective," Working Paper 3 (Beijing: Institute of Latin American Studies, Chinese Academy of Social Sciences, 2002).

57. Manfred Wilhelmy von Wolf and Augusto Soto, "El proceso de reformas en China y la política exterior," in *China y América Latina: Nuevos enfoques sobre cooperación y desarrollo—una segunda ruta de la seda,* edited by Sergio M. Cesarín and Carlos Moneta (Buenos Aires: BID-INTAL, 2005), p. 50.

58. While there have been repeated rumors of bilateral contacts in the field of intelligence, there does not appear to be evidence of a Chinese military deployment in Cuba nor of the sale of sensitive security-related technology or supplies of sophisticated conventional weaponry by Beijing to Havana. It is unlikely that there would be a new Cuban missile crisis now between the United States and China like the one in 1962 between Washington and Moscow. Dominguez, "China's Relations with Latin America."

59. William Ratliff, "Mirroring Taiwan: China and Cuba," China brief (Washington: Jamestown Foundation, 2006; www.jamestown.org/images/pdf/cb_006_010.pdf [December 2007]).

60. Daniel Erikson, "Cuba, China, Venezuela: New Developments," *Cuba in Transition* 15 (2005): 410–18; Gabe Collins and Carlos Ramos-Mrosovsky, "Beijing's Bolivarian Venture," *National Interest,* no. 85 (September–October 2006): 88–92; and George Gedda, "U.S. Orders Ban of Arms Sales to Venezuela," May 15, 2006 (www.globalsecurity.org/org/news/2006/060515-venezuela-arms.htm [December 2007]).

61. U.S. Government Accountability Office, *Energy Security: Issues Related to Potential Reductions in Venezuelan Oil Production* (Washington: U.S. Government Printing Office, 2006).

62. Andy Webb-Vidal, "Venezuelan Bankers Get Rich from Chavez's Revolution," *Financial Times,* August 17, 2006, p. 7 (www.ft.com/cms/s/308b81da-2d42-11db-851d-0000779e2340.html [December 2007]); and Simon Romero, "For Venezuela, as Distrust for U.S. Grows, So Does Trade," *New York Times,* August 16, 2006, p. A3 (www.nytimes.com/2006/08/16/world/americas/16venezuela.htm [December 2007]).

63. William Ratliff, "Pragmatism over Ideology: China's Relations with Venezuela," China brief (Washington: James Foundation, 2006; www.jamestown.org/images/pdf/cb_006_006.pdf [December 2007]), pp. 3–5.

64. The experience of Salvador Allende in Chile was a reformist path to socialism that did not try to export itself to the neighboring countries but was nonetheless ferociously interrupted by a coup d'état in 1973. Bolivia's revolutionary experience of the 1950s, which did not seek to spread beyond its borders, also ended in a coup d'état in 1964.

65. For more on Chávez's Bolivarian Revolution, see Harold A. Trinkunas, "Defining Venezuela's Bolivarian Revolution," *Military Review* 85, no. 4 (2005): 39–44.

66. Banning Garrett and Jonathan Adams, "U.S.-China Cooperation on the Problem of Failing States and Transnational Threats," Special Report 126 (Washington: United States Institute of Peace, 2004; www.usip.org/pubs/specialreports/sr126.html [December 2007]).

67. For more information on the UN Mission to Haiti, see www.un.org/depts/dpko/missions/minustah/ (December 2007).

68. Niklas Swanström, "Narcotics and China: An Old Security Threat from New Sources," *Central and Eurasia Forum Quarterly* 4, no. 1 (2006): 113–31.

69. Rex Hudson, "Terrorist and Organized Crime Groups in the Tri-Border Area (TBA) of South America" (Washington: Federal Research Division, Library of Congress, 2003; www.loc.gov/rr/frd/pdf-files/TerrOrgCrime_TBA.pdf [December 2007]).

70. Sheldon Zhang and Ko-lin Chin, "Characteristics of Chinese Human Smugglers," research brief (Washington: National Institute of Justice, 2004).

71. These figures from the World Health Organization are quoted and analyzed by Luis Esteban G. Manrique, "Un poder paralelo: El crimen organizado en América Latina," *ARI*, July 25, 2006 (Real Instituto Elcano de Estudios Internacionales y Estratégicos; www.realinstitutoelcano.org/analisis/1017/1017_gonzalez_manrique_violencia_america_latina.pdf [December 2007]). The effects of small arms on women and their strategies to reduce levels of violence locally should also be noted. See Emily Schroeder, Vanessa Farr, and Albrecht Schnabel, "Gender Awareness in Research on Small Arms and Light Weapons: A Preliminary Report," working paper (Bern: Swisspeace, 2005; www.iansa.org/women/documents/swisspeace-working-paper2005.pdf [December 2007]).

72. Rachel Stohl, "Fighting the Illicit Trafficking of Small Arms," *SAIS Review* 25, no. 1 (2005): 59–68.

73. Thomas Jackson and others, "Who Takes the Bullet? The Impact of Small Arms Violence," *Understanding the Issues*, no. 3 (2005; www.prio.no/files/file47012_who_takes_the_bullet_the_impact_of_small_arms_violence.pdf?phpsessid=bb2df7cd070a60537b6b4ca7b938b100 [December 2007]); Geneva Graduate Institute for International Studies, *Small Arms Survey 2006: Unfinished Business* (Oxford University Press, 2006); and Lerna K. Yanik, "Guns and Human Rights: Major Powers, Global Arms Transfers, and Human Rights Violations," *Human Rights Quarterly* 28, no. 2 (2006): 357–88.

74. Jubany and Poon, "Recent Chinese Engagement in Latin America and the Caribbean."

75. Willy Lam, "The Fifth Generation of the Communist Party," China brief (Washington: Jamestown Foundation, 2006; www.jamestown.org/print_friendly.php?volume_id=415&issue_id=3605&article_id=2370731 [December 2007]).

76. An Asian report published in 1994 states, "There are four basic kinds of society in Asia: the clean society, the reasonably clean society, the society where corruption is very much a part of life, and the society where corruption is a way of life.... The bulk of Asian countries are societies where corruption is an entrenched way of life." Commission for a New Asia, *Towards a New Asia* (Kuala Lumpur, 1994), p. 53.

77. This became evident when Thomas Shannon, the U.S. assistant secretary of state for Western Hemisphere affairs, visited China just days before President Hu Jintao's 2006 visit to the United States. The purpose of Shannon's trip to Beijing was to gain a better understanding of China's position vis-à-vis Latin America, yet he did not visit Latin America to learn about the other side's views. See Patrick Goodenough, "U.S., China to Discuss Competing Interests in Latin America," *CNS News*, April 10, 2006 (www.cnsnews.com/viewforeignbureaus.asp?page=/foreignbureaus/archive/200604/INT20060410a.html [December 2007]).

78. Indeed, we are not so much in the presence of a revisionist challenger in the international system as of a superpower—the United States—inclined to favor a hegemonic revisionism: it is Washington that seeks to reorganize the rules of the game in world affairs. See Robert Jervis, "The Remaking of a Unipolar World," *Washington Quarterly* 29, no. 3 (2006): 7–19. Steve Chan had already shown in 2004 that the United States, and not China, acted like a revisionist power. See Steve Chan, "Realism, Revisionism, and the Great Powers," *Issues & Studies* 40, no. 1 (2004): 135–72.

MONICA HIRST

5

A South-South Perspective

This chapter focuses on two interconnected dimensions of the China–South American relationship: South-South relations and multilateral diplomacy.[1] When the cold war ended, these two dimensions of the relationship between the People's Republic of China (PRC) and South America strengthened considerably, as China emerged on the international arena as a defender of a multipolar world order and as a key actor vis-à-vis the developing world (for an overview of China's foreign policy priorities during and after the cold war era, see chapter 2, by Jiang Shixue).

The visit by President Yang Shangkun in 1990 to several Latin American countries ushered in a new era of strengthened commercial, technological, and cultural ties with the Southern Cone and dialogue on peaceful coexistence and advocacy of South-South cooperation.[2] Since then a growing diplomatic dynamic, with increasingly frequent visits of high-level officials in both directions, intensified ties and interests on both sides. It is in this context that convergence between the foreign policies of the PRC and Brazil also took on special importance. This chapter includes a section on the importance of Sino-Brazilian relations, highlighting the areas in which bilateral ties have the greatest potential for increased cooperation.

South-South Cooperation, Intermediate States, and Multilateralism

The notion that the developing world should seek to deepen its cooperation agenda is not a recent proposition in the international community. Decolonization in the postwar period, the creation of the nonaligned movement, and the mobilization of intermediate and developing nations in the context of the United Nations—which led to the creation of the United Nations Conference on Trade and Development (UNCTAD) and the formation of the Group of Seventy-Seven (G-77)—are the main antecedents to this process. These earlier experiences of South-South cooperation showed that it was easier to implement cooperative experiences for economic issues than for security issues.

The G-77 was formed in 1964, during the first session of UNCTAD, with the aim of expanding coordination and solidarity among developing nations to establish a new international economic order and expand cooperation in the areas of trade and development.[3] A growing social and economic gap between the developing and developed world has led groups such as the G-77 to implement programs to assist the neediest countries. Although not a member, China uses the G-77 as a forum for projecting its South-South ideas, following the rationale set forth by the group that "South-South cooperation is not an option but an imperative to complement North-South cooperation in order to contribute to the achievement of the internationally agreed development goals, including the Millennium Development Goals."[4]

Beginning in 1991 a China–G-77 agenda was drawn up to encourage cooperation on environmental, economic, and social development issues.[5] In the Marrakech Declaration on South-South Cooperation, the countries of the G-77 stated their intent to "reaffirm the need to address the special concerns of the Least Developed Countries and call for the effective and timely implementation of the Brussels Program of Action for the decade 2001–10. In this regard, taking advantage of economic complementarities among developing countries, we resolve to promote initiatives in favor of LDCs in the context of South-South cooperation, including through, inter alia, triangular mechanisms to better benefit the LDCs."[6]

In a speech at the Thirtieth Annual Meeting of Foreign Ministers of the G-77 in 2006, Li Zhaoxing stated, "China will work with other developing countries to expand avenues of cooperation, create new models of cooperation within the framework of South-South cooperation, and explore a path of sustainable development. As China's economy continues to grow, China will, guided by the principles of sincerity, friendship, equality, mutual benefit, solidarity, cooperation, and common development, do more to help other developing countries to speed up development."[7] In this context, South-South economic initiatives geared toward supporting less developed countries have remained an area of common interest to both China and the intermediate South American states.

The end of the cold war and the expectations placed on multilateralism gave new impetus to interstate coalition building among developing countries.

It is likely that, in addition to the economic factors that drive the coordination of joint initiatives among developing nations, a new wave of politicization could also involve common international security goals. At the same time, South-South cooperation is increasingly characterized by international initiatives led by intermediate states.[8] What sets apart intermediate states is their capacity to react and adopt assertive positions when confronting economic, political, and security issues at the regional and global levels. Although the governments of these countries hope that multilateral institutions will yield a positive influence on the evolution of the international agenda, they act on the assumption that they play a significant role in the process of improving those institutions.

One sign of South-South politicization has been the activity of the G-20. More than twenty member states of the World Trade Organization (WTO), meeting in Cancún in 2003, saw a need to open a new round of global negotiations. Their main concerns have been to curb trade practices that distort the production and marketing of agricultural goods, improved market access, agricultural development, and food security.[9] While China joined the G-20 from the moment it was established, unlike Brazil and India it did not seek a leading role. To some analysts, China is more open to serving as a bridge between the industrialized and the developing nations than to strengthening South-South coalitions such as the G-20.[10] Others saw China as playing a role just as prominent as Brazil and India at Cancún.[11] In any event, the PRC's presence in the G-20 took on political significance because of its economic size and because it is the first coalition that China has joined since its entry into the WTO. China, along with Brazil, Argentina, and India, was part of the core group, ensuring the initiative's cohesion and continuity.

Although China and the South American countries agree on the importance of the South-South cooperation agenda, the Chinese authorities have responded cautiously to initiatives for collective politicization.[12] Whether it is a lack of experience dealing with global issues or its conservative political views, the PRC displays more interest in influencing than in leading the movements of the South on specific demands.

The BRIC and IBSA Groupings

In the context of different interstate arrangements, especially where economic expectations for the twenty-first century are involved, China and Brazil are part of a group of four emerging economic powers that have joined together in a single club: Brazil, Russia, India, and China, a grouping known as BRIC.[13] The economic expectations that led to the creation of this bloc are the central reason why China and Brazil share interests in select multilateral forums, reinforcing the idea that both are perceived by the North as significant players in the global economic agenda.[14] The BRIC countries share some important characteristics: the economic, political, and military traits of intermediate powers or of pivotal emerging markets; the ability and sense of entitlement to influence the international order at both the regional and global levels; and a basic internal cohesion that is conducive to effective state action.[15]

In the case of Brazil and India, participation in the BRIC group does not rule out other coalitions of emerging countries. That is the case with the IBSA (India-Brazil-South Africa) initiative, which involves South Africa and which has become a political and economic coalition that goes far beyond economic speculations. In 2003 India, Brazil, and South Africa signed the Declaration of Brasília, instituting IBSA, a trilateral forum for articulating interests and positions based on common interests. The initiative seeks to pursue five aspirations:

—To represent an affirmative voice of the emerging countries in the debate on globalization,

—To represent a counterpoint to the G-8, which would have even more potential were Russia and China to join,

—To emphasize the value of economic diplomacy as a tool for bringing countries together,

—To bolster the importance of development cooperation on the agendas for international negotiation,

—To bring pressure to bear as a voice of the South in the main multilateral forums (United Nations, International Monetary Fund, World Bank).[16]

The IBSA initiative is innovative insofar as it brings together developing countries that are regional powers. In addition to being a key example of South-South coalition building, it could have an impact in Asia, Africa, and South America. Brazil's active participation underscores the priorities of its current foreign policy. While it may appear confusing, the difference between the BRIC and IBSA approaches on economic issues becomes clear when one overlays variables of hard power and soft power. A clear distinction can be drawn between Brazil and South Africa and the rest of the BRIC countries with regard to international security—they have each chosen policies of nuclear nonproliferation that limit their coercive power in their respective regions. In fact, while China's aspirations as an emerging power may converge with those of South Africa and Brazil, they also present important constraints, since China supports certain premises in world politics criticized by the foreign policies of the latter two countries. This leads to the next section.

China and the United Nations

In recent years the Chinese government has become more interested in strengthening multilateral forums and has adopted a less defensive position about the idea that international institutions and regimes can promote peace and stability.[17] China's participation in UN-led peacekeeping operations is a relevant signal in this regard.[18] However, as an emerging global power China has sought to reconcile this increased involvement with the promotion of a multipolar world order that could more effectively protect its own interests than the strengthening, transforming, and democratizing of the multilateral institutions. This represents a major difference vis-à-vis the approach of other countries, such as India, South Africa, and the main South American states, all of which agree on the urgency of UN reform.

The Chinese government is increasingly more open to proposals for institutional reform and a redefinition of the mission of UN agencies geared toward economic and social issues. This is not the case, however, with regard to Security Council restructuring, a matter toward which China has been notoriously cautious. The dispute on restructuring the Security Council, which centers on whether to increase the number of members and adjust the modalities of rights (permanent or rotating) to voice and to veto power, led to the formation of several coalitions within the organization.[19] The intermediate states played a key role supporting reform, both in the North (countries such as Canada, Norway, and Sweden) and in the South (such as the IBSA bloc).

China, not surprisingly, kept a conservative stance and distanced itself from the reformist positions advocated by the Group of Four (Brazil, India, Germany, and Japan) and by IBSA. The importance of UN authority in international politics is a key factor for China's foreign policy. Beijing places a high value on preserving a hierarchical and discriminatory structure based on veto power in the Security Council and identifies more with an antireformist than with a democratizing position when it comes to membership in that body.[20] The differences between China and the intermediate states were exacerbated in 2005 when coinciding positions between Beijing and Washington were made public and China's cautious silence was replaced by an explicit political veto against any change in the Security Council's structure. Yet it must be underscored that, from the Chinese perspective, the goal was to prevent Japan's entry as a permanent member, not to vote against Brazil's or India's permanent membership.

China's cordial relationship with South America has other implications in the context of the United Nations. The comparative study by Jorge Dominguez of the voting patterns of the main Latin American countries and those of the PRC in the General Assembly reveals a disassociation between the commercial and political dimensions of this relationship.[21] Nonetheless, an analysis of votes suggests at least two interesting findings. In the General Assembly there are more points of convergence between China and South American countries than between these countries and the United States, but in the Security Council the region's convergence with Washington is often greater than that with Beijing.[22]

The PRC's participation in UN peacekeeping missions has been generating new common ground with South America, underscored by the positive results in the collaboration between the South American and Chinese forces in MINUSTAH (the United Nations Stabilization Mission operating in Haiti). This type of synergy helps explain Beijing's support for Venezuela's candidacy in 2006 for the rotating seat of the Group of Latin American and Caribbean Countries (GRULAC) on the Security Council. Venezuela was supported by the ABC countries (Argentina, Brazil, and Chile), the core South American countries responsible for the MINUSTAH. After several rounds of voting to choose between Venezuela and U.S.-backed Guatemala, all resulting in deadlock, Panama was selected as the compromise candidate. Though it is true that China's presence in Latin America is innocuous with respect to the regional security agenda—and thus, as argued in other chapters, it does not represent a threat to U.S. interests—the PRC does at times offer the possibility of acting as an extraregional ally in matters of international politics.

Another important issue regarding PRC–Latin American relations at the United Nations is China's opposition to Taiwan membership. As Juan Gabriel Tokatlian notes in chapter 4, this issue affects relations with the region because Taipei maintains strong diplomatic ties to Latin American countries in an effort to counter Beijing's policies intended to marginalize the island in international relations. The Taiwan question is generally approached through two different perspectives. First, as a zero-sum dynamic, advocated by the PRC since it became a permanent member of the Security Council in 1972. This view, in addition to treating Taiwan as a legacy of the cold war, is linked to the impact of democratization processes on South America's diplomatic options. As a result, some governments in the region chose to forge a close relationship with Taiwan and to distance themselves from the PRC. Second, Taiwan's fight for UN recognition can also be seen as an independent initiative. Rather than seeking to replace the PRC, Taiwan strives for recognition as a distinct sovereign state.[23] As mentioned in chapter 4, Taiwan's diplomatic efforts have focused on Central America and the Caribbean, areas with the greatest U.S. influence.[24]

All countries of South America, with the exception of Paraguay, have aligned with the Chinese government in opposing Taiwan's UN membership.[25] Nevertheless, Taiwan has established bilateral relationships in the region by opening representational offices in those countries to offset the lack of diplomatic recognition.[26] Argentina has been more sensitive to this issue as there are some parallels between the sovereignty problems China faces with Taiwan and those Argentina claims with the Falkland/Malvinas Islands. On the other hand, following what Taiwan calls "the policy of one-and-a-half," several South American countries maintain diplomatic relations with the PRC without giving up the possibility of retaining informal ties with Taiwan, basically on account of economic interests.

Multilateralism and Sino–South American Relations

What, then, is the connection between the economic and the political-diplomatic dimensions of the relationship between China and South America, in particular the ABC countries? There appear to be points of convergence on the new responsibilities associated with the "effective multilateralism" stance assumed by both China and the ABC bloc.[27] The Chinese government has adopted this stance with regard to its foreign policy priorities, as can be seen by its push to isolate Taiwan. In June 1996, for example, China opposed expanding the UN mission in Haiti, based on the support of the Haitian government for Taiwan's membership in the UN. This type of conditionality has been a constant concern for the authorities in charge of MINUSTAH. In 1997 the PRC opposed the proposal to send 155 peacekeepers to oversee the process of disarmament in Guatemala on the same grounds.

For South America (and particularly for the ABC bloc), the sensitive nature of the Taiwan issue also refers to relations between Paraguay and the Taipei government.[28] Ties with Taiwan weaken the central governments as they encourage illicit practices in the public sector. In the Paraguayan case Taiwan's economic influence has a detrimental impact on domestic governability, which affects indirectly the ongoing process of regional integration known as Mercosur. Ironically, the same local political leaders who support ties with Taiwan also advocate a closer relationship with the United States and question whether Paraguay should stay in Mercosur. In Haiti this influence runs up against the UN's reconstruction efforts, which include forces from the ABC countries and from the PRC.[29]

The PRC and the countries of South America share a value for a regionalist approach to foster economic growth and peaceful coexistence among states. This convergence is motivated by the need to offset the presence and potential influence of the United States. China's interest in Latin American regional initiatives also explains its status as an observer in the Rio Group and its practice of consulting with Mercosur, the Andean community, and the Latin American Integration Association (ALADI).[30] It is in this context that scientific and technological cooperation has made China's South-South agenda with various South American countries more concrete. These common interests are even more evident in China's relations with Brazil, as examined more closely in the next section of this chapter.

The Importance of China's Ties with Brazil

In recent years Brazil has placed a strong emphasis on pushing forward the South-South agenda. However, South-South cooperation could prove to be a costly initiative for Brazil, as it requires facing the consequences of collective action and assuming the costs of domestic politics controversies on foreign policy priorities.[31] While China recognizes Brazil as its most important strategic partner in South America, there are nuances in the bilateral relationship. A close connection exists between the expansion of economic ties and the convergence of the political interests of both sides.[32] Also, Brazil's relations with other Asian partners have been affected by China's growing presence in the region. In the 1970s, for example, Japan played an important trade and investment role in Brazil, but it has since been displaced in large part by the PRC.

The Sino-Brazilian relationship has been characterized by a degree of continuity and consistency for several decades.[33] Diplomatic relations were established in the 1970s, when Brazil was still under authoritarian rule, and the basis for the bilateral rapprochement was a shared policy approach to international trade and a pragmatic distancing from the bipolar international order. From the standpoint of Brazil's foreign policy, the move to normalizing relations with China was motivated by the acknowledgment of the importance of its role in international affairs once it became a permanent member of the UN Security Council. Brazil's position was explained by the Brazilian foreign minister in 1974: "On the multilateral level the normalization of relations would eliminate the politically delicate situation for Brazil of not having diplomatic relations with one of the five permanent members of the Security Council."[34]

Sino-Brazilian relations have thus far been based on the principle of nonintervention.[35] During the authoritarian period in Brazil, this principle was used to keep any ideological connotation out of the normalization of relations with China, as it was crucial for the Brazilian government to prevent contact between the PRC and Brazilian opposition groups that identified with the Chinese political system. Today the situation is similar, given the different political models of the two countries, but it is China that wishes to avoid any mention of domestic politics. Nonetheless, in this context, pragmatism and nonideological stances have opened the door for closer bilateral ties. The increasing strategic importance of foreign investment and economic growth for China's foreign interests makes it easier to identify common interests with Brazil, which was formally recognized by China as a strategic partner in 1994. To the sense of continuity in Sino-Brazilian relations one can add the fact that common ground exists between the two nations with regard to working together as poles of attraction in the global economy.

An overview of the evolution of formal political agreements in the last three decades leads to some interesting findings (table 5-1). First, the expansion of the bilateral agenda has been accompanied by a diversification of interests in the last twenty years, with a greater focus on scientific and technological cooperation, including sensitive topics such as nuclear and satellite cooperation.[36] Second, this type of cooperation became much more pronounced starting with the administration of Itamar Franco (1992–95).[37] The third finding is the way these agreements fit in the framework of other important external relations for Brazil. Comparisons have been made with the ties maintained with the United States, Japan, Argentina, and more recently with India.

Brazil negotiated more agreements with China than with the United States, with the exception of the Cardoso years, when nearly half of the U.S. agreements since the 1970s were reached. The figures for Japan suggest its diminishing importance. When Brazilian relations with China were established, both China and Japan maintained a very balanced presence. Ties with Argentina in the final years of the military government were clearly important, and there is a parallel with the Collor and Cardoso administrations. Finally, India has become a new and growing partner for Brazil. While not as important as China, it has come to hold an increasingly prominent place in the last decade, with expanding relations during both the Cardoso and Lula administrations. This stands in sharp contrast to the drop in agreements with the United States and Argentina during Lula's term.

Since the 1990s Sino-Brazilian economic relations have been upgraded, leading to the creation in 2004 of a new institutional framework, the High-Level Coordinating Committee. As China's number-one trading partner in Latin America, Brazil has been increasing its trade with China substantially, with a 20 percent increase from 2004 to 2005. There also has been a significant increase in investment in both directions. In 1993 China and Brazil signed an accord to develop a space program involving five bilateral protocol agreements, which became a paradigm for South-South cooperation.[38] The

Table 5-1. *Agreements between Brazil and China, the United States,*
Argentina, Japan, and India, 1974–2007

Brazilian administration	China	United States	Argentina	Japan	India
Geisel, 1974–79	2	8	1	2	0
Figueiredo, 1979–85	11	10	33	3	0
Sarney, 1985–90	12	6	32	1	2
Collor, 1990–92	4	3	17	0	1
Franco, 1992–95	16	4	13	3	1
Cardoso, 1995–2003	17	26	43	4	8
Lula, first adminis- tration, 2003–07	21	2	29	1	6
Total	83	59	168	14	18

Source: www.mre.gov.br.

joint program focused on satellite production, the first of which was in 1999.
To ensure continued cooperation, Brazil and China signed a broad defense
agreement in 2004 that focused on scientific, military, and technological
exchanges.[39] Although the bilateral scientific cooperation is asymmetrical—
China provides 70 percent of the economic resources and technological
inputs—the number of Sino-Brazilian intercompany and intergovernmental
cooperation initiatives has grown significantly.[40] In the area of energy, so crucial for sustaining China's economic growth, the agreements between Petrobras and Sinopec have expanded since 2004.

In 2005 China was Brazil's third largest export market and its fourth largest
source of imports. These statistics are indicative not only of asymmetries such
as the absolute size of both economies in the world market but also of the relative importance of each country for the other's foreign trade and of the contrast between China's diversified exports and Brazil's concentrated exports.
China's exports include machinery, equipment, and other manufactured
goods—textiles, plastic goods, toys—to the Brazilian market, while Brazil
exports commodities such as soybeans, vegetable oils, iron ore, wood pulp,
timber, and hide products.[41]

It is important to underline that Sino-Brazilian trade relations have not
always been smooth. Brazil's products face the imposition of nontariff barriers hidden in technical standards, as well as in health and administrative regulations. Brazil's difficulties in competing with Chinese manufactured goods,
in both the domestic market and third countries, have increased bilateral disputes. Brazil has brought no fewer than fifteen antidumping cases against

China before the WTO.[42] Brazil is also concerned about losses in its traditional markets, including the United States, the European Union, Japan, and the Mercosur countries.[43] Trade preferences among the Mercosur countries, in addition to suffering from loopholes originating from local protectionist measures, are negatively affected by China's competitiveness.[44]

Trade negotiations and bilateral agreements in global forums expanded following China's entry into the World Trade Organization in 2001. In addition to supporting the PRC's membership, Brazil recognized China as a market economy. These ties do not imply fully convergent interests, since the two countries have very different insertions in the international trade regime. China has achieved much greater openness in its manufactured goods sector and is in a more advantageous position. Brazil faces pressure to expand access to its market for nonagricultural goods but maintains a more defensive posture. In the commodities sector the PRC has maintained a moderate position in response to the demands of the developing countries, but this did not preclude China from joining the Brazilian government in the initiatives of the G-20.[45] Nevertheless, the prospect for a greater convergence between China and Brazil in international trade negotiations is uncertain. Even if both parties share a defensive economic stance vis-à-vis the United States and the European Union in the debate to broaden the global agenda, there are greater commonalities in their views on services than on issues relating to agricultural products.

A deepening of Sino-Brazilian ties could stem from the negotiation of a preferential agreement that would allow for greater coordination between the bilateral economic and trade agenda and initiatives brought forth in multi-lateral economic negotiations. Yet Brazil must also consider its regional commitments. The simultaneous expansion of China's trade with Argentina, though it may help strengthen the China-Mercosur relationship, has become a subtle source of intrabloc tensions as competition for Chinese foreign investment becomes more apparent. When Hu Jintao visited Brazil and Argentina in 2004, this rivalry was exploited by the media in both countries.[46] It is striking to see how China's presence in the Southern Cone unravels ongoing pragmatic preferences for extraregional negotiations. A free trade agreement was signed between China and Chile, just as Chile had signed free trade agreements with the European Union and the United States separately from its Mercosur neighbors. But in the case of Mercosur such agreements have proven difficult to negotiate, as they have been with the European Union and the United States.[47] Some analysts argue that this agreement with Chile has allowed this country to become a "platform" for trade and services with the Southern Cone.[48]

Conclusion

Taking into account the analysis put forth by Tokatlian in chapter 4, together with this chapter's arguments, it is clear that the nature of Chinese–Latin American relations is bifaceted. Like a two-sided coin, one can identify two realities. First, that the bilateral relationship follows the classic dynamics of power politics and strategic interests, in which the region's ties with the United States and the conditions imposed by a triangular geometry constitute an essential dimension. The relationship is shaped by common South-South interests and the possibilities of convergence of the PRC and the region in multilateral forums. In the latter aspect, the Sino-Brazilian agenda has become emblematic. The illusion of a fertile terrain of common interests, however, may obfuscate the uncertainties and even obstacles that limit China's full involvement in a project to strengthen the South-South dimension of the international system, in the terms advocated by several South American states, particularly Brazil.

There is also a striking projection of the Sino-Taiwanese rivalry to Latin America, deepening the North-South divide in the region. Indirectly, this became a factor reinforcing the differentiation between both subregions, with implications in different areas of South America's external relations. In the economic area, a distinction was drawn between a pragmatic cooperation program aimed especially at addressing a short "shopping list" in exchange for political support at the UN—as observed between Taiwan and Paraguay, the Central American countries, and some Caribbean countries—and another fostered by the PRC with Southern Cone countries, which aims to reinforce South-South strategies of economic development and scientific and techno-logical progress. This competition also finds expression in multilateral polit-ical agendas, especially at the United Nations. Examples include the coordination of the positions of the PRC and the South American countries with respect to the renewal of MINUSTAH's mandate and the vote for the GRULAC representative on the Security Council in 2006, when the PRC orig-inally supported Venezuela and the United States and Taiwan supported Guatemala.

Another reality in the Sino–Latin American dynamic is that China's inter-est in identifying areas of cooperation with developing countries and in expanding its array of interstate ties does not necessarily translate into mili-tant political action in favor of the countries of the South when they seek to expand their capacity to influence international decisionmaking. In addition, its action in such coalitions, like the G-20, is cautious and limited compared to its economic weight. China has not been assuming a leadership role by proposing new rules of the game or alternative models of governance for international institutions and regimes, as has been the case of the IBSA countries. Recent studies underscore the uncertainties that still lurk when assessing the horizons of an alliance between China and leading countries in South-South coalitions, such as Brazil.[49]

For Brazil, it is a contradictory fact that China occupies a strategic place for furthering its South-South strategy when at the same time it is not possible for the two to find more common ground on global issues, in view of the differences that persist on the question of UN Security Council reform, on which the Asian countries most in agreement with Brazilian foreign policy—Japan and India—are rivals of the PRC. A paradox that illustrates the asymmetry of Sino-Brazilian relations in international politics is the fact that China's entry in the UN Security Council triggered the establishment of Brazil's diplomatic relations with the PRC in 1974 and that, thirty-two years later, this same power assumes a conservative position that stands in the way of Brazil becoming a permanent member of that same body.

Stronger ties with China are no doubt important for Brazil, both in the medium and long term, in its interest in pursuing a multipolar international order in which the presence of the United States would be less dominant. While this is a point of convergence between Brasília and Beijing, it also gives rise to differences, as shown by such an important issue as reform of the UN Security Council. This is a dividing line that intersects with Brazil's concern to strengthen a South-South agenda for which deepening relations with India—whose differences and tensions with China are not minor—is becoming increasingly important. Yet once again there appear to be more grays than defined colors, for when the issue on the table is nuclear proliferation, the dividing line is between the haves and the have-nots, in which case India and China stand apart from Brazil. At the same time, the Brazilian government's effort to create areas of cooperation in other fields—such as building satellites, in which it is less tied down by commitments to international regimes—reveals a concern to reduce the impact of the strategic inferiority that this dividing line inevitably imposes.

Brazil has revealed a diplomatic capacity for acting in alternative scenarios of interstate coalitions, differentiated by the security and political interests of others. It would be difficult for these spaces to be shared with China, which does not support the Group of Four given its veto against Japan's bid to become a member of the UN Security Council, and at present it is not likely to be in a comfortable position alongside India in the IBSA. Yet one should also consider that India and China share coercive capabilities in global terms and in their respective regions, which Brazil does not have, since it does not belong to the nuclear club. Brazil's defense in South America combines a policy of deterrent capacity along its northern borders with a cooperation agenda with its southern neighbors. In this regard, the possibilities of South-South, BRIC-IBSA convergences run up against limitations that cannot be transposed to the area of international security.

Among potential areas of cooperation between China and some South American countries is development support for the neediest countries. Initiatives of IBSA in education, science and technology, and health, for example, could be strengthened.[50] In addition, a realm of Sino-ABC cooperation is beginning to take shape, fostered by convergent views on multilateralism, mainly through UN peacekeeping operations but also in the fields of technological cooperation and state investment. A link between UN-managed interventionism and the strengthening of less developed countries, and those in chronic institutional failure, may constitute a new form of joint Sino-ABC action convergent with the South-South agenda.

In Sino-Brazilian economic and trade relations, some authors warn of the risk of a simplifying optimism motivated by a horizon of new opportunities that lead to the notion that China is a natural partner of Brazil.[51] Yet strategic partners are not natural partners; theirs are ties built on the basis of reciprocal interests that demand complex and effective negotiations. From an idealized perspective, this partnership could be anchored in political and economic complementarities that strengthen both partners in multilateral forums and in their own growth and development. Brazil has helped bring developing countries together through assertive diplomacy that goes beyond its weight in economic and international security issues; China proceeds with a discretion and caution that belie its importance in the international order. The combination of adequate dosages of diplomatic experience and millenary discipline could contribute to the prospects of a strategic alliance in the twenty-first century.

Notes

1. The author would like to thank Maria Emilia Barsanti for her able research assistance.

2. On that occasion the South American countries visited by the Chinese president were Brazil, Argentina, Chile, and Uruguay. The five principles of peaceful coexistence are mutual respect for territorial integrity and sovereignty, nonaggression, respect for the principle of nonintervention in internal affairs, equality of bilateral rights and benefits, and peaceful coexistence. See "Five Principles of Peaceful Coexistence also Principles for

Development: Chinese Premier," *People's Daily Online,* June 28, 2004 (http://english.peopledaily.com.cn/200406/28/eng20040628_147790.html [December 2007]). For more on China's South-South agenda in Latin America, see Xu Shicheng, "La larga marcha Sur-Sur: China vis-à-vis América Latina," *Foreign Affairs en Español* 3, no. 3 (2003): 95–105.

3. UNCTAD was established in this same context, with the aim of promoting "development-friendly integration of developing countries into the world economy" (www.unctad.org). In 1974 it initiated the debate on a New Economic Order. By 2005 the G-77 had 132 members (its original name was retained due to its historic significance).

4. Marrakech Declaration, Morocco, 2003 (www.g77.org/marrakech/Marrakech-declaration.htm [December 2007]).

5. In March 1991, during the preparatory meeting for the UN Conference on Environment and Development, the G-77 and China issued their first joint position paper. Since then China's cooperation with the G-77 has gradually expanded beyond the areas of the environment and development to include economic and social development and UN financing and budgeting, among others. The first China–G-77 joint declaration was issued during the twentieth G-77 foreign ministers meeting, held in 1996. China contributed $100,000 annually to the G-77 between 1994 and 1996 and contributed double that amount in 1997. "China and the Group of 77," Ministry of Foreign Affairs of the People's Republic of China, November 15, 2000 [www.fmprc.gov.cn/eng/wjb/zzjg/gjs/gjzzyhy/2616/t15326.htm [December 2007]). All currency amounts are in U.S. dollars unless otherwise noted.

6. Marrakech Declaration, Morocco, 2003.

7. "Statement by Chinese Foreign Minister Li Zhaoxing at the 30th Annual Meeting of Ministers of Foreign Affairs of the Group of 77," Ministry of Foreign Relations of the PRC, September 22, 2006 (www.fmprc.gov.cn/eng/zxxx/t273213.htm [December 2007]).

8. Though not casuistic, the concept of an intermediate state still lacks precision. As in many of the categorizations in the field of international relations, the term intermediate state is loaded with ambiguities; its definition includes variables such as population size, geopolitical identity, developing status, the nature of the emerging economy, as well as relevance for regional and international stability.

9. The G-20 was created in August 2003 by twenty-one developing countries during the final stage of preparation for the Fifth Ministerial Conference of the WTO, planned for the following month in Cancún, in view of the difficulty of reaching consensus. Brazil, Argentina, China, and India became the core group articulating a platform designed to bring about negotiations. South Africa, Egypt, China and other Asian countries, Mexico, and most of South America immediately joined the group. Its representation is geographically broad, and its members represent 70 percent of the world's rural population, 60 percent of the world's total population, and 26 percent of agricultural exports. The group's main purpose is to reduce, with a view eventually to eliminating, subsidies for agricultural exports in global trade negotiations.

10. Rosemary Foot, "Chinese Strategies in a U.S. Hegemonic Global Order: Accommodating and Hedging," *International Affairs* 82, no. 1 (2006): 77–94.

11. Amrita Narlikar and Diana Tussie, "The G-20 at the Cancun Ministerial: Developing Countries and Their Evolving Coalitions in the WTO," *World Economy* 27, no. 7 (2004): 947–66.

12. In several speeches (in Argentina, Brazil, and Mexico) President Hu Jintao emphasized that Latin American countries and China are all developing nations and that, as such, they need to foster cooperation and coordination in the current difficult and changing international situation. Yet there are no references to leadership of any kind. He focused on the need to cooperate in the economic, political, and cultural arenas.

13. A report by the Goldman Sachs Global Research Center states that in approximately forty years (if things go right) the BRICs' economies could be larger than those of the G-6. It shows that by 2032 the Indian economy could be larger than Japan's, and that China's economy could be larger than the U.S. economy by 2041. Goldman Sachs Global Researcher, *Dreaming with BRICs: The Path to 2050*, Global Economics Paper 99 (New York: Goldman Sachs Group, 2003).

14. One illustrative example was the presence of Brazil and the PRC, along with South Africa and Mexico, as observers at the G-8 meeting held in St. Petersburg in June 2006.

15. Andrew Hurrell, "Hegemony, Liberalism, and Global Order: What Space for Would-Be Great Powers?" *International Affairs* 82, no. 1 (2006): 1–19.

16. Maria Regina Soares de Lima and Monica Hirst, "Brazil as an Intermediate State and Regional Power: Action, Choice, and Responsibilities," *International Affairs* 82, no. 1 (2006): 21–40.

17. Fernando Delage, "China y el futuro de Asia," *Política Exterior* 102 (November–December 2004): 161–62.

18. Nowadays, China participates in eight peacekeeping missions: in Sudan (UNMIS), Côte d'Ivoire (ONUCI), Liberia (UNMIL), Sierra Leone (UNAMSIL), Western Sahara (MINURSO), Lebanon (FPNUL), and the Middle East (ONUVT); and with police personnel in the mission in Haiti (MINUSTAH). China has approximately 1,487 men in peacekeeping activities. It is the largest contributor to such activities of the permanent members of the Security Council.

19. The idea that this reform process should be accompanied by an increase in the number of permanent members led several states to come forward as natural candidates. Thus alongside the previously excluded industrial powers, Germany and Japan, a group of candidates emerged among intermediate states—Brazil, India, Nigeria, and Egypt—whose permanent membership would lead to a more equitable and representative distribution of the Security Council's core membership. In 2001 the G-4 was formed by Germany, Japan, Brazil, and India as a specific coalition of candidates in favor of the creation of five new permanent seats. In addition to the emergence of individual nominations, candidate states initiated coordinated initiatives to improve preparedness for the responsibilities ahead. For an excellent review of the frustrations

of UN Security Council reform, see Thomas Weiss, "The Illusion of UN Security Council Reform," *Washington Quarterly* 26 (2003): 147–63.

20. Foot, "Chinese Strategies in a U.S. Hegemonic Global Order," p. 87.

21. Jorge I. Dominguez, "China's Relations with Latin America: Shared Gains, Asymmetric Hopes," working paper (Washington: Inter-American Dialogue, 2006), pp. 13–15.

22. United Nations Information Center for Argentina and Uruguay, UN Bibliographic Information System (http://unbisnet.un.org/indexs.htm).

23. Li He, "Rivalry between Taiwan and the PRC in Latin America," *Journal of Chinese Political Science* 10, no. 2 (2005): 77–102.

24. Ibid., p. 88. An analysis of Taiwanese–Latin American economic cooperation can be found in Francisco Luis Peres Expósito, "Taiwan y América Latina: Estrategia de Aproximación y Situación Actual," discussion paper (Madrid: UNISCI, 2004).

25. In 2006 Paraguay repeated the practice of the previous four years of introducing a proposed resolution in the UN General Assembly for Taiwan to rejoin the organization. The arguments in favor of the proposal are based on the economic importance of Taiwan, its population (23 million), and the fact that it maintains diplomatic relations with twenty-five UN member states. Argentina is sensitive to the parallel with the Falkland Islands; the Argentine government claims sovereignty over them just as the PRC claims sovereignty over Taiwan. In reality, the greatest similarity is with Hong Kong, which until 1997 was ruled as a British colony. While for Taiwan self-determination is not in question, in the case of the population of the South Atlantic islands, the option of independence does not enjoy consensus backing.

26. Since 2003 Taiwan has established offices in nine of the eleven South American countries: Argentina, Brazil, Chile, Venezuela, Colombia, Ecuador, Peru, Uruguay, and Bolivia. See Li, "Rivalry."

27. See, among others, Dominguez, "China's Relations with Latin America," pp. 13–15; Monica Hirst, "Crise de Estado e Segurança Regional: Novos Desafios para a América do Sul," in *O século 21 no Brasil e no mundo,* edited by Maria Izabel Valladão de Carvalho and Maria Helena de Castro Santos (Bauru, SP: Edusc, 2006).

28. Emphasis should be placed on the Taiwanese population (approximately 8,000 in Ciudad del Este) and Taiwan's economic presence in the triple border area, which is of great concern due to security issues (organized crime and economic crimes) for Brazil and Argentina. Special mention should be made of the opening, by the Taiwanese, of a regional center for the promotion of CETRA and its support of local companies for the production of auto parts with a view to exporting them to the Mercosur markets. This purpose, however, runs up against the fact that this is an especially problematic area for economic integration, due to the reduced controls on the contraband in automobiles coming from neighboring countries. See Sergio Cesarín, "El Conflicto China-Taiwan y los subsistemas de relaciones en América Latina," *Argentina Global* (Buenos Aires), no. 9 (April–June 2003): 13–15. See also Monica Hirst, "As relações Brasil-Paraguay: baixos incentivos no latu e strictu sensu," *Política Externa* 14,

no. 3 (2005/2006): 11–22; and Fernando Masi, "Paraguai-Brasil e o projecto Mercosul," *Política Externa* 14, no. 3 (2005/2006): 23–30.

29. Since he was elected president of Haiti under the supervision of MINUSTAH, Henri Preval has been strengthening his country's ties with Taiwan, maintaining its previous support for Taiwan rejoining the United Nations as a sovereign member.

30. The PRC is not a member of the Inter-American Development Bank and has been facing the resistance of the United States to entering on conditions similar to those of Japan (1976) and South Korea (2005).

31. For more on this topic, see Lima and Hirst, "Brazil as an Intermediate State and Regional Power," pp. 35–37.

32. Dominguez, "China's Relations with Latin America," p. 3.

33. For Brazil this decision took on great importance, as it was part of guidelines for external action implemented as of 1974 with the Geisel administration, which gave substance to the policy of "responsible pragmatism." In addition to redefining the relationship with the United States, this policy promoted a rapprochement with the third world and positions not compromised by the ideological outlooks of the two superpowers.

34. Arquivo Azeredo da Silveira/CPDOC, *AAS Dispatches with the President,* nos. 15–109, 1974, Report to the President, March 26, 1976.

35. The bilateral understandings make explicit the commitment of noninterference in the internal affairs of other states. Mention should also be made of the discretion maintained by Brazil and the other countries of the region regarding the Tiananmen incident. Stefanie Reiss, "La década del dragón: La diplomacia de China Popular con respecto a América Latina desde 1989," *Desarrollo y Cooperación,* no. 1 (2001): 26–29 (www. colombiainternacional.org/doc%20pdf/ap-decadadragon.pdf [December 2007]).

36. The first understanding in these areas ("Memorandum of Understanding on Cooperation for the Peaceful Uses of Nuclear Energy") dates from May 29, 1984, signed while the military government was still in power in Brazil (Relações Bilaterais—Atos Internacionais Bilaterais; www2.mre.gov.br/dai/bilaterais.htm [December 2007]).

37. By coincidence, Brazilian foreign policy under Franco was led by Celso Amorim, who was again appointed foreign minister by President Lula in 2003.

38. The first agreement for cooperation in space was signed in 1988, during the Sarney administration. See Lílian Fernandes da Cunha, "Em Busca de um Modelo de Cooperação Sul-Sul: O caso da Área Espacial nas Relações entre o Brasil e a República Popular da China (1980–2003)," master's thesis, National University of Brazil (UNB), 2004.

39. The content of this agreement was not publicized, as it was still pending legislative approval.

40. Examples in this regard include the joint venture established in 2001 between the Compania Vale do Rio Doce and the steel producer Baosteel, and the partnership established in 2002 between Embraer and the aeronautics company AVIC2.

41. "China is among the five leading markets for Brazilian exports, accounting for 5.7 percent of the total. Brazil accounts for barely 0.5 percent of Chinese exports. China accounts for 6.2 percent of Brazil's imports (fourth leading market), whereas Brazil accounts for 1.5 percent of China's imports." Lia Valls Pereira, "Relações Comerciais Brasil-China: um parceiro especial?" in *Cuadernos Adenauer* (Konrad Adenauer Foundation), year 7, no. 1 (2006): 129–41, quotation p. 129.

42. Scott Kennedy, "China's Porous Protectionism: The Changing Political Economy of Trade Policy," *Political Science Quarterly* 120, no. 3 (2005): 407–32.

43. The hardest hit products have been home appliances (especially air conditioners), manganese, bicycles, and tools. Lia Valls Pereira and Diego Silveira Maciel, "A concorrência chinesa e as perdas brasileiras," *Conjuntura Econômica* (Rio de Janeiro, FGV) 60, no. 8 (2006): 108–09.

44. It should be noted that, in South America, Peru brought seventeen antidumping actions against China and Argentina brought forty such actions. Kennedy, "China's Porous Protectionism."

45. Lia Valls Pereira and Galeno Tinoco Ferraz Filho, "O acceso da China à OMC: implicações para os interesses brasileiros," final report (Rio de Janeiro: Fundação Centro de Estudos do Comércio Exterior, 2005).

46. "Decepcionado, Kirchner recebe o president chinês," *O Estado de São Paulo*, November 15, 2004 (www. mre.gov.br/portugues/noticiario/nacional/selecao_detalhe3. asp?ID_RESENHA=90767 [December 2007]); and "A Néstor Kichner no le resultará nada fácil agasajar a su colega chinés," *O Estado de São Paulo*, November 16, 2004, p. 12.

47. The FTA between China and Chile was promulgated on August 22, 2006.

48. Sergio Cesarín, "China y América Latina" (Buenos Aires: Nueva Sociedad & Friedrich Ebert Stiftung, 2006).

49. Pereira and Filho, "O acceso da China à OMC."

50. A development fund of $1.3 million was created by IBSA to develop projects to be implemented in Guinea Bissau, Haiti, Laos, and Palestine.

51. Pereira "Relações Comerciais Brasil-China."

PART II

Sino–Latin American
Economic and Energy Issues:
What Lies Ahead?

ROBERT DEVLIN

6 | *China's Economic Rise*

Internationally, China is increasingly perceived as something of an economic juggernaut. In Latin America, China's expansion in the world economy has caused pain in some countries hit by competition in third markets.[1] For raw material exporters, the expanding competitive edge of China is temporarily masked by China's demand for their products. For most countries in Latin America, China represents the potential for increased foreign direct investment (FDI) and for greater strategic cooperation.

In the context of competition and complementarities (see chapter 7, by Francisco González, for a detailed assessment of this subject), China's emergence is often interpreted in narrow terms as market opportunity and challenge. And so it is. However, notwithstanding the market dimension, China's emergence is of greater significance for the region's development. Its increasing competitive prowess is, in effect, a wake-up service for the region. China is just the latest—and too big to go unnoticed—of East Asian countries that have been leapfrogging Latin America in export growth, diversification, and upgrading, all increasingly recognized as key ingredients for sustained growth.

The intangible, natural, and dynamic advantages behind China's increasing ability to compete are not a model for Latin America but rather a motivator to develop, in its own way, a more strategic long-term strategy for innovation and export development. In this context, Latin America also needs to make better use of its inherent advantages in a more systematic fashion. A primary factor in becoming more competitive is the development of a credible public-private sector alliance that allows consensus building for a structured coordination of the main sectors of government, business, labor and academia.

Despite East Asia's fast economic growth, impressive productive transformation, and significant poverty reduction since the 1960s, the region has been largely absent from the Latin American radar screen as an economic model, market, competitor, or partner in cooperation. Beginning in the 1960s, developing East Asia moved to export-led growth from a base of import substitution, partly inspired by Latin America's economic success during the interwar period and the 1950s. In contrast, Latin America persisted with its classic inward-looking substitution strategy, which worked well when international private markets were closed and in a state of trauma but which became increasingly dysfunctional in the postwar era of fast-growing, liberalizing, and globalizing private markets. When crisis, structural reform, and external opening emerged in the 1980s and 1990s, the region's approach was more textbook-like—caricatured in the so-called Washington consensus— than the eclectic formulas observed in developing East Asia.

As a market opportunity, developing Asia was, to a large degree, a missing piece in the Latin America pie charts of trade. North America and Europe, and Latin America itself, traditionally were the places to be. During the reform period, Chile, and to a lesser extent Peru, were exceptions in discovering the Asian market. Meanwhile, developing East Asia was traditionally (with some product exceptions) viewed more as a source of cheap imports than as a competitor at home and abroad. In the 1990s Chile, Mexico, and Peru began to reach out through their participation in the Asia-Pacific Economic Cooperation (APEC) forum.

All this has dramatically altered. Developing Asia is clearly now on the region's mind in all dimensions. And it is China's dramatic economic rise, its thrust into the global public spotlight in the late 1990s, that has served as the catalyst. Indeed, it is China, more so than any of the other countries of East Asia, that is on the minds of Latin Americans at the start of the twenty-first century.

This chapter is divided into four sections. The first section focuses on the Chinese economy, its impressive performance, and the main instruments employed to achieve that performance. The second section examines China's intangible advantages, natural tangible advantages, and dynamic productive factors that have propelled China to the status of major economic actor in the international arena. The third section analyzes some of the main implications of China's economic rise for Latin America, including some of the key elements in China's development, followed by an assessment of Latin America's inherent advantages in the global market. A final section examines a key missing element in Latin America's development strategy: public-private sector strategic alliances geared toward increased competitiveness and export development. Overall, this chapter offers a motivational statement for why and how Latin America might better follow China and East Asia into the league of countries that are rapidly diversifying and upgrading exports for economic growth.

China's Impact

China is becoming an important economic force in Latin America, and its growth is having a significant effect on the volume and prices of many commodities. In many respects, this is good news for the region, especially for raw material exporters in South America. Some analysts caution, however, that this dynamic could have negative repercussions for Latin America in the long run.

As explained in more detail in chapter 7, some countries, particularly in the Caribbean Basin, are already feeling the pinch of Chinese competition in third markets for manufactured goods, and the entire region has experienced domestic pressure in one economic sector or another.[2] Furthermore, the so-called natural resource curse explained by Riordan Roett and Guadalupe Paz in chapter 1, may result in reduced competitiveness in the global market. At the present time, however, expectations are high about new and potentially large flows of Chinese FDI to the region, especially in those countries in which China seeks to secure natural resources for its own economic growth or achieve its geopolitical goals.

Chinese cooperation initiatives, nearly nonexistent before 1990, have been mushrooming in the region, even to the point of creating concern in certain circles in the United States, as noted in several chapters in this volume.[3] And tellingly, after the decline of state interventionist models in the reform period, there is growing interest in bringing back state action to enhance development.

The Growing Ties between China and Latin America

Latin America's growing trade and investment relations with China are well documented.[4] Analysts conclude that China's emergence is both an opportunity and a challenge for the region's growth and development, with the following common highlights:

—The region's total trade with China is still relatively small for both parties but has grown fast (tables 6-1 and 6-2).

—Latin American exports to China are heavily concentrated in commodities. Indeed, only two countries, Mexico and Costa Rica, have noncommodities represented in their basket of top products. China's export basket in Latin America has a larger mix of manufactured goods, which has intensified over time, and the basket is much more diversified (tables 6-3 and 6-4).

Table 6-1. *Latin American Trade with China, 1990 and 2004*
Percent of total trade

Country	1990		2004	
	Export	Import	Export	Import
Argentina	2.0	0.3	7.7	3.7
Bolivia	n.a.	0.9	1.1	1.3
Brazil	1.2	0.5	5.7	5.6
Chile	0.4	1.0	10.5	7.6
Colombia	0.0	0.0	0.9	3.7
Costa Rica	n.a.	0.2	2.7	1.9
Cuba	n.a.	n.a.	n.a.	n.a.
Dominican Republic	n.a.	n.a.	n.a.	n.a.
Ecuador	0.0	0.5	0.7	4.4
El Salvador	0.0	0.4	0.2	4.0
Guatemala	n.a.	0.3	0.7	5.0
Haiti	n.a.	n.a.	n.a.	n.a.
Honduras	n.a.	0.6	n.a.	n.a.
Mexico	0.3	0.4	0.3	2.5
Nicaragua	3.5	0.1	0.4	4.6
Panama	n.a.	6.4	1.2	n.a.
Paraguay	0.0	0.7	2.7	7.6
Peru	1.7	0.9	12.3	4.1
Uruguay	3.9	0.4	3.9	6.7
Venezuela	0.0	0.2	0.6	4.1
Total	0.7	0.8	3.2	4.5

Source: From Comtrade database of the United Nations Statistics Division.
n.a. Not available.

—Most of Latin America greatly lags behind China in export diversification (figure 6-1).

—A commodity boom, fed to a large degree by China's voracious demand for raw materials (China is the world's first, second, or third largest consumer of a wide range of commodities), has improved the region's terms of trade, with South America being the place where most of the winners are concentrated (figure 6-2).

—Export similarity indexes suggest that China and Latin America do not compete head to head much in third markets, with the exception of Mexico and to a much lesser extent Brazil and Costa Rica (table 6-5).[5]

Table 6-2. *China Trade with Latin America, 1990 and 2004*
Percent of total trade

Country	1990		2004	
	Export	Import	Export	Import
Argentina	0.0	0.5	0.1	0.5
Bolivia	0.0	n.a.	0.0	0.0
Brazil	0.2	0.7	0.6	1.0
Chile	0.1	0.1	0.3	0.6
Colombia	0.0	0.0	0.1	0.0
Costa Rica	0.0	n.a.	0.0	0.0
Cuba	0.4	n.a.	0.1	n.a.
Dominican Republic	0.0	n.a.	0.0	n.a.
Ecuador	0.0	0.0	0.1	0.0
El Salvador	0.0	0.0	0.0	0.0
Guatemala	0.0	n.a.	0.1	0.0
Haiti	0.0	n.a.	0.0	n.a.
Honduras	0.0	n.a.	0.0	n..a.
Mexico	0.2	0.1	0.8	0.1
Nicaragua	0.0	0.0	0.0	0.0
Panama	0.2	n.a.	0.4	0.0
Paraguay	0.0	0.0	0.0	0.0
Peru	0.0	0.1	0.1	0.2
Uruguay	0.0	0.1	0.0	0.0
Venezuela	0.0	0.0	0.1	0.0
Total	1.4	1.4	2.3	3.1

Source: See table 6-1.
n.a. Not available.

—Even though China attracts FDI in excess of $1 billion a day, evidence suggests that investment diversion away from Latin America is not a serious problem.[6]

—Information on Chinese FDI in the region is somewhat murky. China is still a relatively small overseas investor. Officially approved direct investment in Latin America was only $77 million in 2005, or less than 1 percent of China's total overseas direct investment that year. The stock in Latin America is about $500 million (table 6-6). Latin America is, relatively speaking, a minor destination for China. The two most important destinations in 2004 were Asia and Africa.

(text continues on p. 123)

Table 6-3. *Top Three Products, Latin America–China Trade, 2004*[a]

Exports to China	Percent	Imports from China	Percent
From Argentina		*To Argentina*	
221 Oil seeds, nuts, kernels	43.9	512 Organic chemicals	15.4
421 Fixed vegetable oils, soft	32.6	719 Machines NES nonelectric	8.2
331 Crude petroleum, etc.	6.0	724 Telecommunications equipment	7.2
From Bolivia		*To Bolivia*	
283 Nonferrous base metal ore, conc.	74.0	599 Chemicals NES	26.1
243 Wood, shaped	6.7	732 Road motor vehicles	9.6
285 Silver and platinum ores	6.1	931 Special transactions	8.5
From Brazil		*To Brazil*	
221 Oil seeds, nuts, kernels	29.8	321 Coal, coke, and briquettes	14.4
281 Iron ore, conc.	20.5	724 Telecommunications apparatus	13.2
421 Fixed vegetable oils, soft	9.1	729 Other electrical machinery and apparatus	6.7
From Chile		*To Chile*	
682 Copper	53.1	841 Clothing not of fur	29.7
283 Nonferrous base metal ore, conc.	25.8	851 Footwear	8.7
251 Pulp and waste paper	10.0	653 Woven textiles, noncotton	6.6
From Colombia		*To Colombia*	
671 Pig iron, etc.	58.0	652 Cotton fabrics, woven	7.8
284 Nonferrous metal scrap	23.9	719 Machines NES nonelectric	6.8
611 Leather	4.7	724 Telecommunications equipment	6.6
From Costa Rica		*To Costa Rica*	
729 Electrical machinery NES	54.6	652 Cotton fabrics, woven	8.8
714 Office machines	28.8	729 Electrical machinery NES	6.8
724 Telecommunications equipment	11.0	851 Footwear	6.4
From Cuba		*To Cuba*	
n.a.	n.a.	724 Telecommunications equipment	11.7
n.a.	n.a.	054 Vegetables, etc., fresh or simply preserved	7.3
n.a.	n.a.	861 Instruments, apparatus	5.5
From Dominican Republic		*To Dominican Republic*	
n.a.	n.a.	653 Woven textiles noncotton	12.9
n.a.	n.a.	719 Machines NES nonelectric	7.7
n.a.	n.a.	652 Cotton fabrics, woven	6.7
From Ecuador		*To Ecuador*	
331 Crude petroleum, etc.	75.9	724 Telecommunications equipment	8.4
332 Petroleum products	11.9	732 Road motor vehicles	6.2
051 Fruit, fresh, nuts, fresh and dry	5.1	718 Machines for special industries	5.5
From El Salvador		*To El Salvador*	
284 Nonferrous metal scrap	70.3	653 Woven textile, noncotton	26.0
031 Fish, fresh or simply preserved	15.4	652 Cotton fabrics, woven	16.7
276 Other crude minerals	6.1	841 Clothing not of fur	12.7

(continued)

Table 6-3. *Top Three Products, Latin America–China Trade, 2004*[a] *(continued)*

Exports to China	Percent	Imports from China	Percent
From Guatemala		*To Guatemala*	
061 Sugar and honey	93.8	653 Woven textiles, noncotton	30.7
652 Cotton fabrics, woven	1.4	652 Cotton fabrics, woven	11.4
724 Plastic materials, etc.	1.4	841 Clothing not of fur	10.6
From Haiti		*To Haiti*	
n.a.	n.a.	629 Rubber articles NES	10.3
n.a.	n.a.	652 Cotton fabrics, woven	6.2
n.a.	n.a.	698 Metal manufactures NES	6.0
From Honduras		*To Honduras*	
n.a.	n.a.	653 Woven textiles, noncotton	23.5
n.a.	n.a.	841 Clothing not of fur	10.6
n.a.	n.a.	652 Cotton fabrics, woven	9.1
From Mexico		*To Mexico*	
714 Office machines	44.4	841 Clothing not of fur	12.5
283 Nonferrous base metal ore, conc.	11.9	714 Office machines	11.2
711 Power machinery, nonelectric	7.1	724 Telecommunications equipment	9.7
From Nicaragua		*To Nicaragua*	
061 Sugar and honey	56.5	652 Cotton fabrics, woven	42.5
611 Leather	32.5	653 Woven textiles, noncotton	23.7
071 Coffee	2.5	841 Clothing not of fur	6.3
From Panama		*To Panama*	
081 Animal feeding stuff	35.8	841 Clothing not of fur	30.4
284 Nonferrous metal scrap	33.9	851 Footwear	11.5
282 Iron and steel scrap	26.0	332 Petroleum products	11.5
From Paraguay		*To Paraguay*	
263 Cotton	76.7	714 Office machines	19.2
611 Leather	14.9	599 Chemicals NES	17.2
243 Wood, shaped	4.2	724 Telecommunications equipment	7.4
From Peru		*To Peru*	
283 Nonferrous base metal ore, conc.	45.1	724 Telecommunications equipment	8.1
081 Animal feeding stuff	34.5	891 Sound recorders, producers	7.2
682 Copper	7.6	653 Woven textiles, noncotton	6.3
From Uruguay		*To Uruguay*	
262 Wool and animal hair	44.6	599 Chemicals NES	10.9
611 Leather	27.2	512 Organic chemicals	8.2
031 Fish fresh and simply preserved	17.4	724 Telecommunications equip	8.2
From Venezuela		*To Venezuela*	
671 Pig iron, etc.	43.7	718 Machines for special industries	9.4
284 Nonferrous metal scrap	26.8	719 Machines NES nonelectric	9.3
513 Inorganic elements, oxides, etc.	14.4	653 Woven textiles, noncotton	8.4

Source: See table 6-1.

a. Based on SITC Rev. 1.

n.a. Not available.

Table 6-4. *Top Three Products, Latin America–China Trade, 1990*[a]

Exports to China	Percent	Imports from China	Percent
From Argentina		*To Argentina*	
041 Wheat, etc., unmilled	46.0	512 Organic chemicals	21.0
421 Fixed vegetable oils, soft	21.1	599 Chemicals NES	11.6
678 Iron and steel tubes and pipes, etc.	13.1	733 Road vehicles, nonmotor	6.5
From Bolivia		*To Bolivia*	
. . .		551 Essential oil, perfume, etc.	26.9
. . .		732 Road motor vehicles	25.1
. . .		864 Watches and clocks	6.3
From Brazil		*To Brazil*	
421 Fixed vegetable oils, soft	32.6	331 Petroleum, crude and partly refined	60.8
671 Pig iron, etc.	14.8	321 Coal, coke, and briquettes	14.4
281 Iron ore, conc.	13.5	221 Oil seeds, nuts, kernels	4.8
From Chile		*To Chile*	
251 Pulp and waste paper	57.0	735 Ships and boats	23.1
283 Nonferrous base metal ore, conc.	26.1	841 Clothing not of fur	17.2
271 Fertilizers, crude	5.1	695 Tools	5.6
From Colombia		*To Colombia*	
051 Fruits, fresh, nuts, fresh or dry	60.2	715 Metalworking machinery	39.5
717 Textile and leather machinery	25.3	722 Electric power machinery, switchgear	26.1
071 Coffee	10.9	512 Organic chemicals	8.7
From Costa Rica		*To Costa Rica*	
. . .		054 Vegetables, etc., fresh or simply preserved	48.9
. . .		698 Metal manufactures NES	10.8
. . .		653 Woven textiles, noncotton	7.2
From Cuba		*To Cuba*	
. . .		013 Meat, tinned NES or prepared	10.2
. . .		054 Vegetables, etc., fresh or simply preserved	8.1
. . .		081 Animal feeding stuff	7.9
From Dominican Republic		*To Dominican Republic*	
. . .		653 Woven textiles, noncotton	31.8
. . .		698 Metal manufactures NES	14.7
. . .		652 Cotton fabrics, woven	7.1
From Ecuador		*To Ecuador*	
292 Crude vegetable materials NES	100.0	695 Tools	16.7
. . .		678 Iron and steel tubes and pipes, etc.	9.4
. . .		698 Metal manufactures NES	8.3
From El Salvador		*To El Salvador*	
031 Fish, fresh or simply preserved	100.0	221 Oil seeds, nuts, kernels	36.3
. . .		698 Metal manufactures NES	24.1
. . .		695 Tools	6.2

(continued)

Table 6-4. *Top Three Products, Latin America–China Trade, 1990*[a] *(continued)*

Exports to China	Percent	Imports from China	Percent
From Guatemala		*To Guatemala*	
...		599 Chemicals NES	11.4
...		652 Cotton fabrics, woven	9.8
...		698 Metal manufactures NES	9.8
From Haiti		*To Haiti*	
...		652 Cotton fabrics, woven	41.8
...		653 Woven textiles, noncotton	15.3
...		541 Medicinal, etc., products	14.0
From Honduras		*To Honduras*	
...		656 Textile, etc., products NES	37.1
...		733 Road vehicles, nonmotor	9.4
...		698 Metal manufactures NES	8.3
From Mexico		*To Mexico*	
512 Organic chemicals	39.0	054 Vegetables, etc., fresh or simply preserved	48.1
581 Plastic materials, etc.	16.1	841 Clothing not of fur	13.9
561 Fertilizers, manufactured	9.9	332 Petroleum products	5.1
From Nicaragua		*To Nicaragua*	
263 Cotton	100.0	054 Vegetables, etc., fresh or simply preserved	53.5
...		599 Chemicals NES	17.5
...		678 Iron and steel tubes and pipes, etc.	13.1
From Panama		*To Panama*	
...		735 Ships and boats	36.7
...		841 Clothing not of fur	26.5
...		656 Textile, etc., products NES	6.3
From Paraguay		*To Paraguay*	
263 Cotton	100.0	851 Footwear	23.3
...		841 Clothing not of fur	15.1
...		724 Telecommunications equipment	6.6
From Peru		*To Peru*	
081 Animal feeding stuff	96.8	321 Coal, coke, and briquettes	40.6
682 Copper	2.6	735 Ships and boats	26.6
292 Crude vegetable materials NES	0.4	541 Medicinal, etc., products	5.0
From Uruguay		*To Uruguay*	
262 Wool and animal hair	89.4	841 Clothing not of fur	31.1
041 Wheat, etc., unmilled	5.7	732 Road motor vehicles	9.9
031 Fish, fresh or simply preserved	4.3	894 Toys, sporting goods, etc.	5.5
From Venezuela		*To Venezuela*	
561 Fertilizers, manufactured	69.4	841 Clothing not of fur	20.5
281 Iron ore, conc.	30.5	541 Medicinal, etc., products	9.1
861 Instruments, apparatus	0.1	276 Other crude minerals	7.9

Source: See table 6-1.
a. Based on SITC Rev.1.
n.a. Not available.

Figure 6-1. *Export Concentration Index, by Country/Group*

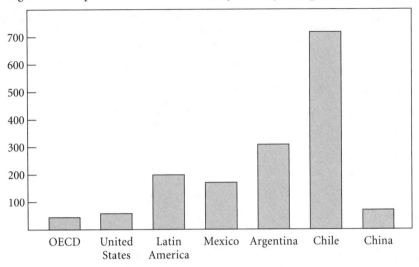

Source: Robert Devlin, Antoni Estevedeordal, Andrés Rodriguez-Clare, eds., *The Emergence of China: Opportunities and Challenges for Latin America and the Caribbean* (Harvard University Press, 2006.

Figure 6-2. *Terms of Trade, Latin America, 1990s and 2005*

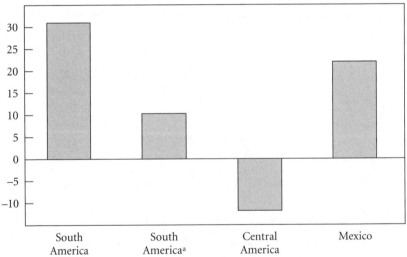

Source: ECLAC, *Latin America and the Caribbean in the World Economy* (Santiago: 2005).
a. Excluding Chile, Bolivia, Venezuela.

Table 6-5. *Export Similarity Index, Latin America and China, 2004*[a]

Country	Index value	Country	Index value
Argentina	7.0	Haiti	3.8
Bolivia	5.9	Honduras	5.1
Brazil	17.4	Mexico	25.1
Chile	5.1	Nicaragua	3.2
Colombia	7.4	Panama	6.4
Costa Rica	13.3	Paraguay	4.1
Cuba	0.3	Peru	4.9
Dominican Republic	11.9	Uruguay	3.8
Ecuador	3.3	Venezuela	2.1
El Salvador	5.0		

Source: See table 6-1.

a. Index constructed at the 3 digit level of SITC Rev. 1. The ESI is defined as

$$ESIij = 100 * \sum c \min (Xci, Xcj),$$

where Xci (Xcj) represents the share of gross exports X of commodity c in total exports of country (j).

Table 6-6. *China's Foreign Direct Investment, Net Flows and Stock, by Country or Region, 2003, 2004, 2005*[a]

Millions of dollars

Country or region	Net flows			Stock		
	2003	2004	2005	2003	2004	2005
Asia	1,499	3,000	4,375	26,559	33,410	40,629
Hong Kong	1,149	2,628	3,420	24,632	30,393	36,507
North America	58	126	321	548	909	1,263
United States	n.a.	120	232	502	665	823
Europe	151	171	505	532	747	1,598
Russia	31	77	203	62	123	466
Oceania	34	120	203	472	544	650
Australia	30	125	193	416	495	587
Africa	75	317	392	491	900	1,595
South Africa	9	18	47	45	59	112
Latin America[b]	22	91	77	396	519	550
Antigua & Barbuda[c]	n.a.	n.a.	n.a.	<1	<1	<1
Argentina[c]	1	1	<1	1	19	4
Bahamas	−1	44	23	44	80	15

(continued)

Table 6-6. *China's Foreign Direct Investment, Net Flows and Stock,*
by Country or Region, 2003, 2004, 2005ᵃ (continued)
Millions of dollars

Country or region	Net flows			Stock		
	2003	2004	2005	2003	2004	2005
Barbados	n.a.	n.a.	n.a.	n.a.	2	2
Belize	n.a.	n.a.	n.a.	n.a.	n.a.	n.a.
Boliviaᶜ	n.a.	n.a.	<1	n.a.	n.a.	<1
Brazil	7	6	15	52	79	81
Chileᶜ	<1	1	2	1	1	4
Colombia	n.a.	5	1	1	7	7
Costa Rica	n.a.	n.a.	n.a.	n.a.	n.a.	n.a.
Cuba	1	n.a.	2	14	15	34
Dominica	n.a.	n.a.	n.a.	n.a.	n.a.	n.a.
Dominican Republic	n.a.	n.a.	n.a.	n.a.	n.a.	n.a.
Ecuadorᶜ	<1	<1	9	1	2	18
El Salvador	n.a.	n.a.	n.a.	n.a.	n.a.	n.a.
Grenada	n.a.	n.a.	n.a.	n.a.	n.a.	n.a.
Guatemala	n.a.	n.a.	n.a.	n.a.	n.a.	n.a.
Guyana	n.a.	n.a.	n.a.	14	13	6
Hondurasᶜ	<1	1		9	6	5
Jamaica	n.a.	n.a.	n.a.	n.a.	n.a.	n.a.
Mexico	n.a.	27	4	97	125	142
Nicaragua	n.a.	n.a.	n.a.	n.a.	n.a.	n.a.
Panamaᶜ	n.a.	<1	8	<1	<1	35
Paraguay	n.a.	n.a.	n.a.	n.a.	n.a.	n.a.
Peruᶜ	<1	<1	1	126	126	129
Saint Lucia	n.a.	n.a.	n.a.	n.a.	n.a.	n.a.
Saint Vincent and Grenadines	6	3	6	6	12	
Suriname	1	1	3	10	10	13
Trinidad and Tobago	n.a.	n.a.	n.a.	n.a.	n.a.	n.a.
Uruguay	1	n.a.	n.a.	1	1	1
Venezuela	6	5	7	19	27	43
Total	2,855	5,498	12,261	33,222	44,777	57,206

Source: Ministry of Commerce of China (http://hzs.mofcom.gov.cn).
a. Nonfinancial sector investment only.
b. Latin America statistics exclude Bermuda, Cayman Islands, Guyana (France), Micronesia, Virgin Islands.
c. <1 indicates less than $1 million.
n.a. Not available.

Figure 6-3. *China–Latin America Cooperation, 1970 to 2004*

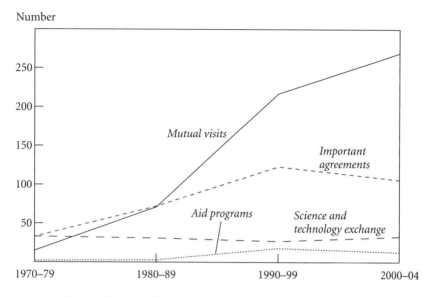

Source: Ministry of Foreign Affairs, PRC.

—China's formal cooperation with Latin America has been notably on the rise since the 1990s (figure 6-3), which corresponds with increased connection via trade.[7]

In sum, as explained by Francisco González in chapter 7, there are both complementary and competitive effects in Latin America's trade with China, with South America benefiting the most from complementarities.

However, as mentioned earlier, the central relevance of China for the region's development is neither competition nor complementarities but rather competitiveness. In short, how can the region improve its competitiveness and move up the export scale for growth? It may be more useful to interpret China's economic surge as a wake-up service for Latin America to raise awareness about the need to diversify and upgrade its exports so as to achieve growth, economic development, and poverty reduction in an era of globalization.

How Did China Do It?

As chapters 2 and 3 note, the Chinese economy was markedly backward in the years following World War II, suffering from rigid central planning, isolation, and ideological turmoil, expressed in socially painful experiments

Table 6-7. *China, Basic Economic Indicators, 1980–2006*

Indicator	1980–89	1990–99	2000–05	2006, first half
Growth rate				
GDP	9.9	10.3	9.5	10.9
Exports of goods	12.9	14.4	25.9	25.2
Imports of goods	14.2	11.5	26.4	21.3
Consumer prices	7.7	7.8	1.2	1.3
Share of GDP				
Fixed investment	26.0	31.9	38.5	39.8
Gross domestic saving	34.8	40.6	42.5	n.a.
Central government fiscal balance	−0.6	−1.0	−2.0	n.a.
Other (U.S.$ billion)				
Foreign direct investment[a]	2.2	29.0	54.5	23.0
Trade balance in goods (customs, China)[b]	−4.4	15.6	39.4	61.4
Trade balance in goods (IMF)[b]	−3.6	18.6	58.4	n.a.
International reserves	4.2	74.3	416.0	941.1
International reserves (months cover for import of goods)	1.8	6.8	11.8	15.4
Total foreign debt, percent of export	n.a.	n.a.	44[c]	n.a.

Sources: Infobank China Content Provider; National Bureau of Statistics of China; State Administration of Foreign Exchange; China Statistical Yearbook 2005, 2001, 1996; International Financial Statistics; People's Bank of China; and World Development Indicators, 2005.

a. The first announced estimate was $60.3 billion of FDI inflows in 2005. This figure did not include the FDI flowing into the financial sectors. The new estimate for 2005 was $72 billion.

b. Exports and imports are FOB in IMF figures. Exports are FOB and imports CIF in China's customs data.

c. 2003 only.

such as the Great Leap Forward and the Cultural Revolution. But since the late 1970s the economy has been on the march, with increasingly spectacular results (see table 6-7). Since 1978 economic growth has averaged more than 9 percent. By 2006 China was the world's fourth largest economy in market prices, was the second largest in purchasing power parity, and had moved into the ranks of middle-income states, with a gross domestic product per capita of some $1,700. Moreover, thanks to China's surge, the world economy has its first growth center outside the member countries of the Organization for Economic Cooperation and Development (OECD). China has been contributing about one-quarter of the growth of the world economy.

Figure 6-4. *China's Delta of Economic Success*

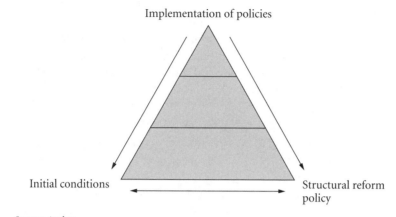

Source: Author.

Behind such growth are unusually high savings and investment ratios as well as a hyperexpansion of exports. The economy, unlike Japan and South Korea in their earlier growth spurts, is relatively open, with trade equivalent to more than 50 percent of GDP, high for a large, continent-sized economy. Meanwhile, FDI inflows exceed $1 billion a day (more than all of Latin America). The economy has abundant shock absorbers in the form of very high rates of domestic savings, a large international reserve, a low foreign debt, and a reasonable fiscal balance. Perhaps most impressive of all is that, since the late 1970s, growth has contributed to lifting more than 400 million Chinese people out of poverty.

In a simplified framework, one can point to a triangular model of successful economic transformation (figure 6-4). At the base of the triangle is the interaction of an injection of market-based structural reforms, beginning in 1978, with some initial conditions. At the top is the critical factor, interaction with the base of strategic policy implementation.

THE INITIAL CONDITIONS. Despite the poor state of the Chinese economy in the late 1970s, some conditions were favorable to growth via market-based structural reform. Some of these were

—Extreme backwardness. In 1978 China had an extremely backward economy. A common feature of economic development is that countries experience catch-up growth spurts when institutional changes introduce more market action that allows gains in efficiency as a country moves to its production possibilities frontier.

—A large, low-wage labor market. A low-wage industrial workforce of more than 400 million at the outset of reforms was conducive to manufacturing and assembly and foreign investment.

—A large domestic market. An economy with nearly one billion consumers and opportunity for economies of scale also provided an incentive for the manufacturing sector to develop and for foreign investment inflows.

—A largely rural population. This facilitated productivity gains through rural-urban migration.

—Some relatively good social indicators. While the economy was in dire shape, one legacy of socialism was progress in areas such as income distribution, education, literacy, health, female participation, and positive trends in birth and mortality rates.

MARKET-BASED REFORMS. Since 1978 China's market-based reforms have been broad in scope and deep in effect (table 6-8). Some of the highlights are as follows:

—Agriculture. The reforms started in agriculture, where commune farming underwent a quasi-privatization through relatively stable assignment of plots to farmers working the land, allowing them to produce and sell what they wanted at market prices after meeting planning targets. These microeconomic incentives, coupled with investments in infrastructure and extension services, helped to significantly raise productivity, output, and rural incomes in the 1980s.

—Town and village enterprises. Rural development and microeconomic incentives were also enhanced in the late 1970s by the rise in the communes of town and village enterprises. Designed to produce goods and services for local demand, these enterprises benefited from rules that allowed household savings to be channeled into local commercial activity. These enterprises, outside the planning process but parallel to the dominant large state enterprises, grew rapidly through the mid-1980s, absorbing rural employment. They were later—in the 1990s—encouraged to evolve into private enterprises, leading the way for more private enterprise in China.[8]

—Trade liberalization. Policies of the late 1970s allowed small-scale export processing contracts from Hong Kong to the mainland. These evolved in the 1980s into export processing zones, which attracted foreign investment. Today the zones account for around 60 percent of exported goods. The closed domestic economy began to open in the mid-1980s through reductions in average tariffs (from over 40 percent to around 12 percent at the beginning of this new century). There was a parallel process in Latin America.[9] The last stage of the opening was the tough conditions accompanying World Trade Organization (WTO) membership for China in December 2001.

Table 6-8. China, Major Structural Reforms, 1978–2005

Year	Policy change
1978	Open Door policy initiated, allowing foreign trade and investment to begin.
1979	Collective farms assign plots to individual families.
1979	Township and village enterprise encouraged.
1980	Special economic zones created for export.
1984	Self-proprietorship (getihu) encouraged, of fewer than eight persons.
1990	Stock exchange started in Shenzhen.
1993	Decision to establish a "socialist market economic system."
1994	Company law introduced.
1994	Multiple exchange rates ended and tax reform introduced.
1995	Shift to contractual terms for staff of state-owned enterprises.
1996	Full convertibility for current account transactions.
1997	Plan to restructure many state-owned enterprises begins.
1998	Program for recapitalization of commercial banks.
1999	Constitutional amendment passed that explicitly recognizes private ownership.
2001	China accedes to the World Trade Organization.
2002	Communist Party endorses role of private sector, inviting entrepreneurs to join.
2003	Decision made to "perfect" the socialist market economic system.
2004	Constitution amended to guarantee private property rights.
2005	Exchange regime reformed.

Source: OECD, *Economic Survey of China* (Paris: 2005); and author.

—Foreign direct investment. In contrast to Japan and Korea, China has relied heavily on direct foreign investment for its economic transformation. Such investment was initially restricted to export processing zones, which accounted for well over 50 percent of exports. In the 1990s China began opening up the domestic economy to foreign investors, a process that has been further cemented by WTO accession.

—State enterprises. State enterprises account for a large share of industrial output and 35 percent of urban employment. Traditionally, they also have had an important role in fiscal income and social welfare systems. In the late 1990s reforms began to give these enterprises better microeconomic incentives, and a process began to restructure firms, to sell off majority stakes, to privatize firms, to merge them, and even to close them down. Much of the focus was on small and medium-size firms that duplicated each other. Large state enterprises have also been subject to reforms but not to much privatization, in part because their employment and welfare systems are an instrument of social stability.[10]

—Financial sector. The banking sector is also undergoing a process of consolidation and recapitalization, coupled with growing foreign competition.

There have been other reforms in the monetary and fiscal arenas, in exchange rates, in stock markets, and in housing. Overall, China has steadily marched toward a market-based economy over the last twenty-five years. A good summary statistic of this advance is that the share of transactions in the economy based on market prices has risen from practically nothing in 1978 to over 90 percent today.[11]

IMPLEMENTATION. While reforms have been extensive and some initial conditions favorable to growth, the real secret to China's success to date may be in how reforms have been implemented. China's experience suggests that the way in which reforms are implemented may be as important as, if not more important than, the reform policies themselves, and Chinese authorities have shown much creativity and local adaptation in introducing the country's market reforms.

China, the Formidable Competitor

One of the key factors in China's impressive economic rise is its growing competitiveness in the global marketplace. Several factors account for this growing ability to compete. These factors can be classified as intangible advantages, natural tangible advantages, and long-term dynamic drivers of new advantage.

Intangible Advantages

China's intangible advantages arise from a combination of political and economic circumstance and strategy. They include a long-term strategic vision, a pragmatic approach, an economic government apparatus that can act coherently through the centralized Communist Party of China (CPC), and an environment of competition.

A LONG-TERM STRATEGIC VISION. Economic actors in China display a strong economic culture of ambition, manifested in a persistent drive to diversify and upgrade products and exports by accumulating new knowledge. China moreover is a place where economic actors tend to know where they want to go, not only today and tomorrow but ten to fifteen years from now. Latin America, in contrast, seems much less forward looking and more absorbed by day-to-day events.[12]

In general terms, the Chinese economy is goal driven, with corresponding incentive structures. For example, major Chinese manufacturing firms, with government encouragement, are no longer satisfied with subcontracting.

They are now driven by the very challenging goal of creating their own international brand recognition.[13] In addition, success in meeting goals allows no time for celebration; new goals are established and profits reinvested to achieve them. Indeed, the current annual growth rate in China of more than 10 percent is being largely driven by reinvested profits.[14]

PRAGMATISM. The Chinese have been very pragmatic in introducing policy reforms. Radical swings in policy are rare. Rather, reforms tend to be introduced cautiously, gradually, and in an evolutionary way. This certainly contrasts with the pendulum swings that so often plague Latin American policies.

One way to interpret the Chinese approach to implementing reform is empirical experimentation.[15] Incremental changes, often led by pilot programs, created lessons that allowed Chinese authorities to make adjustments or midstream corrections and to create or adapt institutions and administrative procedures to sustain the march forward without the crises that have plagued other regions, including Latin America.

Another angle from which to view the strategy is dualism.[16] In effect, market structures come into play at the margin of the old planned economy, as the latter is gradually absorbed by the former. This dualistic approach happens on many fronts, whether trade liberalization, capital account opening, exchange rate reform, state enterprise reform, or other.

A clear example is trade and investment liberalization, which began with enclave export processing zones. Only when there was considerable experience in exporting—with a knowledge of foreign firms and markets coupled with a cushion of accumulated international reserves—did a gradual opening of the highly protected domestic market begin. Moreover, capital account opening has been restricted, following the wisdom of good sequencing that emerged out of Latin America's debt crisis of the early 1980s.[17] Only now, after opening the current account, is China beginning to gradually reform capital account management.

A COHERENT ECONOMIC APPARATUS. Before the reforms, change in China at all levels was typically abrupt and disruptive. However, the reform era has been characterized by smooth transitions and continuity in the evolution of a forward-looking strategic economic vision. The government has been able to intervene in the market to achieve its goals. It is not always efficient or effective, but that ability has been, on balance, an asset in moving the economic transformation forward. In the long term, as the economy develops, it is unlikely that the same extent of state intervention would be helpful, but at the early stages of transformation it has been an important asset.[18]

The power of the Communist Party government exceeds anything that could be imagined in democratic Latin America. However, coherence and the capacity to implement policy are still requisites for development. In Latin American governments, coherence of policy over time has improved, especially for macroeconomic management, but that is not generally the case with sectoral management and incentives, which are important for competitiveness.[19]

China's pragmatic public intervention is not based on any blueprint. It is, however, guided by clear priorities: sustained high growth, productive transformation, and employment generation; social stability in the context of rapid social change; and the hegemony of the Communist Party.

COMPETITION. Considerable competition is driving the Chinese economy. Chinese exporters must adjust to tough competition, especially in their efforts to upgrade. Privatization and economic liberalization have been another source of competition, while localities also compete aggressively to attract investment.

Natural Tangible Advantages

China also benefits from several natural tangible advantages. They include abundant low-cost labor, economies of scale, regional disparities, and membership in the Southeast Asian "neighborhood."

ABUNDANT LOW-COST LABOR. Mauricio Mesquita-Moreira paints a vivid picture of China's labor cost advantage compared to Latin America: China's massive industrial labor force of more than 600 million has much lower wages than Latin American workers.[20] In manufacturing, the difference is significant. Mexico's and Brazil's wages, respectively, have been up to eight and six times higher than China's. In Central America labor costs in the critical textile and apparel sectors are between 30 percent and 300 percent higher, depending on the country.[21] On average, the region's wages are four times higher than those in China.[22] Clearly, competing with China on the basis of labor costs alone will not work.

China has experienced wage pressures on the coast, even given the large surplus labor force in rural areas. The reaction has been to simply move the lowest-wage jobs inland. But China's competitiveness is driven by more than just low wages: in the apparel industry, the workforce is young and fairly well educated, with an average of nine years of education. Meanwhile, despite setbacks in its image regarding quality control, Chinese firms have been known internationally for some time for their quality, reliability, and full package operations.[23]

On the other hand, labor productivity in manufacturing in Mexico and Brazil is higher than China's, according to Mesquita-Moreira.[24] However, the gap in wages with China is greater than the productivity gap. Moreover, labor

Figure 6-5. *Labor Productivity, China and Selected Countries, 2001*

Index

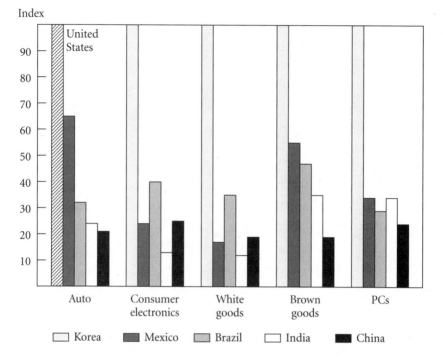

Source: Mauricio Mesquita-Moreira, "Fear of China: Is There a Future for Manufacturing in Latin America?" *World Development* 35, no. 3 (2007): 355–76.

productivity is growing faster in China than in Latin America, so that the productivity gap should be decreasing (figures 6-5 and 6-6).[25]

ECONOMIES OF SCALE. Given its size, China has the ability to capture the benefits of economies of scale at an early stage of development. This serves as a bargaining chip to extract advantages from direct foreign investors and even impose standards based on Chinese technology.[26]

REGIONAL DISPARITIES. Although, on average, China is a low-wage country, there is high regional segmentation of markets. The coast is quite dense in capital and skilled labor; per capita income in Shanghai is higher than in most Latin American countries.[27] This could explain why, with low per capita income, China has a surprisingly large quantity of medium- and high-technology exports that are growing fast and outdistancing those of Latin America (figure 6-7).

Figure 6-6. *Manufacturing Wage Gap, Brazil and Mexico versus China, 1996–2003*

Wage ratio to China[a]

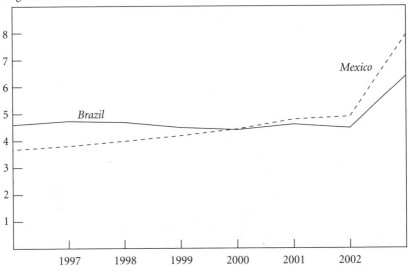

Source: See figure 6-5.
a. Wages are measured in purchasing power parity using current international dollars.

THE NEIGHBORHOOD. China sits in the middle of what might be termed Southeast Asia, Inc. Not surprisingly, China's development approach has some similarities with a broader East Asian model, inspired to some extent by Japan.[28] The neighborhood also was conducive to China's increasing penetration of East Asian production chains that are fragmenting as its neighbors move upstream. While the Caribbean Basin has exploited the North American neighborhood, production chains there in many cases are dependent on trade preferences, a vulnerability discussed later.

Dynamic Productive Factors

Compared with Latin America and other regions of the world, China has some formidable natural advantages. But it is its strategic policy that is setting the stage to move upstream quickly in the years to come. Policies in the areas of education, innovation, investment, and credit have played a significant role in China's rapid development.

EDUCATION. In China there is an impressive push for higher education. Reflecting an ambition to adapt and innovate its way up the production

Figure 6-7. *Technological Content of Exports, China and Latin America, 1990 and 2004*

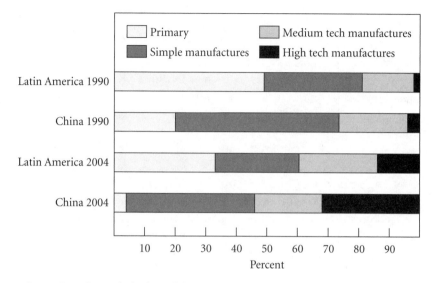

Source: From Comtrade database of the United Nations Statistics Division.

chain, the Chinese expenditure ratio per student between tertiary, secondary, and primary education has been 10:2:1. This is extremely high compared to other countries, including Korea, Chile, Mexico, and the United States.[29]

Enrollment in higher education rose by a factor of 5 in the decade ending in 2004, and exceeds 13 percent of the college-age population.[30] This is low for a middle-income country (Mexico is 21 percent), but the absolute number of higher education graduates is 2.4 million a year, of which roughly 45 percent are in science and engineering.[31] Even more impressive, the country is generating 150,000 masters and doctoral graduates a year, of which 50 percent are in science and engineering.[32] The limited information on test scores in science and math for fourteen-year-olds suggests that Chinese students are competitive internationally. The significant pool of low-wage, competent technical labor has been inducing multinational corporations to establish research and development centers in China.[33]

INNOVATION. China's culture of ambition and desire to move upscale is reflected in a survey that shows that innovation was the second highest priority of Chinese firms, after high quality.[34] China currently is spending at least 1.2 percent of GDP on research and development (R&D). That figure exceeds that of every Latin American country by far (except Brazil's, which is

1 percent) and even tops Spain's.[35] Moreover, the government has a formal goal of 2.5 percent for 2020. The objective is to have 60 percent of the country's growth driven by science and technology by that year.[36]

The number of Chinese researchers as a percent of inhabitants exceeds that of Latin American countries, as do such indicators as the number of the country's researchers in R&D and patent applications placed in the United States. The number of full-time researchers in China already exceeds that of Japan and is close on the heels of the number in the European Union. A 2005 study projects that, by 2015, China will exceed third-ranked Japan in standard indicators of science and technology.[37]

INVESTMENT. China's investment in fixed assets is nearly 40 percent of GDP; the Latin American average is roughly half that.[38] And the Chinese have given high priority to infrastructure development, vital to productivity growth. This is an area in which Latin America has severely lagged. Indeed, China outdistances Latin America (and middle-income countries more generally) in indicators such as access to electricity, paved roads (with more than 30,000 kilometers of automobile routes), and telephone land lines.[39]

CREDIT. Thanks to a high personal savings ratio, China has abundant cheap bank credit, albeit biased toward state financing. In contrast, Latin American firms often face severe credit constraints.

In looking at indicators such as those for investment, higher education, and research and development, it is clear that there can be inefficiencies, and, undoubtedly, there are some. But size does matter. Even if 30 percent of the investment were wasteful, the country's effective investment coefficient would still be relatively high. If 30 percent of the scientists and engineers leaving graduate school were "inept," the country would still be generating 100,000 competent ones a year. If 30 percent of R&D expenditures were wasteful, the more effective expenditures would still be 0.8 percent of GDP—higher than practically all of Latin America.

Implications of China's Economic Rise for Latin America

China's performance and competitive advantages are impressive. But an economy expanding so fast clearly has a high risk of accidents along the way, perhaps even fatal ones. China does face many areas of risk, which create serious vulnerabilities.[40] But given the cushions mentioned earlier, and the fact that Chinese authorities have repeatedly shown themselves to be forward looking, alert, and proactive in dealing with problems (in their own way), it might be wise to give them the benefit of the doubt. Even with the caveat that in economic predictions bubbles occur, most professional estimates have

Figure 6-8. *Growth in Exports of Goods and Services, by Country/Group*

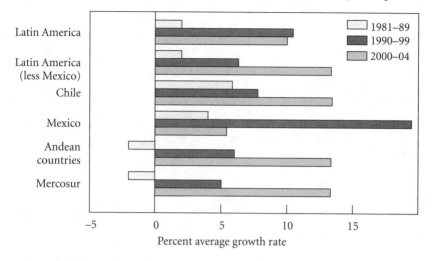

Percent average growth rate

Source: UN Commodity Trade Statistic Database (http://comtrade.un.org).

been reasonably sanguine about China's ability to grow at high rates for years to come.[41,42] Latin America also should remember that if China continues to grow as fast, and given its culture of ambition, the China of tomorrow will not look like the China of today. Among other things, the Chinese economy will be less commodity intensive and more technology intensive, and it will display more consumption and services. The country will also have more geopolitical power.

The World Bank's quarterly report on China in 2006 pointed out that China's trade basket continues to diversify rapidly and move up market.[43] New product varieties are emerging every year, and an expanding private sector is leading the drive. Moreover, import substitution is deepening domestic supply chains, with export processing steadily falling as a share of total exports, now at 50 percent according to the World Bank. Ernest Preeg reports that high-tech information and telecommunication equipment is a leading driver of exports and that "Chinese valued-added for information technology exports will soon reach 70 percent, if it has not already done so."[44]

Latin America's exports have expanded significantly during the reform period, and growth has been especially healthy (figure 6-8). There has been diversification as well. Still, the region's share of world exports has declined sharply since 1950, and after twenty years of reforms, the share is not much different from what it was in 1980 (figure 6-9).[45] The share of manufactured

Figure 6-9. *Share in World Trade, Latin America, East Asia, and China, Selected Years, 1950–2005*

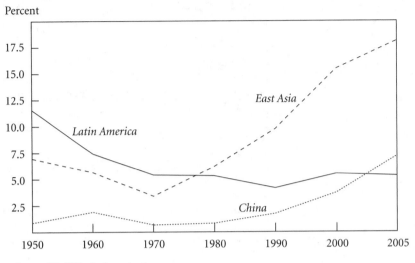

Percent

Source: World Trade Organization.

exports has risen, but as Mesquita-Moreira points out, "Output and exports of manufactures are still dominated by 'mundane' resource and labor intensive goods or are concentrated in the labor intensive links of the value chain; and the region has been having difficulties to increase its limited share of the world market, being thoroughly outperformed by East Asia."[46]

Indeed, China is just one more chapter in an unfolding story of reversed fortunes (figure 6-10).[47] In the early 1950s developing East Asia was economically very backward and war torn. Latin America, in contrast, was the premier growth region in the developing world, inspiring important development theories as well as copycats in Asia and Africa. But in the 1960s East Asia moved toward export-led growth while Latin America stayed in its classic inward-looking import substitution mode, which was quickly becoming outdated as the world economy retook the path of globalization. Growth in the region slowed and then, with few exceptions, became anemic in the crisis and reform periods of the 1980s and 1990s. Beginning in the late 1960s, the first East Asian wave to overtake Latin America in growth included Korea, Singapore, Taiwan, and Hong Kong. The next wave was in the late 1970s and 1980s, which comprised Malaysia, Thailand, and Indonesia. Then in the 1990s, China's advance became noticeable, and on China's heels were India and Vietnam.

Figure 6-10. *Per Capita Income, East Asia and Latin America, 1950 and 2001*

Percent[a]

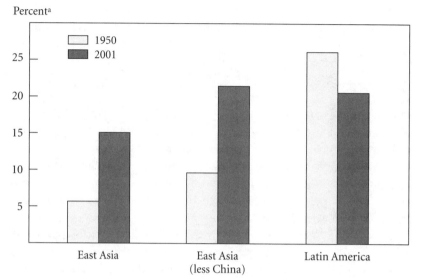

Source: Anthony Elson, "What Happened? Why East Asia Surged Ahead of Latin America and Some Lessons for Economic Policy," *Finance and Development* 43, no. 2 (2006), table 1.
   a. Based on U.S. per capita GDP in purchasing power parity.

Although economic growth in Latin America has been improving, it is nowhere near miracle status:

> If it were just a matter of which region comes first in the growth rankings, this story would be irrelevant for the policy debate in Latin America. But it is not just about rankings. It is about a region that has managed to lift most people out of poverty after three consecutive decades of fast growth (and it is happening again in China) and another region that, despite its efforts to reform, has consistently failed to . . . reduce poverty.[48]

What Should Latin America Do?

Latin America has made major advances in structural reforms. The economies of the region today are more stable, agile, and competitive than they were at the outset of the 1980s crises. But as noted earlier, the region's export-led development has lagged behind East Asia's, and this has contributed to unremarkable growth in the former and strong growth in the latter.

There are no magic formulas for national export diversification and upgrading. Moreover, the potential scope and complexity of the options for achieving these goals are enormous, and selectivity is inevitable. Neither East Asia nor China can be a model for Latin America—the two regions are worlds apart in most ways. It is clear, however, that East Asia's success does offer insights that could be adapted to Latin America. Some of these elements are outlined below.

DEVELOPING LONG-TERM STRATEGIES AND GOALS. Achieving long-term strategies at the national, sectoral, and firm levels is a characteristic not only of China—it can be stylized to depict East Asia's success stories. Persistence and consistency over time, coupled with pragmatism and market testing, are necessary to keep strategies firm yet flexible enough to adapt to changing circumstances. Latin America's difficulty in developing a long-term strategic vision puts it at a disadvantage when competing in a fast-changing and increasingly knowledge-based world economy.

DEVELOPING LOCAL CAPACITY. With or without direct foreign investment, it is important for Latin America to develop local capacities to innovate for the diversification and upgrading of exports. China started out with simple export processing zones, not unlike those in Latin America. These were followed by policies, including joint ventures with FDI, to encourage added domestic value and to increase local capacities (such as science and engineering education and sponsorship of industrial and technological parks). Latin America generally has been slower off the mark in this area.[49]

DEVELOPING A PROACTIVE STATE. The Chinese government has developed a capacity to assist economies and the private sector in developing and realizing long-term strategies. Ensuring fundamental macroeconomic balance is, of course, central, but it is not enough. Private sector export development faces obstacles from market failures of both the static and dynamic type. In Latin America government action, in the form of horizontal and vertical interventions, can assist in ameliorating market failures that constrain export diversification and upgrading. East Asian countries have traditionally valued this role of government. But in the reform period, Latin American emphasis was on government failure and a rollback of public intervention. While the rollback has far from eliminated market tinkering, it has negatively affected capacity and coherence.[50]

SOME FUNDAMENTALS. East Asian governments give a high priority to competitive exchange rates, high saving and investment rates, access to domestic credit, education, and investment in science and technology networks, including R&D expenditures and infrastructure.[51] These areas, so critical to export diversification and upgrading, are all soft spots in the economies of Latin America.

Latin America's Inherent Advantages

Latin America has a number of inherent advantages that need to be better exploited. Some of these include closeness to important markets, abundant natural resources, a tourism industry with significant growth potential, an enormous inflow of remittances from abroad, and potential for greater regional integration benefits.

CLOSENESS TO MAJOR MARKETS. Latin America is geographically closer to wealthy international markets than developing Asia is. However, a 2006 study shows that transport costs are not a particular advantage for the region because the unit values of goods shipped by China (and East Asia) tend to be higher than Latin America's and compensate for most differentials in shipping costs.[52] Labor costs are not competitive either. Where Latin America does have an advantage is "speed to market" for ocean transport. But to exploit this advantage the region must focus on goods that are time sensitive, improve transport infrastructure, develop consolidated containerized regional shipping hubs, and improve business and export processes.[53]

NATURAL RESOURCES. There is increasing evidence that natural resources are not a curse for growth.[54] Successful natural resource exporters have diversified and upgraded beyond commodities, whether by adding knowledge-based linkages (backward and forward) to the base sector activity (such as Australia has) or by adding new higher value exports to the portfolio beyond natural resources (such as Sweden, Finland, and Malaysia have). This requires coherent national innovation systems (plus adaptation encompassing the entire production and marketing chain) that effectively support better or newer private sector export activities. Latin America's innovation systems suffer from incompleteness, fragmentation, and underfinancing.[55]

TOURISM. Latin America has abundant tourist attractions, but with a few exceptions this natural advantage is not fully exploited because of problems with security, infrastructure, coordination, language barriers, and marketing. Moreover, special adjustments will have to be made to capture an expected huge wave of Chinese tourists in the world economy over the next fifteen years.[56] As many as 150 million Chinese citizens already have incomes sufficient for foreign travel.[57]

THE LATIN AMERICAN DIASPORA. The economic impact of the overseas Latin American community is now enormous. Worker remittances, which in 2005 reached 2.3 percent of GDP, might be better invested in export-oriented development. Overlapping cultural roots, language, and tastes create potential new export markets abroad.[58]

REGIONAL INTEGRATION. Asia is only now discovering regional integration, while Latin America has a long tradition and much experience in this area. Regional integration can be a vehicle to enhance competitiveness and develop exports. This comes about through several steps: offering a platform for economies of scale and new export experience; combining factors of production and interindustry trade; attracting foreign investment; cooperating in areas such as infrastructure, education, innovation, and international negotiations; and modernizing institutions.[59]

Unfortunately, subregional integration in Latin America, after much progress in the 1990s, is now languishing. North-South free trade agreements (FTAs) in the region are doing better, but the benefit of rich country preferences has not been without risks. In the case of Mexico, U.S. NAFTA preferences are highest in low-wage industries (figure 6-11), which provides an incentive to diversify exports by allocating resources to these sectors. While Mexico may have a comparative advantage in those sectors with the United States, it may not have an advantage vis-à-vis China and East Asia.

Moreover, the protection of preferences is falling. U.S. preferences are steadily eroding as it expands its FTA network, including to Asia. East Asian countries are increasing their productivity faster than Mexico. Hence preferences are a benefit only if they buy time for national programs that help upgrade exports, a lesson that Mexico is learning because of Chinese competition. Finally, in terms of South-South trade, Chile's example of pursuing FTAs in East Asia, including China, could be a way to open markets and to gain entry to East Asian production chains.

Conclusion: A Missing Page in Latin America's Competitiveness Agenda

Strengthening and improving the quality of countries' growth and integration into the world economy involves export development, product diversification, added value, and new knowledge-based activities. These demands of the world economy require that firms, at the least, have information about access to markets and trends and also to techniques of product differentiation and marketing; that they invest in new activities; and that they adapt technologies to commercial application, have access to credit and skilled labor, and have access to essential public goods. Further, a favorable business environment and sectoral coordination and articulation are essential. Due to

Figure 6-11. *Mexico's Preferential Tariff Margin vis-à-vis China, 1990 and 2000*

Percent[a]

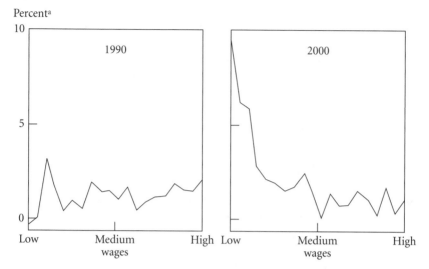

Source: Ernesto López-Córdova, "Economic Integration and Manufacturing Performance in Mexico: Is Chinese Competition to Blame?" Working Paper 23 (Washington: Inter-American Development Bank, 2004).

a. Difference in applied U.S. tariffs.

imperfections, markets do not spontaneously generate this environment, especially in developing countries where factor markets are incomplete.

High participation in the labor-intensive segments of international production does not necessarily lead to technological upgrading and productivity growth or to technological spillovers. Going up the technology ladder is especially difficult when the local suppliers' base is not well developed or when foreign-owned manufacturers, rather than national firms, are the major suppliers of the most sophisticated components and services. Compared to the thriving internationally integrated production systems (IIPS) in East Asia, Latin American systems are still characterized by imported goods and services (often just protracted maquiladoras) with little value added and little integration of enterprises and sectors to global production networks. Latin American systems also lack adequate design, engineering, R&D, and marketing services, which tend to be concentrated in the parent companies of multinational corporations. This lack on the part of the local productive apparatus works to the detriment of national suppliers and endogenous technology capabilities. Even in countries like Brazil, with more integrated production—moving upscale and into IIPS—it has been a slow, limited, and uncertain process.[60] Thus innovation and investment in new export-related activities have been prevented from playing a central role in industrial restructuring and export growth in Latin America.[61] But such innovation has been constrained not only by the supply side; lack of demand is also part of the equation. Innovation and export development are unlikely to take place without support policies and programs emerging from intensive cooperation among the public and private sectors and academia that aim to overcome market failures in information, coordination, technology, and so forth.

In Latin America the public-private nexus tends to be weak or dysfunctional. The private sector operates in a harsh environment with few strategic carrots to encourage upgrading (that is, it is left to its own devices with the risk of suboptimal interface with externalities) or too many ad hoc carrots and too little sticks (resulting in state capture). In contrast, East Asia's private sector has been encouraged by proactive industrial policies with a long-term strategic focus and a better balance of carrots and sticks.

There are now signs in Latin America of a shift in preferences toward a more strategically focused proactive state. The shift may be a result of stories of successful export development in Asia, Oceania, Europe, and North America where the visible hand of proactive public policy is all too apparent. There is still the question, of course, of what type of government intervention will work in Latin America—and how it is to be realized. Latin America had had a long tradition of government intervention in the economy, which involved a top-down approach in the era of domestic import substitution industrialization. That traditional approach must not be resurrected. Nor are ad hoc measures optimal, because they tend to accumulate contradictions over time.

Instead, a close strategic alliance should be formed between the public and private sectors. Each sector can identify binding constraints and formulate support strategies, but neither party has the complete picture in the fast-changing and competitive world of globalization. The private sector has first-hand knowledge of how the market works, its problems, and the effectiveness of public interventions in support of innovation and exports, but the private sector's perspective on market opportunities is partial and fragmented. Although the public sector has less capacity to assess a specific market situation, it can address such larger issues as information barriers, social benefits of private action, coordination, dysfunctional conflicts, and a long-term view that can counteract short-term profit-taking activities. Strategic public-private sector alliances underlie many of the economic successes in East Asia. Even more advanced countries such as New Zealand, Ireland, and Finland have moved in this direction.[62] Subnational entities also frequently use alliances for economic transformation. In Latin America effective and sustained public-private alliances seem to be a missing page in the region's competitiveness agenda.[63] Consensus-based priorities founded on public-private dialogue and evidence-based research of constraints and opportunities are, in the face of limited public resources, essential to guide deployment of public interventions and incentives for new activities. A well-structured alliance can also facilitate checks and balances, public accountability, and timely adjustments.

The private sector pieces of an alliance are ready to be put together. What is missing are public agencies that can engage the private sector without being captured, that have sufficient technical capacity to instill confidence and motivate systematic coordination, and that include building consensus on coherent interventions in support of export development. This also requires public financing with transparency and accountability for results. Latin American countries cannot avoid this new direction if they want more and better exports for transformation and growth. One way the countries might get credible public-private alliances off the ground is by copying from the Chinese playbook: examine insights from other successful experiences; adapt according to local circumstances; start gradually by developing pilot alliance programs for supporting innovation, new export-related activities and upgrading; and adjust and expand according to empirical evaluation of results.

Notes

1. A preliminary version of this chapter was presented at the G-24 meetings in Singapore, September 13–14, 2006. The author especially thanks Zheng Kai for his valuable research assistance. Agustín Cornejo and Andrea de la Fuente also provided research support.

2. China has been a favorite target of antidumping initiatives. See Michael Finger and Julio Nogués, eds., *Safeguards and Antidumping in Latin American Trade Liberalization* (New York: Palgrave, 2006).

3. Stephen Johnson, "Balancing China's Growing Influence in Latin America," Background Paper 8 (Washington: Heritage Foundation, 2005).

4. ECLAC, *Latin America and the Caribbean in the World Economy* (Santiago: 2005); Claudio Loser, "China's Rising Economic Presence in Latin America" (Washington: Inter-American Dialogue, 2005); Inter-American Development Bank, *Periodic Note* (Washington: IADB, Integration Dept., 2006); Robert Devlin, Antoni Estevadeordal, and Andrés Rodríguez-Clare, eds., *The Emergence of China: Opportunities and Challenges for Latin America and the Caribbean* (Harvard University Press, 2006); Jorge Blázquez-Lidoy, Javier Rodríguez, and Javier Santiso, "Angel or Devil? China's Trade Impact on Latin America" (Paris: OECD Development Center, 2006); Lucio Castro,

"China and Latin America," presentation at the University of Westminster, London, February 6, 2006; A. Gottschalk and D. Prates, "The Macroeconomic Challenges of East Asia's Growing Demand for Primary Commodities in Latin America," paper prepared for the G-24, Washington, 2005; Rhys Jenkins and Enrique Dussel Peters, "The Impact of China on Latin America and the Caribbean" (Beijing: DFID, 2006).

5. Mauricio Mesquita-Moreira estimates that the loss of world manufacturing exports to China was relatively modest between 1999 and 2004—less than 2 percent of 2004 manufacturing exports. He is, however, concerned about more recent trends, including penetration of domestic markets. Mauricio Mesquita-Moreira, "Fear of China: Is There a Future for Manufacturing in Latin America?" *World Development* 35, no. 3 (March 2007): 355–76.

6. Kamal Saggi, "Foreign Direct Investment and Development: Lessons from Recent Experience in Latin America" (Southern Methodist University, Department of Economics, 2006).

7. Robert Devlin and Zheng Kai, "Nuevo y Creciente Romance: la Cooperación entre China y América Latina," in *Oportunidades en la Relación Económica y Comercial entre China y México*, edited by Enrique Dussel Peters (Mexico City: Mundi-Prensa México, 2007).

8. The private sector's share of industrial firms is estimated by the OECD at 70 percent. The firms' share in nonfarm business output is estimated at nearly 60 percent. Official figures, based on a narrower universe of registered firms, give a lower estimate of the output share—about a third. OECD, *Economic Survey of China* (Paris: 2005).

9. Inter-American Development Bank, *Beyond Borders: The New Regionalism in Latin America* (Washington: 2002).

10. Chong-En Bai, Jiangyong Lu, and Zhingang Tao, "The Multitask Theory of State Enterprise Reform: Empirical Evidence from China," *American Economic Review* (May 2006): 353–57.

11. OECD, *Economic Survey of China*.

12. One example is that there seemed to be less preparation than one would have expected for the effects of the end of the international Multifiber Agreement.

13. Paul Taylor, "A Show of Strength in Technology," *Financial Times*, July 14, 2006, p. 17.

14. World Bank, *Quarterly Update, August 2006* (Beijing: 2006).

15. Min Zhao, "External Liberalization and the Evolution of China's Exchange Rate System: An Empirical Approach," Research Paper 4 (Beijing: World Bank, n.d.).

16. Yingyi Qian, "How Reform Worked in China" (University of California, Department of Economics, 2002); Eswar Prasad and Raghuran Rajan, "Modernizing China's Growth Paradigm," *American Economic Review* (May 2006): 331–36.

17. *Latin America and the Caribbean: Policies to Improve Linkages with the Global Economy* (Santiago: ECLAC, 1995).

18. Of course, an alternative argument is that all would have performed even better if the state had not intervened so much in the economy. Aside from being a much too broad counterfactual, in the face of the extraordinarily fast sustained growth and

dramatic structural transformations that have taken place, this argument, at least in its simplest form, would not be convincing. Looking toward the future, however, the trade-off may be increasingly relevant for China.

19. Baruj, Kosacoff, and Porta examine trade and investment incentives in the context of Mercosur integration and find many dysfunctional public interventions that accumulate over changes in governments because of a lack of a consensual strategic national vision. Gustavo Baruj, Bernardo Kosacoff, and Fernando Porta, "Políticos Nacionales y la Profundización de Mercosur: El Impacto de las Políticas de Competitividad" (Washington: Inter-American Development Bank, Department of Integration, 2005). Also see Wilson Peres, "El (lento) Reto de las Políticas Industriales en América Latina y el Caribe," Serie Desarrollo Productivo 166 (Santiago: ECLAC, 2005).

20. Mesquita-Moreira, "Fear of China."

21. Arturo Condo, "China's Competitiveness and the Future of the Textile Sector in Latin America," LAEBA Annual Conference, Buenos Aires, 2004.

22. Blázquez-Lidoy, Rodríguez, and Santiso, "Angel or Devil? China's Trade Impact on Latin America."

23. Xingmin Yin, "A Survey on China's Apparel Industry" (Fudan University, Economics Department, 2006).

24. Mesquita-Moreira, "Fear of China."

25. Szirmai, Ren, and Bai point to a labor productivity spurt beginning in the early 1990s that has been fast enough to even reduce the productivity gap with the United States: the gap fell from 95 percent in 1995 to 86 percent in 2002. Adam Szirmai, Rouen Ren, and Manyin Bai, "Chinese Manufacturing Performance in Comparative Perspective, 1980–2002" (Yale University, Economic Growth Center, 2005).

26. Some industries, especially light ones, have not fully taken advantage of economies of scale. See Lin Su and Ren Ruo, "Capital Input in China and the Estimation of TFP Growth," *Journal of World Economy* (China), no. 9 (2005): 61–83.

27. Income data include only people legally registered to live in Shanghai.

28. IADB, *Periodic Note.*

29. Devlin, Estevadeordal, and Rodríguez-Clare, *The Emergence of China.*

30. *China Statistical Yearbook* (Beijing: China Statistics Press, 2005).

31. This includes two-year community college–like programs.

32. *China Statistical Yearbook.* In 2003 graduates with a doctorate numbered 1,440 in Mexico; 7,730 in Brazil; and 6,450 in Spain. In 2001 China matched the highest figure in science and engineering doctorates alone. Ernest Preeg, *The Emerging Chinese Advanced Technology Superstate* (Arlington, Va.: Manufacturers' Alliance and Hudson Institute, 2005).

33. Devlin, Estevadeordal, and Rodríguez-Clare, *The Emergence of China.*

34. Preeg, *The Emerging Chinese Advanced Technology Superstate.*

35. In absolute terms, expenditure in 2004 exceeded that of South Korea, a strong technological player in world markets.

36. "Faking It," *Economist,* May 20, 2006, p. 83.

37. Preeg, *The Emerging Chinese Advanced Technology Superstate.*

38. ECLAC, *Economic Survey of Latin America* (Santiago: 2006).

39. "Slow! Government Obstacles Ahead!" *Economist,* June 17, 2006, pp. 41–42.

40. Some of the critical areas are social tensions over increasing inequality (especially between urban and rural areas); large hidden contingent liabilities (nonperforming loans, pensions, environmental cleanup); widespread inefficiencies in state enterprises; turbid governance of firms and corruption; a possibly overheated economy; compliance with WTO obligations; a rise of protectionism among trading partners; flexibility and appreciation of the exchange rate; global imbalances and a sharp slowdown in the world economy; rebalancing domestic demand with consumption; and management of political demands as more markets bring more satisfying individual preferences.

41. Some point to China overtaking the German and Japanese economies before the end of the next decade. See "Dreaming with BRICs: The Path to 2050," Global Economics Paper 99 (New York: Goldman Sachs, 2003). John Hawksworth, along with Goldman Sachs, projects that China will be by far the world's largest economy by 2050. See John Hawksworth, "The World in 2050" (London: PriceWaterhouseCoopers, 2006).

42. As mentioned earlier, trade is currently the main link between China and Latin America and serves as a potential platform for other investments and cooperation. China means important competition in some countries for certain sectors—for example, textiles and apparel, footwear, electronics—that are now in competition in third markets, or are likely to be in the future, as China further diversifies. China also means a new major booming export market for Latin America. Commodity producing countries focus on this side of China's economy; but should the commodity boom falter, and should commodity producers suffer symptoms of Dutch disease, the competitive aspect of the Chinese phenomenon will gain more attention.

43. World Bank, *Quarterly Update, August 2006.*

44. Ernest Preeg, *Economic Report* (Arlington, Va.: Manufacturers' Alliance, 2006).

45. Corporación Andina de Fomento, *América Latina en el Comercio Global* (Caracas: CAF, 2005). Protectionism in world markets in areas where Latin America has a comparative advantage, such as agriculture, is partly to blame. Inter-American Development Bank, *Beyond Borders.*

46. Mesquita-Moreira, "Fear of China," p. 356.

47. See also Devlin, Estevadeordal, and Rodríguez-Clare, *The Emergence of China.*

48. Ibid.

49. Michael Mortimore, "The Impact of the TNC Strategies on Development in Latin America and the Caribbean," in *Foreign Direct Investment, Income Inequality, and Poverty,* edited by D. W. Velde (London: Overseas Development Institute, 2004).

50. Peres, "El (lento) Reto de las Políticas Industriales en América Latina y el Caribe."

51. Stallings argues that deep domestic financial markets is one of the key factors distinguishing East Asian and Latin American economic performance. Barbara

Stallings, *Finance and Development: Latin America in Comparative Perspective* (Brookings, 2006).

52. Devlin, Estevadeordal, and Rodríguez-Clare, *The Emergence of China.*

53. Because of low volume, ships in the region often must make multiple stops instead of point-to-point transit.

54. Stijns reviews the literature and does some new empirical work that supports this point. Jean-Philippe Stijns, "Natural Resource Abundance and Economic Growth Revisited" (Northeastern University, Department of Economics, 2005).

55. Graciela Moguillansky, "Innovation: The Missing Link in Latin American Countries," paper prepared for LASA annual meeting, January 2006.

56. World Tourism Organization, *Chinese Outward Tourism* (Madrid: 2003).

57. "The Golden Years," *Economist,* May 13, 2006, p. 52.

58. ECLAC, *Economic Survey of Latin America.*

59. Inter-American Development Bank, *Beyond Borders.*

60. Mikio Kuwayama and José E. Durán Lima, "La Calidad de la Inserción Internacional de América Latina y el Caribe en el Comercio Mundial," *Serie Comercio Internacional,* no. 26 (2003): 1–72.

61. Moguillansky, "Innovation."

62. For an analysis of the Australian and New Zealand cases, see Graciela Moguillansky, "Australia y Nueva Zelandia: la Innovación como Eje de la Competitividad," *Serie Comercio Internacional,* no. 72 (2006): 1–64. For Ireland, see Rory O'Donell, "Ireland's Economic Transformation," Working Paper 2 (University of Pittsburgh, Center for West European Studies, 1998); and for a subnational alliance, see Antonio Vázques-Barquero, "Dinámica Productiva y Desarrollo Urbano: La Respuesta de la Ciudad de Vitoria (País Vasco) a los Desafíos de la Globalización" (Santiago: EURE, 1999).

63. When they exist at all they tend to be precarious. See Peres, "El (lento) Reto de las Políticas Industriales en América Latina y el Caribe." They suffer from being one-sided (too much public sector or too much private sector), unsustained, incomplete, underfinanced, or only on paper.

FRANCISCO E. GONZÁLEZ

7

Latin America in the Economic Equation—Winners and Losers: What Can Losers Do?

This chapter highlights why some Latin American countries have benefited more than others in their economic relationships with China and examines whether those affected negatively can contain their losses.[1] By and large, economic gains have been thus far a function of the commodity lottery and the extent to which the Chinese economy and that of individual Latin American countries are complementary or substitutable. However, this is not a permanent equilibrium. As the global marketplace allocates resources and opportunities at lower costs and shorter delivery times, China and the countries of Latin America will need to keep adjusting their short-term political and economic strategies to ensure sharing gains from the expanding global economy. This chapter also highlights the importance of conscious actions that policymakers have undertaken or can undertake to contain losses.

The first section presents the statistics behind the strengthening relationship between China and Latin America to show how the commodity lottery has allocated gains and losses for individual Latin American countries. The second section highlights the extent of losses suffered by countries such as Mexico and the Central American republics whose economic outputs are more substitutes for than complements of the Chinese economy and evaluates policy alternatives that could limit their losses.

Winners and Losers

As several authors in this volume indicate, between 1990 and 2004 China doubled its participation in the world economy. China's gross domestic product as a proportion of world GDP in purchasing power parity rose from less than 7 percent in 1990 to more than 15 percent in 2006. Chinese exports as a percentage of world exports grew from 2 percent in 1990 to over 8 percent in 2006. Likewise, Chinese absorption of world foreign direct investment (FDI) grew from 2 percent in 1990 to over 5 percent in 2006.[2] These numbers reflect China's transformation in less than three decades from an agricultural, semi-autarkic economy to the world's manufacturing workshop and one of its leading exporters of manufactured goods.

Latin America, like other regions richly endowed with natural resources such as Africa and the Middle East, has become an important link in China's chain of production. The Chinese economy's appetite for commodities and energy will remain undiminished in the foreseeable future, and it is reasonable to assume that the booming trade between China and Latin America will continue.[3] This boom is relatively recent. In 1990 Chinese imports from Latin America amounted to only $1.5 billion. By 2005 they had grown eighteenfold, reaching $27 billion that year.[4] The annual growth of imports between 2000 and 2004 (42 percent) was almost double the growth of Chinese imports from the rest of the world (26 percent).[5] Chinese exports to Latin America increased even more, from $1.3 billion in 1990 to $23.3 billion in 2005.[6] Although estimates by Chinese sources are lower than Western ones (the PRC General Administration of Customs estimates that imports from Latin America went from $1.5 billion in 1991 to $10.5 billion in 2004, while Chinese exports to Latin America in the same period went from $795 million to $14 billion),[7] Western and Chinese sources agree on one point: Latin America, once a net exporter to China, has become a net importer. Latin America's trade deficits with China thus far have been relatively modest because trade between both parties is a small proportion of their total trade.[8] In fact, the bulk of recent exports from both China and Latin American countries remains strongly tied to U.S. and European Union markets (table 7-1).

Latin American countries currently stand to lose more from China's tough competition for the same high-income consumer markets than from their deficits in bilateral trading relations. One of the most comprehensive studies to date, by Robert Devlin, Antoni Estevadeordal, and Andrés Rodríguez-Clare, confirms that the China–Latin America economic relationship can be seen as a function of competition for the U.S. market. Thus, while the U.S. market export similarity index (ESI) between China and Mexico rose continuously between the early 1970s and 2001, denoting more overlapped trade patterns and thus stronger competition, the ESI between China and countries like Chile, Peru, and Argentina remained relatively low.[9] The case of Mexico is different. Given its extreme export concentration on the U.S. market, its

Table 7-1. *Share of Exports, Top Five Destinations, Seven Exporting Countries, 2006*
Percent

Rank of trade partner	China	Mexico	United States	Brazil	Argentina[a]	Chile[a]	Peru
1	U.S. (21)	U.S. (85)	Canada (22)	EU (22)	EU (17)	EU (23)	U.S. (24)
2	EU (19)	EU(4)	EU (21)	U.S. (18)	Brazil (16)	U.S. (16)	EU (19)
3	Hong Kong (16)	Canada (2)	Mexico (13)	Argentina (8)	Chile (11)	Japan (12)	China (10)
4	Japan (9)	Colombia (1)	Japan (6)	China (6)	U.S. (11)	China (11)	Switzerland (7)
5	Korea (5)	Venezuela (0.7)	China (5)	Mexico (3)	China (8)	Korea (6)	Canada (7)

Source: Based on World Trade Organization, statistics database, trade profiles (http://stat.wto.org/country profile/wsdbcountrypfview.aspx?language=e&country [December 2007]).
a. Data refer to 2005.

survival depends on retaining competitive access to it. China's top export market is also the United States, but its trade is much more diversified, having important stakes in both European Union and Asian markets. The South American countries export similar proportions to the United States and the European Union, and they all have China among the top five as a destination for their exports. In turn, more than one-third of U.S. exports go to its trading partners in NAFTA, but it also holds important stakes in the European Union and Asian markets.

Devlin, Estevadeordal, and Rodríguez-Clare use the United States as a benchmark to compare China and Latin American trade competition on the assumption that the relative openness and attractiveness of the U.S. economy is a good proxy to capture countries' domestic production and their exports. To this economic justification can be added the geopolitical one related to the traditional hegemonic U.S. presence in the Western Hemisphere. An accurate assessment of the China–Latin America economic relationship has to include how much it affects the United States and what actions the latter has taken or is ready to take to influence that relationship. So it is more fruitful to assess the China–Latin America relationship as a China–Latin America–U.S. triangle, in which trade flows are part of a more complex politicoeconomic quest. In the case of the United States, it is for hemispheric hegemony. In the case of China, it is for securing raw commodities and energy to further its fast-paced economic modernization and flex its muscles internationally. In the case of Latin American countries, it is for reigniting and sustaining economic growth to address gross inequality and poverty and social and political polarization.

In addition to the two indicators (trade concentration or diversification by export destinations and the ESI) that show increased competition from Chinese exports for some Latin American countries (Mexico) but not for others (Argentina, Chile, Peru), we need to know more about countries' export structures and main export products. The term *commodity lottery,* used by Victor Bulmer-Thomas to account for individual Latin American countries' integration into the world economy by the commodities they specialize in exporting, can be used to understand the China–Latin America–U.S. triangle.[10] The commodity lottery is composed of the random allocation of natural resource endowments. Different commodities stimulate different forward and backward linkages, face different demand elasticity, and are either unique or can be substituted synthetically.

Given the economic revolution in China, and its concomitant high demand for raw materials and energy, natural resource exporters in Latin America should benefit from China's rise, as Robert Devlin notes in chapter 6. In contrast, countries whose production structure and exports resemble China's, that is, countries dominated by unskilled, labor-intensive manufacturing, will compete for markets and incur losses due to strong Chinese competitiveness. Competition should be particularly fierce over U.S. market share, the world's largest market for the light manufactures produced by China, Mexico, and the Central American republics. How complementary or substitutable are China's and individual Latin American economies?

The most similar export structures by economic sector currently are those of China, Mexico, and the United States (figure 7-1). Next, Brazil's and Argentina's economies, on the one hand, and Chile's and Peru's, on the other, are similar. The three-sector division presented is too aggregate to specify export competition within each of the sectors; for example, consider those U.S. manufacturing exports that are way up the value chain of production compared with those of China and Mexico. The top ten U.S. exports are all manufactures and include technology-intensive items such as semiconductors, computer accessories, and pharmaceutical preparations, as well as heavy manufacturing from the aircraft and auto industries and industrial and electrical machines.[11] China's top ten exports are all manufactured goods, too, and include heavy manufacturing such as electrical equipment and machinery, power generation equipment, and iron and steel; and unskilled, labor-intensive light manufactures (textiles/apparel, furniture, toys, and footwear).[12] Likewise, with the exception of crude oil, Mexico's top ten exports are manufactures, too, and include the auto industry, electrical equipment, and

Figure 7-1. *Exports by Economic Sector, China, the United States, and Selected Latin American Countries, 2006*

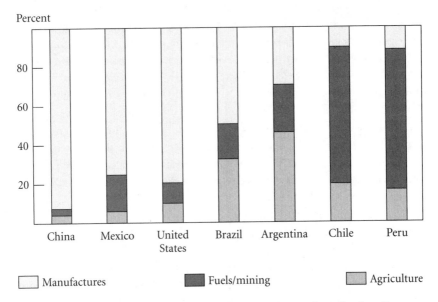

Percent

Source: Based on World Trade Organization, statistics database, trade profiles (http://stat.wto.org/countryprofile/wsdbcountrypfview.aspx?language=e&country [December 2007]).

telecommunications.[13] Within the manufacturing sector there are technology-intensive niches in which the U.S. economy remains complementary with the Chinese and Mexican economies, but in unskilled, labor-intensive sectors the economies are more substitutable and, therefore, competitors.

In contrast to China, Mexico, and the United States, whose top ten exports are manufactures, Chile's, Argentina's, and Peru's are natural resources and related processed products.[14] These countries have the most complementary economic structures vis-à-vis China. Chile's exports remain dominated by copper and its derivatives, although natural resources such as lumber, fish, and grapes are among this country's top ten exports. Peru's exports are heavily concentrated on mining, but it also has textiles and apparel, petroleum products, and coffee among its top ten exports. Argentina concentrates on the export of agriculture and livestock products, although it also exports crude oil, petroleum products, and natural gas.[15]

Even though the natural resource exporting economies of Argentina and Chile are among the most complementary with the Chinese economy, they have also suffered losses due to competition with the latter. In the period 1995–2004, Argentina's manufacturing sector initiated 31 antidumping WTO investigations into the Chinese mechanics and transport sectors, the highest number by Argentina against any country.[16] During the same period Chile invoked the rules of origin 396 times (in total, not only against China) in sectors such as textiles, metals, plastics, chemicals and rubber. China was found guilty in 22 investigations and suffered penalties in 15.[17]

Brazil benefits from natural resource exports to China. Among Brazil's top exports are fuels; mining products such as iron ore; petroleum products and crude oil; and soybeans, vegetable oils, poultry, and meat.[18] The two countries have launched cooperation ventures in heavy industry (steel, oil, ethanol, aeronautics) and in knowledge-intensive activities (space satellites, biotechnology, information technology, medicine, and new materials).[19] Brazil also has a strong domestic manufacturing base, which faces competition from China. Since 1989 Brazil has implemented 101 antidumping and safeguard measures, 20 percent of them targeting Chinese manufacturing imports.[20] Even though countries in Latin America exporting natural resources have experienced pressure from Chinese competitiveness, by and large their bilateral trading relationship has translated into net gains. All have sustained trade surpluses with China since it joined the WTO in 2001 (figure 7-2). Before this date, they experienced modest deficits in their bilateral trade with China.

China's integration into the world trading system has provided natural resource exporters in South America an opportunity to diversify their export destinations beyond the United States and the European Union into East Asia. The greatest beneficiaries from recent bilateral trade have been Chile and Peru, whose economies are the most complementary with China. In particular, the global commodities boom since 2004 has translated into a boom in mining exports for these countries. This boom has been fueled by China, which in 2005 "accounted for almost half of the world's consumption of metallurgical coal, over 40 percent of thermal coal and iron ore consumption, and more than 20 percent of steel, aluminum, copper, and zinc consumption."[21]

Although Argentina and Brazil have also benefited from this boom, their surplus trade balances with China reached a zenith in 2003 and have declined since then. These reductions are a result of China's strategy to square its trading balance sheet with its largest suppliers of raw materials in the region. This is one of the reasons that President Hu Jintao of China spent almost two weeks touring South America after the Asia-Pacific Economic Cooperation (APEC) summit in Chile in November 2004. As various authors in this volume point

Figure 7-2. South American Natural Resource Exporters, Trade Balance with China, 1995–2005

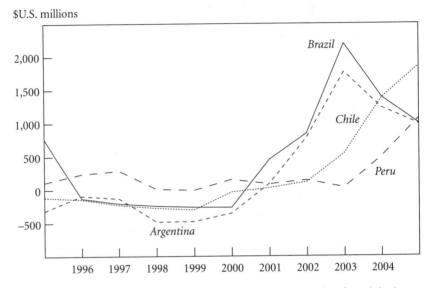

$U.S. millions

Source: Based on Asociación Latinoamericana de Integración (ALADI) trade statistics (www.aladi.org).

out, one of President Hu's main political objectives was to secure support for the One China policy, but his main economic objective was to get South American countries to recognize his country as a market economy.[22] Responding to promises of Chinese investment in infrastructure and more open access for South American exports to its domestic market, Argentina, Brazil, Chile, and Peru extended market economy status to China.[23] As a consequence, these countries now find it much harder to apply antidumping safeguards against cheap Chinese manufacturing imports. Brazilian and Argentine manufacturers in textiles, footwear, and toys have been hard hit by the influx of cheap Chinese imports. Moreover, the promised Chinese investment in South America has not materialized (see Jiang Shixue's analysis in chapter 2 about this controversial issue).[24]

In stark contrast with the gains of natural resource exporters, Mexico and the Central American countries have suffered net losses from their economic relationship with China. These losses have been twofold. Mexico and the Central American countries have experienced growing deficits in their bilateral trade with China. They have also lost market share to China in the United States, their main export market. Mexico's trade balance with China has deteriorated significantly since the latter joined the WTO in 2001, jumping from $3 billion in 2001 to $14.5 billion in 2005 and $23 billion in the first quarter of 2007.[25] Central America has also suffered growing trade deficits with China since the 1990s, although its bilateral trade remains small.[26] These deficits are growing because Mexico and the Central American countries geared "their production and commercial specialization since the 1990s to the transformation of imported inputs that are sold in the United States."[27] The result for Mexico and Central America has been a concentrated trade profile, whose manufacturing exports to the U.S. market have competed head-to-head with those of China.

The commodity lottery helps to explain the distribution of gains and losses for Latin American countries derived from the global economic rise of China. Natural resource exporters have benefited from Chinese demand for raw materials, while exporters of labor-intensive manufactures produced by unskilled labor and overdependent on the U.S. market, such as Mexico and Central America, have incurred important losses. However, the evidence in this section also suggests that the commodity lottery need not apply only on a country-by-country basis, such as Chile is winning and Mexico is losing. It can also apply by economic sector, as seen in the opposition and complaints by manufacturing leaders in Argentina and Brazil against cheaper Chinese imports. These complaints and demands for state protection against Chinese competitiveness and market takeover have occurred in strong natural resource exporting countries. From this perspective, manufacturers in Brazil and Argentina who have been harmed by Chinese competition share more with Mexican and Central American manufacturers than with their domestic compatriots who have been making big windfalls from Chinese demand for raw materials.

However good an explanation the commodity lottery is, its structural character (natural endowments determine winners and losers) should not convey impotence (there is no point in doing anything about changing the status quo because whatever we do, our natural endowments will keep determining our trading gains or losses). The commodity lottery is not a fixed equation. Sound public policy and strategic domestic and international actions by leaders of affected countries, no matter how small and dependent, can influence how their economy integrates into the expanding global economy. The next section evaluates the extent of losses suffered by the Mexican and Central American manufacturing sectors as a result of fierce economic competition with China. It also evaluates the success or failure of government policy responses to contain or reverse these losses and discusses alternatives that could make such policy responses more effective.

Policy Options for Losers

To assess the evolution of Chinese competition in export manufacturing it is important to understand the central role of the state in the economic revolution started under Deng Xiaoping in 1978 (see chapter 2 for an overview of Deng's reform policies). Since then, one of the most effective catch-up tools has been the Chinese state's strategic selection of production sectors, which it has promoted within a long-term time frame. The first selection of favored sectors was established in 1981. It included such various sectors as agriculture, energy, information technology, and space technology. After obtaining poor results, the government shifted its strategy in 1988 with a program, known as TORCH, to promote ten high-technology manufacturing sectors. By 1996 this program had yielded promising results, and the state modified its strategy in its Ninth Quinquennial Plan and in its Long-Term Objectives' Profile to 2010. This adjustment focused Chinese state support on the auto industry and on the electronics and telecommunications, machinery, petrochemical, chemical, steel, and construction sectors.[28]

Today, as one analyst points out, "China already knows what it wants by 2020 and, most importantly, it has a plan to achieve this."[29] The aims are to quadruple GDP and to achieve an average annual growth of 7 percent, a GDP per capita of $5,000 for the country's 1.5 billion inhabitants, and a 45 percent integration component for its high-technology exports (double today's integration component), in addition to implementing an aggressive program to establish 50 transnational companies, 500 medium-size firms, and 5,000 small and medium-size firms capable of competing in the global economy.[30]

However, wishing for something and achieving it are not the same thing. Even so, China's record since the 1980s has been impressive. During that decade, around half of Chinese exports were oil and raw materials; by the 1990s a majority of its exports were concentrated in apparel and textiles; and since the second half of the 1990s auto parts and electronics have taken the lead.[31] These statistics show China's success in moving up the value chain in manufacturing exports. Most economists consider such a progression crucial for emerging economies to make relative gains in the process of globalization.[32]

Given such an aggressive, well-planned strategy for economic expansion, it is not surprising that China's manufacturing competitors in Latin America, especially Mexico and the Central American republics, live in fear of Chinese competitiveness. However, Mexico and Central America do not face the same challenge. Analyses suggest that only Mexico shares the trade specialization patterns of emerging Asian giants like China and India. The Andean and Central American countries are somewhere in between. The Southern Cone countries, as shown also in the previous section, have moved in a different direction.[33] Other analyses, using the first ten chapters in the *Standard International Trade Classification*, also conclude that China and the Central American countries are more complementary than China and Mexico, whose economies are more substitutes.[34] Mexico's top ten exports, with the exception of oil, are all manufactures that compete with Chinese manufacturing exports.[35] But the top exports of the Central American countries are bananas, coffee, other tropical fruits, raw sugar (beet and cane), and other miscellaneous food preparations.[36] Since 2002 China has become Mexico's second largest source of imports, with a big influx of auto parts, electronics, toys, and footwear, all of which have hurt local producers who traditionally supply the domestic market. The Chinese economic powerhouse has not achieved the same penetration into Central America.[37]

Mexico and Central America do share an important structural characteristic: economic dependence on exporting to the U.S. market. The corollary is that while China has made great inroads into the U.S. market, this is a problem shared by Mexico and the Central American countries. Any assessment of how much China's competition has hurt Mexican and Central American manufacturing exports must include an analysis of the main trends in the sectors, moving up the value chain, starting with textiles and apparel and moving on to electronics and computers.

The Textiles and Apparel Sector

Chinese leaders in the 1980s decided that it was better to carry out export trials before opening up to international markets. This strategy allowed them to promote the unskilled, labor-intensive industrial model, geared initially toward the assembly of imported inputs into finished goods for reexport. The model, widely known in Spanish as the maquiladora industry (assembly of parts for reexport of finished products), is a niche in which China had a comparative advantage. China first nurtured this comparative advantage in textiles and apparel. Between the mid-1980s and the mid-1990s, this sector became the engine of China's massive industrialization.[38]

The Chinese strategy was based on identifying and putting together an exporting platform before tackling international competition. As noted in prior chapters, this strategy was the complete opposite of the free market reforms scheme, later known as the Washington consensus, adopted by Latin American governments in the wake of the region's financial and economic collapse in 1982. The policies under the Washington consensus were one size fits all; liberalization was carried out wholesale without export trials.[39] Such trials should be fundamental, as the Chinese case suggests, because only industrial activities that make promising gains once exposed to international competition could help Latin American societies cope with the transition from relatively closed and protected economies to open and cutthroat economies. Even worse, decisions to promote the textiles and apparel sector in Mexico, Central America, and the Caribbean were not guided by the purpose of identifying comparative advantages. Rather, they were "an outgrowth of preferential U.S. trade policies. Indeed, the United States, facing strong competition from low-cost Asian producers, enacted a series of trade preferences for Mexico and countries in the Caribbean Basin Initiative (CBI) to complement U.S. industry and help make it more competitive."[40]

U.S. trade policy changed in 1986 when section 807 of the trade law gave preferential market access to U.S. firms, which imported garments sewn abroad but with fabrics cut in the United States. This amendment removed quotas on exports of apparel assembled from fabrics cut and formed in the United States to CBI countries and, in 1988, to Mexico.[41] After NAFTA went into effect in January 1994 garments sewn in any of the signatory countries became eligible for duty-free and quota-free treatment, as long as the yarn and fabrics were produced in a signatory country. Demands to gain parity with NAFTA from CBI countries culminated in the passage of the Caribbean Basin Trade Partnership Act (CBTPA) in May 2000. The U.S. Congress passed the Dominican Republic–Central American Free Trade Agreement (D.R.–CAFTA) in July 2005, which, it should be noted, does not provide new tariff cuts for textile and apparel products that already enter the United States duty free under the CBTPA. The CBTPA expires in September 2008.[42]

Basing the promotion of textile and apparel maquiladoras on the preferential access granted by U.S. trade law rather than on solid comparative advantages could accentuate rigidities over time, which might hurt competitiveness for Mexico and the Central American and Caribbean countries included in the CBI. Such promotion has yielded medium-term gains for these countries, and the sector has "generated exports and good jobs," according to some authors.[43] The textiles and apparel value chain has been broken down territorially, with the most capital- and skill-intensive processes remaining in the United States and those requiring unskilled labor being relocated to its southern neighbors, resulting in a regional cluster.[44] The fate of all the contributors to this value chain, be they U.S. or Mexican, Central American or Caribbean businessmen and governments, are linked: all rise or fall together.

U.S. businesses could relocate the unskilled, labor-intensive links of the chain to other developing regions, if these countries were seen as losing their competitive edge. China's fierce competition in textiles and apparel has been a function of its edge in cheaper production costs as well as in luring U.S. businesses to relocate operations to its thriving coastal cities. China's special economic zones provide fiscal incentives, joint ventures' facilities, cheap supply of labor, electricity, and diversity of component suppliers.[45]

As mentioned earlier, the main reason that Mexico and Central American/Caribbean countries are vulnerable to Chinese competition in this sector is the extreme concentration of exports on a single market, the United States. Unlike China, whose average share of textiles and apparel exports to the United States was only 12 percent in 2001, the average share for Mexico and the countries included in the CBI was above 90 percent.[46] This was before China's final accession to the WTO and before the elimination of quotas under the Multifiber Agreement (MFA) in 2005.[47]

As expected, textiles and apparel imports from China have surged since the elimination of quotas, and such growth has been at the expense of Mexico and the Central American countries.[48] However, China's takeover of the U.S. market has not affected producers across the board. While El Salvador has reported a decline in textile exports since the ending of quotas by the WTO and the opening up of the market to cheap Chinese imports, Nicaragua has become the second fastest growing exporter of apparel to the United States.[49] Besides its preferential access to the U.S. market under CAFTA, which neighboring countries also enjoy, Nicaragua has the lowest labor costs in the region.[50] Similarly, some areas in Mexico have been affected more negatively than others by the end of the MFA quotas. Some maquiladora cities along the Mexico-U.S. border, like Ciudad Juárez, have suffered employment losses since early 2005.[51] But regions offering the process known as full package, in which suppliers not only assemble a product but also purchase basic inputs, cut the fabric, design the product, package it, and deliver it to the retailer, have retained their U.S. market share. This is the case of the industrial cluster of La Laguna, around the city of Torreón, which continues to supply almost half of the jeans imported into the United States.[52]

Another major problem for Mexican textile and apparel producers for the domestic market is the smuggling of cheap Chinese clothing into Mexico. Chinese producers have become major exporters of cheap counterfeit versions of designer clothes, which have swamped the Mexican clothing market. Some estimates suggest that up to 58 percent of clothing sales in Mexico are the product of this illicit market, with only 20 percent made in Mexico and 22 percent legal imports.[53] The topic of Chinese smuggling was high on the agenda of meetings between the Mexican president, Vicente Fox, and China's prime minister, Wen Jiabao, during the latter's visit to Mexico in December 2003. According to President Fox, by 2003 the Mexican government had lost more than $3 billion in taxable revenue due to the wholesale smuggling of Chinese clothing.[54]

Textile and apparel specialists argue that if Mexico and Central America cannot compete with China on production costs, they must cultivate their "proximity to the U.S. advantage." Fast delivery is essential in the textiles and apparel sector. Given the mercurial timeliness of fashion, retailers dislike big inventories, expect fast turnover of their goods, and "require apparel suppliers to replenish basic and fashion products on a weekly basis."[55] Proximity to the United States is a comparative advantage for Mexico and Central America only if their speed to market satisfies the lean retailing model that prevails in this sector.

The Electronics and Computer Sector

Moving up the value chain of production, China's share of the electronic and computer sector in the global market went from only 0.04 percent in 1985 to 8.80 percent in 2001.[56] This rise was a direct consequence of strategic planning by the Chinese state, with its high-technology TORCH program. Compared to textiles and apparel, China's electronics and computer sector is still low, but it has already surpassed Mexico's, which went from 0.25 percent to 4.50 percent in the same period.[57] In Central America only Costa Rica has a share of this sector, thanks to a big Intel semiconductor assembly and test plant built in 1996.

Unlike the textiles and apparel sector, in which trade liberalization was completed only after the end of the MFA in 2005, the electronics and computer sector has been liberalized since the 1990s. Open markets created incentives for firms in developed countries to transfer parts of their value chains to developing countries, where production costs were much lower. As a consequence, U.S. and EU participation in the global market for electronics and computers saw a dramatic fall, from 80 percent in 1985 to 40 percent in 2001.[58] American and European firms still command the heights in the industry in terms of sale of finished products and brand recognition, but much of their value chain has been outsourced. How much do Mexico and Costa Rica stand to lose from Chinese incursion into this sector?

The Mexican government started investing in high-technology sectors in the 1940s. Under the import substitution industrialization development model, Mexican firms manufactured radios and televisions and their component parts. The government started investing in the computer industry in the 1970s. This program was intended to serve the domestic market and to help Mexico compete internationally. The program was quite successful; it attracted investment and production plants from computing giants IBM and

Hewlett Packard. Despite Mexico's poor economic performance after the 1982 external debt crisis, the sector exhibited healthy growth. By 1987 half of domestic production supplied all of the domestic computer market; the other half was exported to the United States and Canada. The city of Guadalajara became the Mexican "Silicon Valley," and foreign investment surged, making Mexico the eleventh leading world exporter of high-technology products in the world economy by 2001.[59]

Enter China. Its TORCH program established high-technology industrial parks and state support to assemble computers, to increase the percentage of Chinese components in such computers, and to produce other hardware such as monitors, printers, and hard disks. The Chinese government also supports development in the software industry; in 2002 thirty-five universities offered computer programming degrees. Transnational corporations have been invited to establish joint ventures: the main U.S., European, Japanese, and Taiwanese computer manufacturers have joined local Chinese firms such as Juawei, CSMC Corporation, and ZTE.[60]

Mexico still has some comparative advantages over China in the electronics and computer sector, in particular, proximity to the U.S. market. High-tech shipments from China to the United States take fifteen days. Similar shipments take twelve days from Japan and twenty-three days from Malaysia. Shipments from Guadalajara to the United States, however, take only one day. China still retains the upper hand when it comes to labor costs in this sector. Mexican wages are $2.40 an hour, whereas China's are only $0.95.[61] This is one of the main reasons Mexico lost an opportunity to become a major supplier to the big electronics and computer transnational corporations. Despite its industrial base before the establishment of transnational electronics and computer firms in its territory, no linkage between domestic and foreign firms took place. Between 1994 and 2002, 97 percent of all investment in Guadalajara's electronics sector was from foreign sources. As a consequence, thirteen of twenty-five Mexican firms that operated in Guadalajara in 1997 had closed down by 2005.[62]

The electronics sector in Costa Rica developed differently. When the CBI granted preferential market access to Central American and Caribbean goods, Costa Rica diversified its export base, previously concentrated on exporting coffee and other agricultural products. The Costa Rica Investment Board (CINDE), made up of local businessmen and supported by the Costa Rican government through U.S. Agency for International Development grants, helped to link up domestic and foreign investors.[63] In the early 1990s CINDE members realized that Costa Rica was losing its competitiveness in unskilled, labor-intensive activities vis-à-vis other CBI member countries and Mexico. In

1993 CINDE started promoting Costa Rica as a country whose relatively high human capital and comparatively high regional infrastructure and socioeconomic development could become a strong base for exporting electronics and telecommunications goods.[64]

This strategy paid off when Intel chose to build a $300 million semiconductor assembly and test (A&T) plant in Costa Rica in 1996. Its decision was based on Costa Rica's nonunion, probusiness environment, its favorable attitude toward FDI, its location, and its transportation infrastructure. The Costa Rican government was also responsive to concerns voiced by Intel.[65] Thanks to Intel, FDI in high-tech manufacturing in Costa Rica has more than doubled since 1996; it is now almost two-thirds of total foreign investment (the rest is in agriculture and trade).[66]

What has been the net result of Intel's operations in Costa Rica? On the positive side, Costa Rica became the biggest exporter per capita in Latin America between 1999 and 2001, because of Intel's exports. In addition, Intel employs 3,200 workers at salaries substantially higher than average salaries for workers in apparel or agriculture.[67] It also has helped develop the Costa Rican communications infrastructure, has forced the government to reorient its goals and priorities toward meeting demands from a global corporation, and has spurred the creation of a local support industry: 460 firms supply Intel with materials and services.[68]

On the negative side, only 2 percent of the value added of Intel's exports contains local materials, so the backward linkages remain weak. Despite Costa Rica's efforts to attract other high-tech global companies, none has set up shop in the country. Due to excess capacity and a fall in world demand, Motorola and DSC/Alcatel shut down their component operations in that country.[69]

Intel's operations in Costa Rica remain to a large extent maquiladora activity. For high-technology firms to set up shop in a country or region, they need "a more developed support industry of international and local vendors to enhance their supply chains and promulgate a full clustering effect."[70] This is happening in Shanghai, Malaysia, Singapore, and Ireland but not in Latin America.[71] Mexico and Costa Rica will face even tougher competition in this sector in the future. The higher concentration of electronics and computer firms in Southeast Asia and China means that their costs, logistics, and growing consumer markets (since 2002 China has been the second biggest consumer market for personal computers in the world after the United States) make them highly attractive places for high-tech giants to set up shop.[72] Intel itself has an assembly and testing plant in Shanghai and is constructing a new one in Sichuan, which started to package and test advanced multicore microprocessors in early 2007.[73]

Policy recommendations in this area are easily spelled out but difficult to implement. The experts argue that high-tech FDI on its own is not enough to help develop the electronics and computer sector. Domestic linkage is crucial to attracting and keeping high-tech FDI and to raising a country's potential for adding domestic value to exports that can compete in the global marketplace. It should be easier for bigger economies such as Mexico than for smaller ones like Costa Rica to develop domestic linkage capability.[74] Recent evidence suggests that competitive pressure from China has forced the Mexican electronics and computer sector to restructure in such a way.[75] As a consequence, the outlook for the sector is better today than it was in the 2001–04 period. This development has taken the form of a shift from "low-mix/high-volume manufacturing to high-mix/low-volume manufacturing . . . broader range of services including design, logistics, and after-sales service . . . and significant investment in capacity expansion in organic growth as opposed to acquisition."[76] These changes can be interpreted as a deliberate "smartening up" to try to move away from maquiladora activity and into the equivalent of a full-package strategy with strong indigenous components.

Conclusion

As the other authors in this volume note, China's rise to global economic prominence has had a strong impact in Latin America. Thus far the commodity lottery helps to explain the most general trends according to which natural resource exporting countries, such as Chile and Peru, have experienced big windfalls in their growing relationship with China. Countries with a mixed export structure that includes raw materials and a manufacturing component, such as Brazil and Argentina, have experienced gains in the former sector and losses in the latter. And economies that rely on the export of labor-intensive manufactured goods to the United States, like Mexico and Central America, have been affected negatively by China's penetration into the U.S. market. The commodity lottery has had a sector-by-sector effect; in general terms Latin American natural resource exporters have benefited, while manufacturers have lost.

China's economic development strategy, based on moving gradually up the value chain of production, has created a conundrum for Latin American manufacturers. Starting at the bottom end of the value chain, China has become a leading exporter of textiles and apparel, in the process harming Mexican and Central American producers. Experts argue that Mexico and Central America should exploit their proximity to the United States to regain comparative advantage. To do this, they have to master full packaging and speed-to-market processes. The policy recommendation in this area can be summarized as follows: beating Chinese competition in textiles and apparel will require faster and more thorough production processes.

China also has positioned itself aggressively in the electronics and computer sector by moving up the value chain. Having started from a tiny base, China has established a strong export industry and has used its location in Asia to purchase inputs cheaply and assemble final products at a highly competitive price. The experts argue that if Mexico and Costa Rica want to retain a competitive presence in this sector, they have to integrate it more efficiently. More indigenous value added, plus exporting lower volumes of more sophisticated goods, is necessary if these countries are to withstand Chinese competition, whose main comparative advantage remains its continued capacity to bring down costs.

In the meantime, China continues to work on moving up the value chain. The auto and auto-parts industries provide an example. Beijing announced a plan to designate eight cities as special zones for assembly and export of cars.[77] Thus far China's experience in this sector is spotty. As noted by one analyst, "Chinese automakers must recognize that Europe expects cars that meet regional standards and fulfill expectations of demanding customers. Simply manufacturing cars is not enough to be successful in Europe."[78] Managers and workers in the Mexican auto industry, the country's second largest export sector after oil, might breathe a sigh of relief after reading this. The big three U.S. car manufactures have continued expanding their operations into Mexico, as have Nissan and Volkswagen.[79]

The auto industry is a sector in which Mexico's proximity to the United States, the largest car market in the world, remains of paramount importance. Heavy goods, such as cars, are expensive to transport long distances, and the fact that the United States and Mexico are in the same time zones makes it much easier for multinational firms with operations in both countries to coordinate.[80] If the big auto-manufacturing firms set up shop in China, it would probably be to supply the immense potential domestic market rather than to export cars. Still, it is premature to write off China's most recent attempt to move up the value chain in automobile production given its cost advantage in manufacturing.

If Mexico and the countries of Central America that export manufactures to the United States are to stay in business, they must find ways to speed up their production and make it more efficient, smarter, and more integrated than the Chinese competition. This is, of course, easier said than done, but the expanding global economy does not wait long before choosing winners and losers. One of the few ways in which these complex objectives could be pursued in a sustained way would be through a revival of industrial policy. This area of economic planning was stigmatized by rent seeking, bureaucratization, and inefficiency in the wake of the critique mounted by the Washington consensus against state intervention in the economies of developing countries. However, as one analyst notes, it is strikingly obvious that when Chinese and Latin American exporters meet, the ensuing confrontation is not between two similar actors but rather between a Latin American company or entrepreneur and Chinese exporters backed by a comprehensive strategy and the full force and support of the Chinese state, which has made trade policy a top state endeavor.[81]

The revival of industrial policy in Latin America need not mean returning to the failed policies of the ISI years. Rather, it points to the creation of a smart state, which helps promote the competitiveness of the private sector while giving it relative autonomy. As Robert Devlin states in chapter 6, a missing piece in Latin America's economic development in the recent past is the development of public-private partnerships to increase international competitiveness. Such a strategy is crucial: economic plans need medium- to long-term time horizons; economic activity needs to be rewarded for its performance in the global marketplace; and nonpartisan research and coordination is needed to help private actors discover niches, forge strategic partnerships, and upgrade business operations.[82] China has done this with smashing success. Why can't Latin America do the same?

Notes

1. For invaluable research assistance, the author thanks Sarah Johnston-Gardner, Katherine Fennell, and Alejandro Carrión-Menéndez.

2. José Luis Machinea, "World Economic Situation and China's Impact on Latin America and the Caribbean," Latin American Iron and Steel Congress, Caracas, October 31, 2005; International Monetary Fund (IMF) Data & Statistics (www.inf.org); World Trade Organization (WTO) Statistics Database (www.wto.org); and United Nations Conference on Trade and Development (UNCTAD), China Statistics (www. unctad.org).

3. IMF, *World Economic Outlook 2006* (www.imf.org/external/pubs/ft/weo/2006/02/pdf/c2.pdf [December 2007]), pp. 49–52; *Economist*, "China: Coming Out" (www.economist.com/surveys/displaystory.cfm?story_id= 5623226 [December 2007]); Oxford Analytica, *China: A Five-Year Outlook* (www.oxan.com/cr/projects/outlook/china2.asp [December 2007]).

4. Robert Devlin, Antoni Estevadeordal, and Andrés Rodríguez-Clare, eds., *The Emergence of China: Opportunities and Challenges for Latin America and the Caribbean* (Harvard University Press, 2006), p. 126; Alexander B. Hammer and James A. Kilpatrick, "Distinctive Patterns and Prospects in China–Latin America Trade, 1999–2005," *Journal*

of International Commerce and Economics, U.S. International Trade Commission (September 2006): 7.

5. Economic Commission for Latin America and the Caribbean (ECLAC), "China Seeking to Strengthen Economic Ties with Latin America and the Caribbean," Press release, September 6, 2005 (www.eclac.org).

6. Devlin, Estevadeordal, and Rodríguez-Clare, *The Emergence of China*, p. 126; Hammer and Kilpatrick, "Distinctive Patterns," p. 11.

7. Arturo Oropeza García, *China: entre el Reto y la Oportunidad* (Mexico City: UNAM, 2006), p. 253.

8. This analysis concentrates on merchandise trade and does not include other fundamental aspects of the economic relationship between China and Latin America such as competition for foreign direct investment and services trade.

9. Devlin, Estevadeordal, and Rodríguez-Clare, *The Emergence of China*, pp. 117–23.

10. Victor Bulmer-Thomas, *The Economic History of Latin America since Independence* (Cambridge University Press, 1994), p. 15.

11. U.S. Census Bureau (www.census.gov/foreign-trade/statistics/product/enduse/exports/c0000.html [December 2007]).

12. U.S.-China Business Council (www.uschina.org/statistics/tradetable.html [December 2007]).

13. ECLAC.

14. The main processed Chilean products are frozen fish, wood pulp, and wine; Argentina's are vegetable oils, frozen meat, and leather products.

15. ECLAC.

16. Oropeza, *China*, p. 262.

17. Ibid., pp. 264–65.

18. ECLAC.

19. Oropeza, *China*, pp. 256–59.

20. Ibid., p. 258.

21. Mark Thirlwell, "The High Price of Feeding the Hungry Dragon," *Financial Times*, April 27, 2006, p. 13.

22. Jorge Domínguez and others, "China's Relations with Latin America: Shared Gains, Asymmetric Hopes," working paper (Washington: Inter-American Dialogue, 2006), p. 23.

23. Adam Thomson, "Granting of Market-Economy Status to China Opens Argentina's Door to Investment," *Financial Times*, November 19, 2004, p. 12.

24. Domínguez and others, "China's Relations with Latin America," p. 23; Jonathan Wheatley, "Brazil Says China Deal Is Falling Short of Its Hopes," *Financial Times*, October 3, 2005, p. 1.

25. ALADI (www.aladi.org).

26. Secretaría de Integración Económica Centroamericana (www.sieca.org.gt/publico/ca_en_cifras/monografias_de_comercio/china_continental/ca_resumen_de_la_balaza_comercial.htm [December 2007]).

27. Enrique Dussel Peters and Liu Xue Dong, "China: competencia comercial con México y Centroamérica," summary by Alma Rosa Cruz Zamorano, in *Comercio Exterior*, March 2005, p. 286.

28. Oropeza, *China*, pp. 288–89.

29. Ibid., p. 290.

30. Ibid.

31. Dussel Peters and Liu, "China," p. 283.

32. Mauricio Mesquita-Moreira, "Fear of China: Is There a Future for Manufacturing in Latin America?" *World Development* 35, no. 3 (March 2007): 355–76; Enrique Dussel Peters and Liu Xue Dong, *Oportunidades y retos económicos de China para México y Centroamérica* (Santiago: ECLAC, 2004), p. 7; Daniel H. Rosen, "How China is Eating Mexico's Lunch," *International Economy*, Spring 2003, p. 25.

33. Daniel Lederman, Marcelo Olarreaga, and Eliana Rubiano, "Specialization and Adjustment during the Growth of China and India: The Latin American Experience," Policy Research Working Paper no. 4318 (Washington : World Bank, 2007), pp. 7–8.

34. Dussel Peters and Liu, "China," p. 283.

35. Ibid., p. 285. From 1990 to 2003 more than half (55 percent) of Mexican exports to the United States have been in electronics, autos, and autoparts, sectors in which the country competes directly with China.

36. ECLAC.

37. Dussel Peters and Liu, "China," pp. 285–86.

38. Ibid., p. 286.

39. Oropeza, *China*, p. 302.

40. Devlin, Estevadeordal, and Rodríguez-Clare, *The Emergence of China*, p. 176.

41. The nineteen countries currently included in the CBI are Antigua and Barbuda, Aruba, Bahamas, Barbados, Belize, British Virgin Islands, Costa Rica, Dominica, Grenada, Guyana, Haiti, Jamaica, Montserrat, Netherlands Antilles, Panama, St. Kitts and Nevis, St. Lucia, St. Vincent and the Grenadines, Trinidad and Tobago (www.ustr. gov/Trade_Development/Preference_Programs/CBI/Section_Index.html [December 2007]).

42. Jennifer Bair and Enrique Dussel Peters, "Global Commodity Chains and Endogenous Growth: Export Dynamism and Development in Mexico and Honduras," *World Development* 34, no. 2 (2006): 203–21.

43. Devlin, Estevadeordal, and Rodríguez-Clare, *The Emergence of China*, pp. 177–78.

44. Ibid.

45. U.S. General Accounting Office, Report to Congressional Requesters, "International Trade: Mexico's Maquiladora Decline Affects U.S.-Mexico Border Communities and Trade; Recovery Depends in Part on Mexico's Actions," July 2003 (www.gao. gov/new.items/d03891.pdf#search= percent22US percent20GAO percent20report percent20international percent20trade percent20mexico's percent20maquiladora percent20decline percent22 [December 2007]).

46. Devlin, Estevadeordal, and Rodríguez-Clare, *The Emergence of China*, figure 7.5.

47. The MFA gave the United States, Canada, and the European Union a multilateral instrument to limit imports of yarn, fabric, and clothing from developing countries through the imposition of quotas. The consequences of such quotas forced the price of imported textiles and apparel up, while creating incentives for the domestic production of such goods. Under WTO rules, the MFA was phased out. On January 1, 2005, the last stage of this process was completed, although the United States can still use "safeguards" against dumping until 2008. U.S. Department of Agriculture (www.usda.gov).

48. Frederick Abernathy, Anthony Volpe, and David Weil, "The Future of the Apparel and Textile Industries: Prospects for Public and Private Actors" (Harvard Center for Textile and Apparel Research, 2005), p. 21.

49. "Feeding a Dragon," *Latin Finance*, September 22, 2006 (www.latinfinance.com); "As China's Apparel Exports Grow, So Do Nicaragua's," *Logistics Today News*, April 6, 2005.

50. Devlin, Estevadeordal, and Rodríguez-Clare, *The Emergence of China*, table 7.2.

51. María Esperanza Sánchez, "México: las maquiladoras," *BBC Mundo.com* (http://news.bbc.co.uk/hi/spanish/specials/newsid_4308000/4308603.stm [December 2007]).

52. Abernathy, Volpe, and Weil, "The Future of the Apparel and Textile Industries," pp. 21–22.

53. Dussel Peters and Liu, "China," pp. 286–87.

54. BBC, "México y China dialogan," December 13, 2003 (http://news.bbc.co.uk/hi/spanish/latin_america/newsid_3315000/3315523.stm [December 2007]).

55. Abernathy, Volpe, and Weil, "The Future of the Apparel and Textile Industries," p. 1.

56. Dussel Peters and Liu, "China," p. 287.

57. Ibid.

58. Ibid.

59. Eva A. Paus and Kevin P. Gallagher, "The Missing Links between Foreign Investment and Development: Lessons from Costa Rica and Mexico" (Tufts University, Global Development and Environment Institute, 2006), pp. 14–16 (www.ase.tufts.edu/gdae/pubs/wp/06-01missinglinks.pdf [December 2007]).

60. Dussel Peters and Liu, "China," pp. 287–88.

61. Paus and Gallagher, "The Missing Links between Foreign Investment and Development," pp. 16–17.

62. Ibid., p. 24.

63. For information, see www.outsourcingcostarica.com.

64. Andrés Rodríguez-Clare, "Costa Rica's Development Strategy Based on Human Capital and Technology: How It Got There, the Impact of INTEL, and Lessons for Other Countries," UNDP Human Development Report (New York: United Nations, 2001), pp. 4–8.

65. Ibid., pp. 9–10.

66. CINDE (www.cinde.org/eng-20anos.shtml [December 2007]).

67. Intel, "Intel Costa Rica Celebrates 10 Years of Innovation, Commitment, and Excellence," Intel-Costa Rica (www.intel.com/community/costarica/spotlight.htm).

68. CINDE.

69. World Bank/MIGA, "The Impact of Intel in Costa Rica: Nine Years after the Decision to Invest" (Washington: 2006), pp. 16–20 (www.fdi.net/documents/worldbank/databases/investing_in_development/intelcr/ [December 2007]).

70. Ibid., p. 27.

71. Ibid.

72. Dussel Peters and Liu, "China," p. 289.

73. World Bank/MIGA, "The Impact of Intel in Costa Rica," p. 27 and appendix 4.

74. Paus and Gallagher, "The Missing Links between Foreign Investment and Development," p. 27.

75. Mariana Via Urista and Bruce Rayner, "The New Mexico Option," *EMS Now*, Sept. 12, 2006 (www.emsnow.com/npps/story.cfm?id=21788 [December 2007]).

76. Ibid.

77. Richard McGregor, "Beijing Puts Eight Cities on Frontline in Big Push on Car Exports," *Financial Times*, August 18, 2006, p. 6.

78. Wim Oude Weernink, "If Chinese Are Serious, They Must Deliver," *Automotive News Europe*, June 26, 2006, p. 10.

79. Elisabeth Malkin, "In Mexico, Automaking Is a Growth Industry," *New York Times*, July 21, 2006, p. C1.

80. Byron Pope, "China vs. Mexico," *Ward's Auto World*, June 1, 2006, p. 20; Chuang Peck Ming, "Nearshoring: Better than Outsourcing," *Business Times Singapore*, September 9, 2006.

81. Oropeza, *China*, p. 303.

82. Alice H. Amsden, *The Rise of "The Rest": Challenges to the West from Late-Industrializing Economies* (Oxford University Press, 2003); Peter Evans, *Embedded Autonomy: States and Industrial Transformation* (Princeton University Press, 1995).

LUISA PALACIOS

8

Latin America as China's Energy Supplier

Oil trade flows have not experienced the same surge as other commodities driving Latin America's trade explosion with China in recent years, nor is a surge likely to occur in the foreseeable future. Not only does the outlook for oil production and consumption raise questions about the region's own energy balances, but it is clear that Latin America's oil exports to the People's Republic of China (PRC), while still modest, are just one piece in the large puzzle of China's quest for energy sources worldwide. That said, Chinese energy links with Latin America have different manifestations depending on whether you are examining trade flows or investment flows. Looking at the energy relationship between China and Latin America only in terms of trade flows misses another aspect of this relationship: Latin America is increasingly a destination for Chinese energy investment, as China seeks to diversify from a declining oil resource base at home and goes in search of opportunities abroad.

In 2006 China accounted for 9 percent of the world's crude oil consumption and 7 percent of the world's oil imports, while the United States accounted for 24 percent of the world's consumption and 26 percent of world imports.[1] Although today's figures continue to underscore the importance of the United States as the world's greatest consumer of oil, these figures provide an incomplete picture of what is in store for oil markets as we look ahead. What matters most for oil producers and for Sino–Latin American energy relations is not where China is today but how it compares with its position in the world at the start of the twenty-first century and where it is likely to be in 2030.

China's oil demand increased by more than 55 percent between 2000 and 2006. In 2003 China overtook Japan as the second largest consumer of oil in the world, but it remains the third largest importer after Japan because China

170

produces just over 50 percent of its domestic oil requirements (this ranking treats EU countries separately). In comparison the U.S. share of world oil demand slightly decreased from 25 percent in 1996 to 24 percent in 2006; in absolute numbers, U.S. oil consumption increased by only about 5 percent in the 2000–06 period. The U.S. Energy Information Administration (EIA) projects that the growth in China's oil demand will average 3.5 percent annually—the highest growth rate in the world—and that it will reach approximately 16 million barrels a day by 2030.[2] This means that China is projected to account for 28 percent of the overall increase in world liquid fuels consumption between 2004 and 2030 and for 14 percent of total world oil consumption in 2030, almost doubling its 2004 market share.[3]

Two factors are behind these projections. First, China's rapid economic growth and urbanization, coupled with the increasing modernization of its transportation system, will contribute to the PRC's increase in consumption. Second, China's domestic production is expected to decrease in the next decades, even as its oil demand grows, so it will be forced to import more than 70 percent of its oil requirements in 2030, compared to almost 50 percent in 2006 (in comparison, the United States currently imports about 65 percent of its total oil requirements, crude and products combined).[4]

How the world satisfies increased demand from China (and developing Asia as a whole), and at what price, is one of the most important challenges energy markets face in the coming years. This oil dependence is already generating important questions about Chinese foreign energy policy. In its quest to secure energy resources China is competing not only with the traditional oil importers from the Organization for Economic Cooperation and Development (OECD) but also from the emerging consumers of developing nations such as India and Brazil.

In this context, Latin America's role as an energy supplier for China will depend not only on the evolution of Chinese oil demand and supply but also on Latin America's supply and demand dynamics and regulatory frameworks. This chapter examines the evolution of oil flows in Latin America and seeks to shed some light on current trends in Latin America's oil sector, including the region's role in satisfying China's growing energy demand.

Oil Dynamics in Latin America: How Does China Fit In?

Given current oil flows, it is difficult to make the case that Latin America will become a highly strategic region for China's energy security needs. According to the *BP Statistical Review of World Energy 2007*, Latin America represented around 7 percent of Chinese oil imports in 2006: 262,000 barrels a day of the 3.9 million barrels a day that China imports (figure 8-1). Most of Chinese oil imports come from the Persian Gulf, imports that satisfy just over 38 percent of Chinese oil requirements. While China has diversified its oil sources, these efforts have focused on Russia and West Africa, regions with greater proximity and thus lower transportation costs. In fact, it is evident that the United States dominates Latin America's oil export flows by far, absorbing 77 percent of the region's oil exports (figure 8-2). Europe is the second leading destination, with a share of 11 percent of exports, while China absorbs a mere 5 percent.

China's significant oil demand means that every oil-exporting country in the world will theoretically contribute to its energy security, albeit to different degrees. Nevertheless, it will always make more economic sense for net oil balances in the oil-exporting Latin American countries to remain in the Western Hemisphere, with oil flows to China and Asia increasing only at the margin. It is unlikely that we will see considerable increases in Latin America's oil exports to China, with the exception of Venezuela, because, as detailed in the sections below, Latin America's own energy needs and those of the United States will continue absorbing the bulk of the region's oil. Most of China's oil import increases will continue to come from the Persian Gulf instead.

Will Latin America Continue to Be a Net Exporter of Oil?

One possible constraint on the potential increase of oil flows to China are Latin America's oil balances. The region continues to be a net oil exporter, with external sales of almost 6 million barrels a day, which represented 11 percent of world exports in 2006. But increased economic growth in the region has already led to higher oil consumption in some countries. Between 2000 and 2006 oil production capacity in the region rose 2.9 percent, as oil consumption increased by 5 percent.[5]

The region's 416,000-barrel-a-day consumption increase in the 2000–06 period was concentrated in Mexico, Venezuela, Brazil, and Ecuador. These four countries accounted for 50 percent of the increase in oil demand in that period, an amount 1.6 times higher than all of Latin America's oil exports to China in 2006. Ironically, this positive economic growth is very much a function of China's rise as a consumer of commodities.

Another element that could impact oil balances going forward is the legal framework for investment in the oil sector. While Colombia, Brazil, and Peru have taken a market-oriented approach in developing their hydrocarbon sectors, this is not the case in Venezuela, Mexico, and even in Ecuador and Argentina. This last group faces various and differing institutional, political, and legal challenges that could cloud their oil production outlook and affect

Figure 8-1. *Chinese Oil Imports, by Country of Origin, 2006*

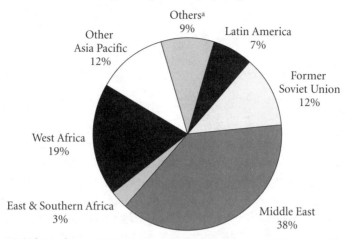

Source: British Petroleum, *BP Statistical Review of World Energy, June 2007* (London, 2007), p. 20.
a. Others include Australasia, Canada, Europe, Japan, North Africa, Singapore, and the United States.

aggregate production levels. The challenges could also limit significant increases in oil flows to China.

In Mexico constitutional impediments to private sector participation in the oil sector will constrain domestic oil production. Mexico will eventually need to open its hydrocarbon sector to private sector participation, but that is unlikely to happen in a very significant way in the near future.[6] Price distortions in

Figure 8-2. *Latin American Oil Exports, by Country of Destination, 2006*

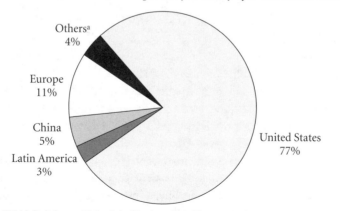

Source: British Petroleum, *BP Statistical Review of World Energy, June 2007* (London, 2007), p. 20.
a. Others include Africa, Australasia, Canada, Japan, Singapore, and other Asia Pacific countries.

Argentina's domestic energy policy have kept oil and gas prices at artificially low levels and have led to overconsumption and underinvestment in exploration and production oil and gas activities, all factors that, without significant policy reforms, stand to endanger the country's position as a net exporter of hydrocarbons. In Ecuador political instability in conjunction with the April 2006 hydrocarbon law reform increasing the government's share of oil revenue, as well as the expropriation of Occidental fields in May 2006, has weakened the country's investment outlook.[7]

In Venezuela the nationalization of oil resources will constrain any meaningful increases in oil production. But how this can affect oil flows to China is a more complex issue, given Venezuela's overtures to increase its ties with China. And given oil production constraints in this Andean country, the main concerns with such a rapprochement center on the possible redirection of oil flows from the United States to China. The implications of the Venezuela connection for the Sino–Latin American–U.S. energy relationship—a triangular dynamic addressed by several authors in this volume—merits a more in-depth analysis, which is offered later in this chapter.

The Emergence of National Oil Companies

As noted earlier, current Sino–Latin American oil flows do not tell a very compelling story about the relevance of Latin America's energy resources for Chinese demand growth, despite the widespread belief, also mentioned in other chapters of this volume, that China's interest in Latin America is largely driven by an energy security strategy. Latin America's own growing oil demand, concomitant with significant supply constraints in terms of the institutional framework for oil investments, adds an element of uncertainty. While it is clear that Latin America will continue to be a net exporter of energy resources, it is uncertain to what extent, as the region becomes a growing consumer of its own oil.

Beyond these medium-term considerations, Latin America will continue to play an important role for energy investments, despite the regulatory and institutional constraints that persist in some countries, mainly because the region remains open for business, especially at the upstream level (with the notable exception of Mexico). Even with only 14 percent of the world's oil production, Latin America will continue to attract the attention of international oil companies because the major Persian Gulf producers remain relatively closed at the upstream level, particularly for exploration and production of crude oil. Latin America will need international investment capital to further develop its participation in the sector. Despite recent signs of resource nationalism in the region—particularly in Venezuela, Bolivia, and Ecuador—

and even with tougher fiscal and contractual conditions, the region remains relatively open for companies that wish to access oil reserves and develop production. In fact, the very distinct characteristics of oil sectors in different countries have attracted oil companies of all sizes and nationalities, including the Chinese national oil companies (NOCs).

So far international oil markets have seen a growing international exposure by the NOCs of oil-producing countries, which emerged from the nationalization events of the 1970s. These include Kuwait's KPC, Venezuela's PDVSA, and Saudi Arabia's Saudi Aramco, all of which have moved to acquire downstream (refining and distribution) assets in consumer markets to complement their own upstream assets.

The new trend in the oil industry is the emergence of the large oil consumers of tomorrow—namely, China and India—and the internationalization of their NOCs, which are trying to acquire exactly what they lack: access to oil reserves and production capability. The NOCs of emerging-market, oil-importing countries are simply emulating the model followed by the international oil companies (IOCs) and the NOCs of the Group of Seven (G-7) countries in the past.

China's National Oil Companies: Leading the Drive for New Foreign Investment in Latin America

China's petroleum industry underwent an important restructuring process when a dramatic reorganization of state-owned oil and gas assets led to the creation in 1998 of two vertically integrated firms, the China National Petroleum Corporation (CNPC) and the China Petroleum and Chemical Corporation (Sinopec Group).[8] Originally, CNPC had been involved mainly in upstream production and exploration activities in mainland China, while Sinopec was involved mainly in downstream refining and distribution. The reorganization transferred assets between the two, transforming them into vertically integrated regional entities.[9]

In 1999 CNPC formed a holding company, PetroChina, into which it transferred most of its assets for exploration and production, refining and marketing, and chemicals and natural gas businesses inside of China. It was the first step in launching an offering of shares in the international market. In April 2000 the company made an initial public offering on the New York and Hong Kong stock exchanges. Today, PetroChina is China's largest oil company, sharing ninth place worldwide with Mexico's PEMEX, according to the *Petroleum Intelligence Weekly*'s 2005 oil company list.[10] This is the highest ranking reached by any Chinese oil company.

The restructuring of the Chinese oil companies and a subsequent increase in financing capabilities led to an important internationalization of Chinese NOCs in early 2000. By the end of 2005, CNPC, for example, owned oil and gas assets in twenty-three countries. These produced 35.82 million metric tons of crude oil (34 percent of the company's oil production), of which equity oil participation was 20 million metric tons.[11] Sinopec has bid on more than thirty international contracts, resulting in ownership of more than 200,000 tons of equity crude in the Middle East, Africa, Central Asia, South America, and Australia.[12] More than any other Chinese NOC, Sinopec, China's largest refiner, needs to expand overseas upstream opportunities— the company currently imports nearly 60 percent of the crude it needs for its refining facilities.

Two additional players in the Chinese energy sector with assets abroad are worth mentioning: the China National Offshore Oil Corporation (CNOOC), which engages primarily in the exploration, development, and production of crude oil and natural gas off China's shores and accounts for roughly 10 percent of China's oil production; and a smaller company, Sinochem, which is concentrated on the downstream sector in China.[13] CNOOC has also engaged in an internationalization strategy since early 2000. Starting from zero in 2001, the company's overseas acquisitions represented 10 percent of the company's total reserves, more than 20 percent of gas production, and 7 percent of total oil production by 2005.[14] CNOOC's international presence is concentrated in Indonesia and Australia. Sinochem, the fourth largest Chinese state-owned oil company, has been actively developing an international strategy. Today, Sinochem holds oil and gas exploration and development rights in Ecuador, Tunisia, and the United Arab Emirates.[15] CNOOC and the previously mentioned Sinopec carried out initial public offerings of stock between 2000 and 2002, bringing in billions of dollars in foreign capital.

China's NOCs are undergoing an important internationalization process. They are expected to concentrate on acquisition of and access to upstream assets, given domestic needs for crude resources. According to PetroChina's 2004 annual report, "The Company will continue to accelerate the implementation of its overseas business development strategy. It will expand overseas operations and will actively seek opportunities to develop its overseas oil and gas exploration and development business. It will also expand international trade and grow its overseas business by way of mergers and acquisitions or joint ventures."[16]

Making space in international markets for the Chinese NOCs, as well as other NOCs from emerging-market countries, represents a challenge for the more mature IOCs in the G-7 countries. NOCs from the emerging markets have an interesting card to play: the strategic partnership among NOCs supported by their governments. Brazil's Petrobras and India's ONGC are pursuing this strategy, as are Chinese NOCs. But China's situation is spotlighted because of its available capital and the government's aggressive strategy to meet future import needs. As a result, the Sino–Latin American energy link has many layers and actors. The Chinese government clearly does have an overall policy to secure access to energy supply sources in the region, and numerous visits by Chinese and Latin American officials underscore the fact that this energy relationship is being brokered at the highest diplomatic levels. But the Chinese companies involved have their own business objectives, and in dealing with other countries they are acting on behalf of their companies' interests and their own international standing as much as they are securing Chinese access to oil resources.[17]

Because private investors now own a portion (albeit small) of these companies' shares, they face the discipline of financial markets in terms of growth and profitability. In sum, Chinese NOCs share the government's incentives for access to resources, but they also pursue business objectives. Increased Chinese investments in Latin America thus are expected to lead to some diversion of oil flows to the Asian continent. But it is conceivable as well that Chinese companies with important international assets might in the future engage in international arbitrage that would result in some of this Chinese oil from the region ending up in the United States. This is why Sino–Latin American energy ties are not only about trade but, increasingly, also about Chinese NOCs' access to energy assets worldwide.

Chinese NOCs in Latin America

The headlines generated by Chinese investments in Latin America and the PRC's potential oil investment deals in the region have sparked concerns in the United States.[18] Most of these concerns center on the notion that Chinese investments will end up diverting oil flows in the Western Hemisphere from their current U.S. destination to China. Although there is a growing presence of NOCs throughout Latin America, there is little reason to believe that they will replace Chevron, Petrobras, or Repsol-YPF as the most important players in the region. Chinese investments in Latin America represent the emergence of a new player looking to occupy a space. In this sense, China is not alone. Latin America has seen other actors emerge in the region in recent years, including small and medium-size Latin American–owned oil companies. Thus Chinese NOCs are not the only new kids on the block: they are simply the most visible because they have the greatest investment capacity.

All this attention overshadows the fact that, as in other sectors, the Chinese have been better at signing memoranda of understanding (MOUs) than at actual investment of capital, and Chinese energy investments in Latin America pale in comparison with investments in other parts of the world. For example, in 2005 China acquired the Canadian-run PetroKazakstan for $4.18 billion, the largest overseas acquisition made by a Chinese company to date.[19] That said, some of China's energy investments in Latin America are in the process of becoming increasingly valuable assets for the PRC, as it moves slowly to gain a presence in the region's energy scene.

ECUADOR: THE LEADING RECIPIENT OF CHINESE ENERGY INVESTMENT IN LATIN AMERICA. While the potential for Chinese investment in Venezuela has drawn more attention, Ecuador has been the most important recipient of Chinese energy investments in Latin America. The $1.42 billion acquisition of Canadian-based Encana assets in Ecuador at the end of 2005 gave CNPC and Sinopec a major foothold in Ecuador's oil sector. The Encana purchase, which was carried out through Andes Petroleum, a joint venture between CNPC and Sinopec, granted the Chinese access to the following:[20]

—100 percent of the Tarapoa block in the Oriente Basin,

—40 percent nonoperating economic interest in block 15 in the Oriente Basin, which, after the government's seizure, was indemnified by Encana to the Chinese consortium,[21]

—majority operating interest in blocks 14, 17, and Shiripuno, also in the Oriente Basin,

—36 percent stake in the OCP pipeline, making the Chinese consortium the largest equity stakeholder in the pipeline.[22]

Before the Encana purchase, CNPC had a participation contract with PetroEcuador for block 11 in the Amazon region in Ecuador, which launched production in December 2005. The Encana acquisition put the Chinese producers on Ecuador's oil map. Given the expropriation of Occidental's (Oxy) block, with this acquisition the Chinese consortium now accounts for 12 percent of Ecuador's oil production (excluding its participation in block 15). The Chinese also recently bid in Ecuador's marginal field auction announced on September 2006, in addition to expressing an interest in Oxy's block 15 if Ecuador decides to auction it. But Oxy's lawsuit before the International Centre for Settlement and Investment Disputes (ICSID) demanding compensation and return of its assets in Ecuador will probably deter the government from auctioning block 15 any time soon. In addition to CNPC and Sinopec, other Chinese actors participated in the Ecuadorian oil auction. Also, Sinochem acquired 14 percent of block 16 in December 2003 from Conoco-Phillips, for approximately $100 million, and the private conglomerate GUPC has been actively engaged in talks with the Ecuadorian government about investments in the oil sector.[23]

Until 2005 almost 70 percent of Ecuador's oil exports were shipped to the United States, with Central America and Peru as the second and third most important destinations. Exports to China represented less than 1 percent of total Ecuadorian oil exports in 2004. The Encana purchase will provide an interesting test on how Chinese local ownership will affect the distribution of oil assets in Latin America. According to the central bank of Ecuador, in the first nine months of 2006 oil exports to China represented almost 3 percent of total crude oil exports, a more than threefold increase in volume from 2004. Yet increased oil flows to China have so far not affected trade with the United States in terms of the overall percentage of Ecuador's exports to that country, although in terms of volume exports to the United States actually went up by 28 percent in late 2006 compared to the year before. Ecuador's location on the Pacific Ocean also gives it an advantage with China in terms of transportation costs. However, Ecuador's production, 530 million barrels a day, limits its importance in terms of overall oil flows to China.[24]

SINO-BRAZILIAN ENERGY LINKS: LITTLE BUT MUTUAL INTEREST THUS FAR. Brazil signed a strategic agreement of cooperation with Sinopec in May 2004, when Petrobras first opened its offices in China. A few months later, in February 2005, Petrobras signed an MOU for joint business ventures with the powerful CNPC, eventually leading to the announcement of construction of the 300-kilometer Cabiúnas-Vitória natural gas (Gascav) pipeline. The deal, signed in April 2006 between Petrobras and Sinopec, was worth $239 million.

The Sino-Brazilian energy links are probably of equal interest to Brazil as they are to China with regard to the potential of increasing each actor's presence in a growing consumer market. Because Brazil is self-sufficient in terms of crude oil and has a surplus in petroleum products, its energy ties with China are primarily about investment in a growing emerging market and not necessarily about securing oil flows. China's main demand, however, is for crude oil rather than for petroleum products (petroleum product imports represent around 20 percent of Chinese net total oil imports). And so while the Chinese continue exploring opportunities in Brazil, the Brazilians likewise continue to look for ways to do business in China. But thus far actual investment between the two countries has failed to materialize in any substantial way.

CHINA'S ENERGY PRESENCE IN OTHER COUNTRIES. The experience with promised Chinese investment in other Latin American countries, like Bolivia, Colombia, and Peru, has been mixed. In Bolivia the $1.5 billion investment by Shengli International Petroleum Development Co., Ltd., in the country's hydrocarbon sector, which was announced in 2004, has not materialized.[25] This is partly due to Bolivia's own political instability, which has postponed investments in the country not only by the Chinese NOCs but also by other IOCs. While such investments may yet materialize, Bolivia does not seem like an ideal destination for Chinese investment because Bolivia's natural gas opportunities are greater than those in the crude oil industry. Chinese energy demands are concentrated on fuel oil and coal; natural gas represents less than 10 percent of its energy requirements. With the exception of Trinidad and Tobago, which is light years ahead in the liquefied natural gas trade, most of the gas trade in Latin America is through pipelines to neighboring countries, mostly in the Southern Cone among Bolivia, Brazil, Argentina, and Chile. Peru is next in line for these exports, with the Camisea project, but its completion is not expected until 2010.

While Bolivia has only obtained promises, Colombia is beginning to see actual investments. In April 2005 the national hydrocarbon agency signed an MOU with the China National Oil Development Corporation (CNODC), a subsidiary of CNPC, for exploration and production.[26] In September 2006 Sinopec took a 50 percent stake in a Colombian-based exploration and production firm called Omimex for about $800 million. Sinopec did this in conjunction with India's Ongc Videsh, the first joint acquisition by rivals in Latin America's energy market.[27] Colombia has also seen a significant increase in oil foreign direct investment, most of it involving highly attractive exploration contracts. Although Colombia's government has remained open to foreign investment, thus far Chinese investment has been limited to production rather than to riskier exploration activities.

The Chinese are more active in Peru than in Colombia, Bolivia, or even Brazil. In 2004 the Argentine oil company PlusPetrol sold 45 percent of its Peruvian unit, PlusPetrol Norte, to CNPC, for some $200 million. At the time PlusPetrol Norte was the main crude oil producer in Peru, with an output of 21 billion barrels in 2003, 63 percent of the total crude oil output. Since then the company's oil production has declined, but it remains the most important crude producer in the country, representing 40 percent of total production. In 2005 Peru signed two contracts with CNPC for the exploitation of blocks 111 and 113 in the jungles of Peru.[28]

In the Sino–Latin American equation, Venezuela, an important player in the energy field, is of keen interest to the United States. Because of the potentially serious diplomatic and political implications of the China-Venezuela energy relationship, the subject warrants a separate examination, included in the section below.

Sino-Venezuelan Energy Ties: A Benign or Threatening Force for Regional Stability?

No other country sparks more nervousness about Chinese access to Latin America's energy assets than Venezuela. Venezuelan president Hugo Chávez's attempts to increase oil flows to China have faced substantial scrutiny, especially from the United States. China's interest in Venezuela coincided with the latter's repeated threats to halt shipments to the United States, the destination for 60 percent of its oil exports. This threat first appeared on the radar screens of U.S. policymakers at the end of 2004, and it has since been repeated numerous times by the Chávez government. Although today the threats of disruption have lost some resonance, initially they sparked such concern that Senator Richard Lugar, chairman of the U.S. Senate Foreign Relations Committee, requested a study about the potential effects on the United States in the event that a disruption in supply of crude oil and refined oil products from Venezuela did materialize.

The U.S. Government Accountability Office released its report on June 27, 2006.[29] The report focuses on the cost to the U.S. economy should Venezuela impose an oil embargo. It also cites a significant increase in expenditures for Venezuela with respect to higher transportation costs and the lack of adequate refining capacity outside the United States for Venezuela's distinctive heavy crude, high-sulfur oil.[30] Though the probability of a complete disruption of Venezuela's oil flows to the United States is not zero, this is clearly an extreme scenario that is unlikely absent extraordinary diplomatic developments. The more likely scenario is for Venezuela's energy policy to increasingly favor gradual diversification away from the U.S. market.

The triangular aspect of Sino–Latin American–U.S. energy relations is quite evident in the Venezuelan case. The U.S. role is relevant because of the diplomatic implications for China should Venezuela pursue its desire to increase its energy ties with the PRC. The more intense Venezuela's anti-U.S. campaign becomes, the more costly it will be for the Chinese government to deepen its ties with Venezuela, as it is not in China's interest to alienate the United States.[31]

Overall, the complex energy relationship between China and Venezuela has been contaminated by the antiimperialistic rhetoric of Chávez's foreign policy. Yet Chinese energy policy and foreign policy vis-à-vis the United States acts as a constraint on Chávez's desire to become "a reliable oil supplier to China." Should these diplomatic tensions subside, energy cooperation between Venezuela and China could conceivably become much more significant. Otherwise, the relationship is likely to continue to move forward but probably more slowly than would otherwise be the case, as argued in the following sections.

Sino-Venezuelan energy relations can be divided into two main areas: the oil trade and the investment component. Though perhaps simply two sides of the same coin, in the case of Venezuela the two issues should be addressed separately. While Chinese investments in Venezuela will grow with increased flows between the two countries, oil flows also depend on the government's policy to increase production in the state-owned Petróleos de Venezuela, S.A. (PDVSA), and to speed up the execution of its oil policies.

SINO-VENEZUELAN ENERGY TRADE: SUBSTITUTING U.S. OIL FLOWS? December 2004 marked the beginning of President Hugo Chávez's China oil diplomacy. During a state visit to China, Chávez successfully negotiated an MOU directed at increasing energy ties between the two countries. In June 2005 a supply agreement was reached under which Venezuela would send 30,000 barrels a day of fuel oil to China for one year, and a few months later PDVSA opened an office in Beijing to evaluate investment opportunities in China.

PDVSA stated in August 2005 that Venezuelan exports to China would likely reach 300,000 barrels a day of crude oil and petroleum products in the near future and that both governments were working toward achieving this goal.[32] This was an aggressive target. According to PDVSA reports, Venezuela's oil exports to China reached 12,300 barrels a day in 2004 and averaged 68,800 barrels a day in the first half of 2005. In November 2005 Venezuela negotiated a new one-year supply agreement with China for 100,000 barrels a day of crude oil and a two-year supply agreement for 60,000 barrels a day of fuel oil.[33]

It is believed that Venezuela's oil exports to China in 2006 reached 150,000 barrels a day and that in 2007 these flows increased to at least 200,000 barrels a day. The Chinese government has stated that Venezuela is today China's seventh most important oil supplier.[34] In August 2006 an agreement between the two governments stated a goal of increasing Venezuela's exports to China to 500,000 barrels a day by 2009 (almost equivalent to Venezuela's estimated domestic consumption). At that time, PDVSA reported that oil flows to China were already at 150,000 barrels a day.[35] It is not clear how domestic production could increase, because recent nationalizations and renegotiation of oil contracts with private operators have clouded the environment for oil investment and delayed project execution. Therefore, to accomplish its goal of increasing oil exports to China to 500,000 barrels a day by 2009, Venezuela would have no choice but to reduce oil exports to other markets.

Regulatory restrictions for private investment matter because until 2005 private companies produced approximately 40 percent of the country's oil. Thus an increase in oil exports to China would mean diversion from other destinations, such as the United States and other countries in Latin America. The Venezuelan government has stated an objective of increasing its own oil production to 5.85 million barrels a day by 2012, yet it is not even clear what the current level of oil production is in Venezuela, and estimates vary widely.

The U.S. Department of Energy estimated Venezuela's crude oil output at 2.54 million barrels a day in the second quarter of 2006, in line with OPEC figures of 2.55 million barrels a day for September 2006.[36] Official Venezuelan government figures are 3.3 million barrels a day, with PDVSA's own production estimated at 2.9 million barrels a day.[37] According to the EIA, Venezuela supplied almost 1.5 million barrels a day to the United States in 2006, representing close to 11 percent of U.S. oil imports that year. Domestic demand in Venezuela in 2006 was estimated at almost 600,000 barrels a day, and Venezuela oil exports to the Caribbean (PetroCaribe) and Central American countries applying discount programs should be around 200,000 barrels a day, and Cuba alone is believed to receive 100,000 barrels a day.

Venezuela's current contracts to supply crude oil to the country's refining facilities in the United States (Citgo) and other refineries abroad would force PDVSA to divert oil flows from somewhere else in order to increase exports to China.[38] Venezuela sought majority control of the four heavy crude oil joint ventures in the Orinoco Belt in which PDVSA had a minority share.[39] In obtaining majority control over commercialization of the crude, it is not inconceivable that PDVSA might try to divert some of these oil flows to China if PDVSA were really serious about doing it at any cost. However, significant legal repercussions could result from such a move.

Despite Venezuela's ambitious target of increasing its oil exports to China to 500,000 barrels a day by 2009, even assuming stable oil production the United States will likely remain the most important market for Venezuela's oil in the foreseeable future. However, it is not inconceivable to see current oil flows gradually increase.

The economic realities make Venezuela's political goal of supplying more oil to China a difficult enterprise, at least in the short term. As explained earlier, there is no excess supply that Venezuela can easily shift to China without compromising existing customers. Furthermore, many experts highlight the technical impediments to shifting a significant part of oil flows to China, including transportation costs and the ability of Chinese refineries to process Venezuelan heavy crude oil. In comparison, the United States is a natural market for Venezuelan oil because of its proximity—travel time by tanker to the U.S. Gulf Coast is only five days, compared to thirty to forty days to the Middle East.[40] Moreover, Venezuela's refineries in the United States are particularly suitable for refining large volumes of heavy, sour (high-sulfur) crude oil, a large part of Venezuela's oil exports. Perhaps more than anything else, the fact that Chinese refineries require adaptation to process Venezuelan oil makes Venezuela's goal to increase its oil exports to China by about 500,000 barrels a day by 2009 an ambitious objective. But not an impossible one.

CHINESE INVESTMENTS IN VENEZUELA: MOVING AT DIFFERENT PACES. Judging by the number of MOUs that China and Venezuela have signed recently (twelve in August 2006 and seventeen in January 2005), China's investments in Venezuela should be substantial. However, the Chinese seem to be proceeding with caution, and their actual investments in Venezuela are rising, yet at a slow pace.

China's most important investment in Venezuela materialized on April 17, 2001, when CNPC and PDVSA reached an agreement to produce Orimulsion, a patented fuel developed by PDVSA. Orimulsion is made from natural bitumen and water and marketed as an alternative to coal or fuel oil for power plants. A joint-venture company, Sinovensa, was established with CNPC holding 70 percent equity in the project. Sinovensa was originally expected to produce 80,000 barrels a day of Orimulsion, a figure not included in the country's output quota because Orimulsion does not qualify as crude oil. However, the Venezuelan government has been phasing out production of Orimulsion on the grounds that it is only modestly profitable as a business venture. In September 2006 Venezuela decided to halt production of Orimulsion altogether by the end of that year. Sinovensa is to be restructured under the new hydro-carbons law to produce instead extra-heavy crude and lighter crude mixes.[41] As a result, China's share of oil production in Venezuela will increase simply because the output coming from Sinovensa will qualify as crude oil.

Also in 2006 PDVSA's subsidiary, Corporación Venezolana de Petróleo (CVP), signed an agreement with CNPC to develop the Junín 4 heavy crude oil block in the Orinoco belt. CNPC had already signed an MOU with Venezuela for this block for the certification of reserves in early 2005. Venezuela also invited Brazil, India, Iran, and Russia to participate. PDVSA projects that production at Junín could reach 200,000 barrels a day by 2010, though analysts remain skeptical about the technological capacity of the Chinese and others to develop this crude market given its complexity.

CNPC has also obtained production rights to more conventional oil in the Caracoles and Intercampo fields, which predate the Chávez era as they were assigned during the 1997 third auction round. Venezuela estimates production at the Intercampo and Caracoles fields at 25,000 barrels a day, giving CNPC 1 percent of Venezuela's oil production in 2005. Like other investors in Venezuela, the Chinese had to convert these operating rights into joint companies with PDVSA in 2006. An agreement made in September 2005 to expand conventional oil operations was signed between PDVSA and CNPC. The agreement focused on the development of the Zumano field, which PDVSA estimates could produce up to 50,000 barrels a day, but this agreement is still at the definition phase. Sinopec also signed its first agreement in August 2006 for oil production in the Posa field in Paria Gulf.

The Venezuelan government not only wants to increase its energy trade with China but wants the Chinese to take on a more important share of Venezuela's oil production.[42] More recently, the Venezuelan government also added another dimension to its energy links with China when Chávez signed a series of agreements during his fourth visit to the PRC geared toward increased PDVSA investments in Chinese supplies and technology as well as products and services.[43] The Venezuelan and Chinese governments have also agreed on creating a $6 billion fund ($4 billion coming from China and the rest from Venezuela) to finance oil projects in both countries.

In sum, Venezuela's rhetoric continues to focus on market diversification away from the United States, increasing energy ties with China, and allowing into Venezuela nontraditional IOCs and NOCs from countries that are less than friendly with the United States. While the timelines to achieve these goals might be ambitious, there is at least a political will to slowly continue with this process.

Conclusion

Concerns about the growing energy ties between Latin America and China have led to very different conclusions about the implications of this relationship. Venezuela's drive to strengthen its energy links with China amid threats to halt oil flows to the United States has led to more scrutiny of Chinese operations in Latin America's energy scene than is warranted by actual Chinese investments in the region. However, minimizing the potential for energy cooperation between Latin America and China is risky because the Chinese are becoming important producers in Peru and Ecuador, they have recently acquired assets in Colombia, they are set to participate in Brazil's energy infrastructure, and they have investments in Venezuela. The evidence shows that the Chinese are slowly gaining a foothold in Latin America's energy scene, not as a replacement for other actors, but as new investors.

Latin America's importance in the Chinese energy matrix is not likely to arise from becoming a strategic supplier of oil to China. The Middle East already dominates Chinese oil imports, and their share of Chinese oil imports is expected to increase in the future. While increased Chinese investments in Latin America's energy sector may lead to a limited rise in interregional oil flows, the United States will continue to absorb the bulk of Latin America's oil flows, even in the unlikely event that Venezuela reaches its goal of increasing exports to China to 500,000 barrels a day by 2009. Moreover, Latin America's increased energy consumption due to high economic growth rates in the past years raises questions about the region's energy balances. This growing demand is taking place despite slower growth on the production side, especially in the case of those countries following more nationalistic policies at home.

In sum, Latin America is not poised to become a significant oil supplier to China; rather, Latin America is just part of the Chinese quest for energy sources worldwide. But Latin America's limited trade potential with China masks the more important role that Latin America plays as a destination for Chinese oil investments. While most of the focus on China's role in world oil markets is based on demand dynamics, equally important for Sino–Latin American energy relations is how China's supply sources evolve. Uncertainty about the stability or potential slight decreases in future Chinese oil production is leading companies to pursue an aggressive diversification of their asset portfolios into upstream opportunities abroad, given the limited opportunities at home. While resource nationalism in Latin America has constrained the bountiful opportunities presented in the 1990s when the region was liberalizing its oil sector, Latin America's upstream sector, with the exception of Mexico's, is still open for business. Moreover, resource nationalism in Latin America can play to the advantage of Chinese and other NOCs, given their flexibility in dealing with governments.

NOCs from China and other emerging-market countries are simply following the same strategies that their European counterparts followed some decades ago, and the growing space they are likely to occupy internationally remains one of the most interesting challenges ahead for the industry. While Chinese NOCs have been given special attention, they are certainly not the only new players in the region, nor are they likely to become the most important. The Latin American energy scene is evolving in interesting ways, with China's presence being just one of the new developments. Ultimately, Latin America cannot avoid being an appealing region for the Chinese oil companies to expand their diversification portfolio as part of their internationalization strategy.

Notes

1. These figures are estimated by the author based on *BP Statistical Review of World Energy 2007* (www.bp.com).

2. Energy Information Administration, *International Energy Outlook, 2007* (U.S. Department of Energy, 2007), p. 22.

3. Ibid.; and International Energy Agency, *World Energy Outlook, 2004* (Paris: 2004).

4. The EIA estimates in its energy outlook that China's conventional oil production will decline to 3.3 million barrels a day in 2030. See Energy Information Administration, *International Energy Outlook, 2007*, p. 32. It is too early to tell whether recent oil discoveries will bolster production in the future; for more on these oil discoveries, see Wing-Gar Cheng, "PetroChina Makes Major Oil Discoveries," *Energy Bulletin,* May 27, 2004 (www.energybulletin.net/364.html [December 2007]).

5. These figures are estimated by the author based on *BP Statistical Review of World Energy 2007* (www.bp.com).

6. For a discussion of the institutional constraints seen in Mexico's energy sector, see Luisa Palacios, "Explaining Policy Choice in the Oil Industry: A Look at Rentier Institutions in Mexico and Venezuela (1988–1999)," Ph.D. dissertation, Johns Hopkins University, 2001.

7. "Ecuador: Poverty and Debt in the Time of Oil," *Energy Economist* 16, no. 298 (August 2006): 16–18.

8. The Sinopec Group is the major shareholder (71.23 percent) of the Chinese Petroleum and Chemical Corporation Sinopec Corp., which resulted after a reorganization of the holding company in 2000; see Sinopec, *Annual Report, 2005* (www.sinopec.com).

9. Sinopec transferred four northern refineries to CNPC, and CNPC transferred eight southern oil fields to Sinopec. Still, CNPC has a disproportionate share of oil production capacity: 2.20 million barrels a day, compared to Sinopec's 0.75 million barrels a day. Sinopec has somewhat more refining capacity than CNPC.

10. Energy Intelligence (www.energyintel.com).

11. CNPC produced 105.95 million metric tons of crude oil in 2005 and 36.7 billion cubic meters of gas. Overseas, CNPC has claimed 162 million metric tons of recoverable oil reserves and produced 35.82 million metric tons of oil (34 percent of total production) and 4.02 billion cubic meters of gas (10 percent of total production). Just taking into account equity oil production, overseas production accounted for 18 percent of total production and 8 percent of gas production (www.cnpc.com.cn/eng/).

12. Sinopec's contracts abroad include the natural gas risk exploration project in block B in Saudi Arabia, the farm in the block 3/7 E&P project in Sudan, and the acquisition of six blocks from FIOC in Kazakhstan and two blocks from Central Asia Company.

13. China Star was also among the four most important NOCs in China but was bought by Sinopec in 2001.

14. See www.cnoocltd.com.

15. See www.sinochem.com.

16. See www.petrochina.com.

17. Chinese energy specialist, interview by author, New York, October 2005.

18. Daniel P. Erikson, "A Dragon in the Andes? China, Venezuela, and U.S. Energy Security," *Military Review* 83 (July 2006): 83–89.

19. Xinhua, "PetroChina Acquisition of 67% Interest in PetroKazakstan Completed," *Shanghai Zoom Intelligence Co., Ltd.,* January 9, 2007 (www.zoomchina.com. cn/new/content/view/20778/255 [December 2007]).

20. See www.encana.com.

21. According to Encana, the seizure of block 15 "was an event requiring indemnification under the terms of EnCana's sale agreement with Andes Petroleum Company. The purchaser requested payment and EnCana paid the maximum amount in the third quarter, calculated in accordance with the terms of the agreements, of approximately $265 million" (www.encana.com).

22. The shareholders of the OCP pipeline with an estimated capacity of 450,000 barrels a day are Occidental, China's Andes Petroleum, Spain's Repsol-YPF, Brazil's Petrobras, Italy's Agip, and France's Perenco.

23. Repsol is the major shareholder of block 16. See "Sinochem invierte en campo ecuatoriano," *Diario Hoy,* December 16, 2003 (www.hoy.com.ec). See also "Ecuador Hopes for More China Energy Investment," *Reuters News,* June 1, 2006 (www. reuters.com).

24. These figures are estimated by the author based on *BP Statistical Review of World Energy 2007.*

25. Agencia Boliviana de Información, September 2, 2004.

26. Agencia Nacional de Hidrocarburos (www.anh.gov.co).

27. Omimex is reported to produce about 20,000 barrels a day. The firm's most significant oil investment is in Nare, which it operates with Ecopetrol, Colombia's NOC.

28. These figures are estimated by the author based on *BP Statistical Review of World Energy 2006.*

29. U.S.Government Accountability Office, *Issues Related to Potential Reductions in Venezuelan Oil Production,* Report to the Chairman, Committee on Foreign Relations, U.S. Senate (GAO-06-668), June 2006.

30. Ibid., p. 27.

31. Medley Global Advisors, "Venezuela: Aiming at Washington, Hitting Beijing," June 27, 2005 (www.medleyadvisors.com).

32. PDVSA, "Venezuela y China fortalecen relaciones estratégicas en el área de hidrocarburos," press release, August 24, 2005 (www.pdvsa.com).

33. PDVSA, "PDVSA y China National Petroleum Corporation firman contratos para suministro de hidrocarburos," press release, November 14, 2005 (www. pdvsa.com).

34. Xinhua, "Venezuela Crude Oil Exports to China Increase in Q1 2007," May 28, 2007.

35. PDVSA, "PDVSA-China consolidará diversificación del Mercado petrolero en Asia," press release, August 22, 2005 (www.pdvsa.com). It is unclear whether the oil import numbers reported by Venezuela are accurate, since the EIA reports that China imported 69,600 barrels a day of crude oil from Venezuela during the first half of 2006, from 27,500 barrels a day during the same period in 2005 (EIA, *Country Analysis Briefs,* September 2006). The 150,000-barrel-a-day number given by Venezuela does include petroleum products; but in the context of the country having significant issues with its refining facilities at home, it is still unclear whether the numbers are correct.

36. EIA, *International Petroleum Monthly* (www.eia.doe.gov); and OPEC, *Monthly Bulletin,* September 2006 (www.opec.org).

37. These figures correspond to PDVSA's financial statements for 2005.

38. PDVSA states that Citgo has more than 1 million barrels a day of refining capacity. It also has 335,000 barrels a day of refining capacity through a long-term lease in Curaçao, 250,000 barrels a day of equity refining capacity at Ruhr OEL in Germany, and 30,000 barrels a day at Ab Nynas Petroleum (which has assets throughout Europe).

39. The four heavy oil Orinoco joint ventures with estimated production of 600,000 barrels a day of synthetic crude are Petrozuata (ConocoPhillips owns 50.1 percent, PDVSA owns 49.9 percent); Cerro Negro (Exxon Mobil owns 41.67 percent, BP owns 16.66 percent, and PDVSA owns 41.67 percent); Sincor (PDVSA owns 38 percent, Statoil owns 15 percent); Hamaca-Ameriven (ConocoPhillips owns 40 percent, Chevron owns 30 percent, and PDVSA owns 30 percent).

40. Government Accountability Office, "Issues Related to Potential Reductions in Venezuelan Oil Production," p. 1.

41. Business News Americas, "Govt stops orimulsion output," September 27, 2006 (www.bnamericas.com).

42. PDVSA, "Venezuela y China concretan proyectos energéticos para el desarrollo de sus pueblos," press release, August 28, 2006 (www.pdvsa.com).

43. The planned investments include the acquisition of thirteen Chinese rigs with all the personnel training required. In addition, PDVSA signed an MOU with the Chinese State Shipbuilding Corporation (CSSC) and China Shipbuilding Industry Corporation (CSIC) for the construction of eighteen oil tankers to expand PDVSA's fleet. A technical bilateral team was formed to study the prospects for ethanol production in Venezuela using the Chinese experience in the area of biofuels. Finally, Venezuela also intends to use Chinese technology for the production of solar panels. Energy minister Rafael Ramírez also announced plans to improve China's ability to refine Venezuelan crude, which tends to be heavier and higher in sulfur than crude from other countries.

PART III

The Broader Context: Lessons for Latin America from China's Role in Southeast Asia and Africa

JOSHUA KURLANTZICK

9

China's Growing Influence in Southeast Asia

In November 2000 Jiang Zemin made his first visit to Cambodia. Arriving at the airport in Phnom Penh, Cambodia's capital, the owlish and normally stiff leader of the People's Republic of China (PRC) offered a brief greeting to his Cambodian hosts.[1] He was whisked into a motorcade, which rumbled through the streets, avoiding the cavernous ruts that dotted Sihanouk Boulevard, a main street. Most mornings, activity in Phnom Penh all but stops when the morning heat begins to rise. But on this morning, the city resembled one in a devoutly Catholic nation during a papal visit. More than 100,000 Cambodian children lined the streets, many in threadbare school uniforms. They waved tiny Cambodian and Chinese flags or small photographs of Jiang's face. They cheered and screamed for Jiang as his open car toured the city.[2]

However, Jiang's route that day did not take him past one of the city's main sites: Tuol Sleng, an old school where, between 1975 and 1979, Cambodia's Maoist Khmer Rouge regime incarcerated tens of thousands of average Cambodians, usually on trumped-up charges of spying for foreign countries. At Tuol Sleng, the Khmer Rouge brutally tortured their victims before killing them.

During the Khmer Rouge's murderous four-year reign—a regime responsible for the death of as many as 2 million Cambodians—China served as the system's major foreign patron. Beijing sent the Khmer Rouge more than 15,000 military advisers and provided the bulk of the Khmer Rouge's external aid.[3] Even in 2000 China still protected its old ally. Long after the Khmer Rouge had been toppled, and although polls revealed that more than 95 percent of Cambodians wanted an international tribunal to try the Khmer

Rouge officials who were still alive, Beijing quietly worked to forestall such a tribunal.[4] Son Chhay, a Cambodian politician who accompanied Cambodian leader Prince Norodom Ranariddh on a visit to China in 2000, stated that on the trip, "the Chinese emphasized that the tribunal should only have Cambodian judges," which would make effective justice more difficult; "they [the Chinese] were careful, but their intention was clear," said Son Chhay.[5] Standing alongside Jiang, the Cambodian prime minister, Hun Sen, did not mention the Khmer Rouge era or the tribunal. Instead, he praised Jiang's "historic" visit to Phnom Penh and called China's relations with Cambodia "a precious gift."[6] A beaming Jiang replied that he was "overwhelmed by friendship and joy" and promised closer ties between the two countries.[7]

True to Jiang's word, within five years China had become the most important foreign influence in Cambodia, and Hun Sen shuttled to and from Beijing constantly. Beijing became Cambodia's major provider of foreign aid.[8] In addition, Chinese language programs proliferated in downtown Phnom Penh—one Chinese-language school alone drew 10,000 students.[9] Although older Cambodians who still remember the Khmer Rouge remained suspicious of China, their sons and daughters, who once would have headed to Australia, France, or the United States for higher education, now turned to universities in Shanghai and Beijing. By 2006 Chinese newspapers, films, television, and radio had become increasingly popular, and thousands of Chinese entrepreneurs had moved into Phnom Penh and northern Cambodia, creating entire villages of recent migrants.[10] If Hun Sen had concerns about China's influence in Cambodia, he kept them quiet.

But Cambodia is hardly unique. Since the late 1990s perceptions of China in Southeast Asia have shifted significantly, to the point that elites and the general public in most nations in the region now view China as a constructive actor and possibly as the preeminent regional power.[11] China's image transformation in Southeast Asia is due to a variety of factors. On the one hand, China has benefited from missteps by the United States and Japan. These range from Washington's and Tokyo's delayed response to the late 1990s Asian financial crisis to Washington's focus on counterterrorism in Southeast Asia after September 11, 2001, a focus not shared by all nations in the region. On the other hand, China's image transformation in Southeast Asia is also due, in large part, to skillful diplomacy and an increase in "soft power"—the ability to influence countries by persuasion rather than coercion—in the region. As China becomes more influential in Latin America, the use of soft power and strategic diplomacy is also becoming more evident, boosting China's influence there as it has already done in its own neighborhood, Southeast Asia.

China as a Regional Power in Southeast Asia

Until the past decade, China exerted only minimal influence in Southeast Asia and the rest of the world. The Chinese imperial court's treatment of mainland Southeast Asia as vassal states, and the modern history of Maoist China supporting communists in Thailand, Malaysia, and most disastrously Cambodia left a residue of mistrust in the region. China's limited engagement with Southeast Asia foundered on Beijing's continuing claims to the South China Sea, China's suspicion of the region's multilateral forums, and Asian nations' concern that China's ongoing economic growth would siphon foreign investment away from their countries. In general terms, China's foreign policy tools remained weak throughout the second half of the twentieth century. The PRC was not a major international aid provider. In addition, its diplomatic corps was filled with older, less sophisticated envoys, while its public diplomacy was little more than blunt, crude propaganda. And China's economy, though rapidly growing, could not yet match other major powers as a driver of regional trade flows.

But things began to change in the late 1990s. China's breakneck economic growth finally began to foster greater confidence within the Chinese public and the country's leadership.[12] Furthermore, after the Tiananmen crackdown in 1989 and subsequent sanctions from Washington, China's policymakers recognized that the PRC could not rely solely on its relationship with the United States but should develop relations with its neighbors and with other vital regions of the globe, including Latin America. Just as important, and as explained in other chapters in this volume, Beijing made the decision to begin searching for equity stakes in oil, gas, and other natural resources overseas.[13]

The year 1997 marked China's emergence as a major influence in neighboring Southeast Asia, the first part of the globe to feel the impact of China's more proactive foreign policy. Whether or not Beijing believed the United States and Japan fumbled their responses to the 1997 financial meltdown in the region through delayed action, China's own response proved savvy. Beijing refused to devalue its currency, which would have exacerbated the devaluations in Thailand and Indonesia, and instead portrayed its decision as standing up for other Asian nations. After the crisis, the secretary general of one of the main regional organizations, the Association of Southeast Asian Nations (ASEAN), stated that China's role during this crisis was exemplary:

> While Japan has failed to rise to the occasion, China, its rival for regional leadership, has been making all the right moves. Beijing has accepted

the realities and responsibilities of being a full player in the global economy. . . . And, when the financial crisis hit Thailand, China stepped forward with an aid package of $1 billion. But perhaps Beijing's biggest contribution to restoring economic stability to the region is not what it has done but what it has refrained from doing. China has demonstrated impressive restraint in not devaluing its currency, despite intense pressure to do so. Such a devaluation could be devastating for China's neighbors, triggering a further spiral of currency devaluations in the region.[14]

After the financial crisis, Beijing has employed several strategies to continue boosting its influence in Southeast Asia. One such strategy was the increased use of South-South diplomacy. As explained in several chapters in this volume, in particular chapter 5, China's South-South rhetoric focused on the potential for mutually beneficial relations among developing nations in the context of respect for sovereignty, economic paradigms, governance, and political culture. In its relations with other regions, from Southeast Asia to Africa to Latin America, China has pursued a campaign of reassurance to the rest of the world that China's "peaceful rise" is not a threat. Also as part of this strategy, China began portraying itself as the natural leader and guardian of developing countries. China's foreign policy priorities, as other authors in this volume note, have increasingly reached geopolitical dimensions. In this sense, maintaining stable relations in Southeast Asia is a key factor for China's diplomatic and economic success in other regions.

In a reversal of previous foreign policy practices, Beijing no longer seems opposed to actively participating in multilateral organizations, which were previously seen by older Chinese leaders as constraints on China's power. For example, China works closely with its ASEAN peers toward the goals of strengthening the organization and initiating far more joint projects with ASEAN than with other partners like Japan and the United States.[15] In Latin America, China has also shown interest in participating in international organizations, for example by joining the Organization of American States as an observer.

In Asia, in particular, the Chinese government has made "becoming friends and partners with neighbors" a top strategic priority, and a noticeable improvement in Sino-ASEAN relations has taken place since the late 1990s.[16] As one scholar states, "It is too early to tell whether a greater focus on peripheral countries reflects China's long-term intentions to outmaneuver Japan and establish its own sphere of influence in East Asia that excludes the United States, or reflects a desire to increase intraregional economic cooperation and political stability solely for the sake of China's economic modernization."[17]

Over the past several years China has used this win-win rhetoric in Southeast Asia to end nearly all of its old border disputes. In 2003 China signed on to the ASEAN Treaty of Amity and Cooperation, which commits to mutual respect among signatory countries with regard to sovereignty and equality.[18] Beijing has also agreed to create a code of conduct on the South China Sea and has signed bilateral cooperative agreements with several Asian states. Considered one of the greatest diplomatic successes in the region in recent years, China committed through the ASEAN Treaty of Amity and Cooperation to resolving land disputes with Laos and Vietnam plus disputes with Vietnam and other countries over maritime borders in the South China Sea. Some of the disputed areas are valuable because of their proximity to shipping lanes, possible oil and natural gas resources, and important fishing resources in the region's waters. Although, as one analyst states, China's steps toward solving these disputes could very well be motivated solely by its own interests, such as stabilizing its periphery, "these actions have also signaled to other regional actors that China is willing to negotiate, compromise, and behave responsibly, and that it is not determined to seize every piece of territory in the region. Although some states, especially the Philippines and Vietnam, remain wary and suspicious of how a more powerful China might try to resolve remaining territorial disputes, even these countries welcome China's more moderate behavior."[19]

China has also reached out to nations whose bilateral relations with the United States are strained. In the case of the Philippines, for example, after President Gloria Macapagal-Arroyo pulled Philippine troops out of Iraq in 2004 as part of a deal to win the freedom of a Philippine hostage, the United States cut its financial assistance to Manila. Shortly after that, China invited Macapagal-Arroyo for a state visit, aggressively wooing the Philippine leader by offering greater cooperation and aid.[20] However, as some authors in this volume note, the triangular aspect of Sino–Latin American–U.S. relations in effect curtails China's dealings with anti-American leaders like Venezuela's Chávez.

China's foreign policy rhetoric sometimes builds on the fact that elites and the general public in newly democratic nations often resent U.S. criticism of their human rights records. In Mexico, for example, when a former opposition party was democratically elected for the first time in decades, the government was angered when U.S. officials criticized Mexican authorities for alleged use of torture in a case involving a detained U.S. citizen charged for murder.[21] Beijing responded by engaging Mexican officials on the issue of human rights and diplomacy, effectively portraying both China and Mexico as unfair targets of American criticism.

Another major component of Beijing's appeal to developing nations is the portrayal of China as a potential model of successful economic growth (for more on this, see chapter 2). Though China does not openly advertise its model, it implicitly suggests to foreign officials and technocrats how it has used top-down control to further development and reduce poverty, while political reform takes a backseat to economic restructuring. As one official stated regarding the PRC's socioeconomic model in a white paper issued by the Chinese government: "China . . . has created a miracle by feeding nearly 22 percent of the world's population on less than 10 percent of the world's arable land. The living standards of its 1.3 billion people are constantly improving. The Chinese government has lifted 220 million people out of poverty."[22] This can be a particularly attractive model in regions hit hard by financial crises and where some segments of the population have turned against neoliberal policies.

China's New Diplomatic Tools in a Changing International Context

As China's engagement with the world becomes more sophisticated, its diplomatic tools have become more sophisticated as well. In the past decade, China has intensified its diplomatic offensive, which—as outlined in chapters 2 and 3 with respect to Sino–Latin American relations—has focused on selling the image of a country experiencing a peaceful rise. In this respect, one of China's most successful tools is its participation in multilateral forums. One analyst describes this new tool in China's foreign policy as follows:

> China's shift in its approach toward regional multilateral organizations, from suspicion to acceptance and active involvement, has made it easier for ASEAN leaders to believe that China may be starting to play a more constructive role in the region and might continue to do so as it grows more powerful. Although skeptics argue that nothing substantial has been accomplished through these institutions, ASEAN leaders understand that the goal of these institutions is to foster consultation and dialogue, and only through such a process can parties build the mutual trust and confidence that are necessary to resolve problems.[23]

China's tools of economic influence have also become more sophisticated. China's foreign aid system has undergone a transformation, although it still remains relatively opaque. According to a study of Chinese aid by Henry Yep of the National Defense University, in 2003 China's aid to the Philippines was roughly four times greater than American aid, its aid to Laos was three times greater, its aid to Indonesia was nearly double, and its aid to Cambodia was comparable to U.S. aid.[24] Since that study, China's assistance to Cambodia has vastly outstripped American assistance. Similarly, in Latin America an analysis shows that Beijing's aid grew from almost nothing a decade ago to at least $700 million in 2004, in some cases using debt restructuring mechanisms to complement its aid packages, such as a ten-year extension on Cuban loans as part of a set of agreements signed during President Hu's visit to that country in November 2004.[25]

There are signs that Beijing is seeking to make its aid policies more transparent. China has established a partnership with the Department for International Development (DFID), the British aid organization, in order to professionalize Chinese assistance.[26] Yet making China's aid completely transparent may not be in Beijing's interest, as it could eliminate Beijing's advantage in countries like Cambodia, Burma, and Venezuela, where other donors' policies limit interactions with those governments. As in the later days of the Soviet Union when ordinary citizens questioned why Moscow was supporting certain regimes around the world while the domestic economy stagnated, full disclosure of China's aid could elicit an angry response by the poor in China, as the country faces serious domestic economic and social problems.

Beijing has revamped its aid programs to tie assistance to discrete policy goals, including promoting Chinese companies abroad, cultivating important political actors, and bolstering China's positive image. In Thailand, for example, Chinese assistance has been employed for the kind of lobbying so familiar in Washington; these efforts aim to attract important elected Thai officials to China on study trips and conferences.[27] Beijing has also purchased surplus Thai agricultural products to placate Thai farmers worried about the potential impact of the China-ASEAN free trade agreement.[28]

China's embrace of free trade, and its promotion of the idea that it will become a major source of foreign direct investment, plays an important role in bolstering its image. In addition to the China-ASEAN free trade agreement, Beijing is negotiating closer bilateral trade ties and economic partnerships with individual Southeast Asian states. It is estimated that, as a result of the China-ASEAN free trade agreement, Southeast Asia's total trade with China will soon eclipse the region's trade with the United States or Japan. Although China's free trade deals tend not to be as comprehensive as deals signed by the United States, China's approach does allow Beijing to present itself as a faster-moving trade partner than Washington.

On official visits overseas, Chinese leaders often set targets for future Chinese investment in these regions. The targets, usually projecting five or even ten years into the future, tend to be enormous, obscuring the fact that current

Chinese foreign direct investment in regions like Southeast Asia and Latin America still lags far behind investment from the United States and other wealthy countries like Japan. During a meeting in 2005 between a Chinese business delegation and the Indonesian minister of finance Jusuf Anwar, the Chinese allegedly stated that their investment in Indonesia would triple within five years, to as much as $20 billion.[29] Similarly, when Hu Jintao visited Brazil in 2004, he allegedly pledged $100 billion in investment funds in the region within the next decade, also stating that the annual trade volume between China and Brazil would double within three years (other chapters in this volume further explain this controversial statement by President Hu).[30]

As mentioned in various parts of this volume, much of China's new investment in Southeast Asia, Latin America, and other regions has focused on securing access to commodities. According to one energy specialist, Beijing is attempting to "secure the entire supply chain in critical industries."[31] The Chinese government wants to control the entire process, from taking commodities out of the ground to shipping them back to China, because it does not trust world markets to ensure continuous supplies of key resources. It is purchasing stakes in important oil and gas firms abroad, constructing the infrastructure necessary to get those industries' resources to port, and building close relations with refiners and shippers.

Just as in other parts of the world, China's use of soft power in Southeast Asia includes the promotion of cultural exchanges. China has begun hosting overseas scholars, emulating the programs sponsored for decades by the U.S. State Department.[32] Beijing has also created a Chinese version of the Peace Corps, run by the China Association of Youth Volunteers, to send Chinese youth on volunteer service projects to developing nations like Laos and Burma.[33] Another important component of China's public image campaign is its growing international media reach. Xinhua newswire has greatly expanded its output in languages other than English and Chinese, and China's CCTV television stations have significantly expanded their reach overseas.

China's new public diplomacy also includes the organization of informal business and cultural summits that bring opinion leaders to China. These exchanges allow China to emphasize in a subtle fashion its role as a potential partner for investment and trade and its increasingly prominent position as a leader. Some meetings, like the Boao Forum for Asia, bring together Asian business people to events similar to Davos world economic forums. People involved in China's new informal summits report that the central government prefers that non-Chinese representatives head the summits, serving as president or organizer, to give the impression that China plays a nonpartisan role. However, China usually has full control of the list of attendees.[34]

As China expands its public diplomacy, it has inevitably found the need to develop its diplomatic corps. The Chinese Ministry of Foreign Affairs has begun to retire older, more ideological diplomats, replacing them with a young generation of envoys who speak better English and more local languages. China is able to keep its diplomats in one place for longer periods of time, because unlike U.S. Foreign Service officers who have a say in where they would like to be posted, the Chinese Ministry of Foreign Affairs can mandate postings.[35] Top Chinese diplomats often serve three or even four tours in some countries, as they rise to the rank of ambassador and build their language skills, while developing extensive contacts in the local business and political communities.

Promotion of Chinese culture and Chinese language studies are also major components of China's new public diplomacy tools. The Chinese government has launched several initiatives to increase Mandarin instruction—for example, Beijing now funds at least the first year of what it calls Confucius Institutes, Chinese language and culture schools created at leading local universities, which are now found throughout Asia, Latin America, and around the globe. According to Chinese sources, China plans to open at least a hundred Confucius Institutes by 2010.[36] These institutes are reminiscent of the British Council or the Alliance Française, which promote British and French culture without being explicitly linked, at least in people's minds, to Whitehall or the Élysée Palace. Beijing has also tried to promote the instruction of Mandarin and Chinese culture in overseas primary schools. It has signed agreements with countries like Thailand to help integrate Chinese children into public school curricula and has helped students in poor nations like Cambodia so they can attend private local Chinese-language primary schools.

Parallel to promoting Chinese studies in other nations, Beijing has tried to lure more foreign students to China. The Ministry of Education has done so by advertising Chinese universities abroad, by increasing financial aid, and by relaxing visa policies for foreign students.[37] Unfortunately, in the aftermath of the September 11, 2001, terrorist attacks, the United States has severely tightened student visa policies, making it far more difficult for students from Southeast Asia to attend school in the United States.[38]

Some of this cultural outreach has been targeted at ethnic Chinese already living outside China—there are, for example, between 30 million and 40 million ethnic Chinese in Southeast Asia. In recent years, Beijing has rebuilt relations with ethnic Chinese organizations around the globe, from cultural associations to clan organizations to business chambers, and has pushed these diaspora Chinese to help boost relations between China and the developing world by hosting meetings like the World Chinese Entrepreneurs Convention or sending important ministers to visit ethnic Chinese abroad. According to Hong Liu of the National University of Singapore, in 2001 top officials from Beijing's Overseas Chinese Affairs Office visited more than twenty countries to hold meetings with leaders of diaspora Chinese communities.[39]

Finally, over the past decade the Chinese government not only lifted restrictions on migration within China but also made it much easier for Chinese to leave the country for business and tourism. Partly as a result, Chinese migration, sometimes on overstayed short-term visas, is transforming the demographic makeup of northern mainland Southeast Asia, from Burma to Vietnam, as well as parts of other regions, like eastern Africa and some nations in Latin America. Because of outward migration, new Chinese migrants now dominate entire towns in places like Luang Namtha, in northern Laos.[40] The recent migrants are much more attuned to trends in China than older generations of ethnic Chinese, and they also have created a kind of renminbi zone in northern mainland Southeast Asia, where the RMB serves as a de facto second currency.[41]

Assessing China's Success in Its Southeast Asia Foreign Policy

To measure the success or failure of China's growing relations with Southeast Asia, it is important to understand China's goals in the region. One goal is simply to maintain peace on China's periphery. Peace allows China's economy to continue growing, relatively poor border provinces like Yunnan in southwestern China to build economic links to Southeast Asia, and China to gain access to resources.

Beijing also wishes to reduce Taiwan's influence. Ultimately, China would like to reduce Taiwan's informal diplomacy with other countries. Beijing also wants to change regional perceptions of China, so it is seen as a positive, benign actor. Finally, and most important, China may want to shift influence away from the United States, creating its own sphere of influence, a kind of Chinese Monroe Doctrine for Southeast Asia.[42] In this scenario, countries would subordinate their interests to China's and would think twice about supporting the United States should there be any conflict in the region.

Beijing clearly has been successful in its efforts to maintain peace and to boost its image as a nonthreatening emerging power. Outside of Singapore and Vietnam, it is almost impossible to find Southeast Asian leaders or major media outlets today who question China's rise and the potential impact of its economic gains in the region, in sharp contrast to only a few years ago.[43] Between 2000 and 2005 China's trade with the region grew by 20–30 percent annually, and Chinese officials predict that trade will reach $200 billion a year by the end of the decade.[44] Yet Southeast Asian leaders take pains to downplay the possible negative effects of the growth in trade, even though China's exports overlap by more than 50 percent with those of Thailand, Indonesia, Malaysia, and the Philippines and China's growth could threaten the electronics and textile industries, major drivers of economic growth in Malaysia and Indonesia, for example.

Chinese entrepreneurs and policymakers are increasingly given the type of welcome and access in Southeast Asia that was once reserved for U.S. and Japanese elites. For example, Chinese premier Wen Jiabao was warmly received during a visit in 2003 to Indonesia, but when President Bush visited Indonesia the same year, many cultural and political leaders refused to meet with him for fear of being publicly tainted.[45]

On the economic front, some policymakers and some segments of the public in Southeast Asia seem convinced that if they learn from China's model of economic growth, they can duplicate China's success in promoting development and combating poverty. In Vietnam and Laos, for example, younger policymakers regularly study the "Chinese model" of slowly opening the economy while retaining control of the political system.[46]

Polling data in Southeast Asia suggest that many in the region view China as a benign presence and one to be emulated, in sharp contrast to current regional views of the United States. An analysis of the elite Southeast Asian media reveals that whereas as recently as the 1990s leading newspapers frequently criticized China's economic and security policies, today such commentary is rare.[47] Studies in other regions of the world increasingly concur with this view, including surveys of Latin American public opinion. A comprehensive 2005 BBC poll of twenty-two nations found that 48 percent of those polled thought China's role in the world was positive, while 30 percent viewed China's role as negative, though follow-up polls have shown more mixed results.[48] Steven Kull, director of the organization that conducted the poll for the BBC, notes that "it is quite remarkable that, with its growing economic power, China is viewed as so benign, especially by its Asian neighbors that it could threaten or seek to dominate."[49]

Another sign of China's positive image and rising influence in the region is the growing popularity of study-abroad programs in China. Between 2002 and 2004 Cambodian students in China grew by nearly 20 percent, Indonesian students by nearly 50 percent, and Vietnamese students by nearly 90 percent.[50] In Indonesia demand for Chinese language instruction has become so great that the country faces a shortage of some 100,000 Chinese language instructors.[51] A similar dynamic is taking place in Latin America. Reportedly, the demand for Chinese language instruction in Argentina tripled in 2005, and the new Mandarin language program at the University of Buenos Aires had a total enrollment of more than a thousand in just two years of operation.[52]

Another way to measure China's growing power is by looking at the position of ethnic Chinese minorities in a region. Even though many diaspora Chinese have little connection to mainland China, public perception of China affects public perceptions of diaspora Chinese, particularly in regions close to China like Southeast Asia. In many cases, the identity of diaspora Chinese today is positive because of China's positive image and because, rightly or wrongly, some non-Chinese view diaspora Chinese as potential links to China. In Thailand leading politicians now tout their Chinese heritage, advertising their ability to bolster ties with Beijing.[53] In Indonesia, where only a decade ago ethnic Chinese played minor roles in politics and where riots targeting ethnic Chinese laid waste to Jakarta, a wide spectrum of ethnic Chinese now provides input into government policymaking.[54] In Latin America, where large ethnic Chinese communities are limited to a few nations, such as Panama, it remains too early to tell whether perceptions of ethnic Chinese have changed.

Another sign of China's successful engagement is the number of governments in Southeast Asia and other regions that are slashing even informal links to Taiwan. In the 1990s leaders from many countries that officially recognized Beijing would travel to Taipei for informal visits, as the former Malaysian prime minister, Mahathir Mohamad, did in 1997. They also often allowed Taiwan to open Taipei economic and cultural offices in their countries; these offices served as informal embassies. One of the first Southeast Asian countries to break informal ties with the Taiwanese was Cambodia, when in 1998 the Cambodian prime minister, Hun Sen, announced that a Taiwanese informal embassy was no longer welcome in Phnom Penh. Later, other Asian countries halted the practice of informal visits to Taiwan.[55] As several authors in this volume note, Beijing has also enjoyed some success in isolating Taiwan from Latin America.[56]

Some countries have also shown their willingness to isolate other perceived enemies of China. For example, at the request of the Chinese government, Cambodia barred the Dalai Lama from attending a Buddhism conference in 2002. In 2001 the Thai government prodded Falun Gong (the spiritual movement that frightened the Chinese government by holding the largest coordinated demonstrations in China since the Tiananmen protests of 1989) to cancel an international meeting in Bangkok. Explaining Thailand's actions, Thailand's police minister bluntly told reporters, "We want to keep good relations with China."[57] The Bangkok government has also deported or arrested Falun Gong members for protesting in front of the Chinese embassy; following in its footsteps, Indonesia has prohibited marches by Falun Gong supporters and has arrested Falun Gong activists, while Malaysia has filed charges against nine Malaysian Falun Gong adherents.

Ultimately, China's soft power can be used to persuade other nations to take actions they otherwise might not. Measured this way, China's influence in the region clearly has increased. Although ASEAN is obviously meant to take its members' interests into account first, diplomats say that in the past three years consensus at ASEAN meetings has been delayed as member nations analyze how Beijing will react to any decision.[58] For example, although Chinese dams on the upper portion of the Mekong River, the major waterway in mainland Southeast Asia, may be contributing to decreased water flows and decimating downstream nations, China's growing influence, including its aid to nations like Cambodia and Laos, has kept a lid on Southeast Asian leaders' complaints about China's policies.[59]

Conclusion: What Will the Future Bring?

What will China's charm offensive mean in the long run for Southeast Asia and for regions like Latin America? There are signs that China's rising power, and its growing engagement with the world, will prompt Beijing to wield its influence responsibly. In the past decade Beijing has sent Chinese peacekeepers under the United Nations flag to places like Haiti, a dramatic break with China's history of nonparticipation in UN missions. China has also begun to mediate other nations' disputes, a task generally reserved for responsible great powers. After anti-Thai riots in Cambodia led to a break in relations between Cambodia and Thailand in 2003, the Chinese ambassador in Phnom Penh issued a statement asking Cambodia and Thailand to try to resolve their dispute. The Chinese vice foreign minister, Wang Yi, called in the Thai and Cambodian representatives in Beijing and helped them talk through their grievances. In private the Chinese minister then warned the two neighbors to normalize relations as soon as possible. Soon after, the two sides began a reconciliation process.[60] Similarly, and more recently, China has begun to play a limited role in helping mediate the unrest in Burma.

China also has proven influential on nontraditional security issues, working with Southeast Asian states to address drug trafficking and human trafficking. One regional expert on human trafficking lauds Beijing for taking progressive stances on human trafficking education, stances that have put pressure on governments in Cambodia and Laos to do the same.[61] The U.S.

Drug Enforcement Administration has recognized that China understands the threat posed by drug trafficking. In the past decade Beijing signed several important UN drug conventions, hosted major multinational meetings in China on drug control, and started training Asian prosecutors on combating transnational crimes like drug trafficking.[62]

After facing international criticism in 2003 for covering up an outbreak of SARS (severe acute respiratory syndrome)—an outbreak that soon spread across the world—the Chinese government began using its influence to promote cooperation in fighting dangerous diseases. As avian bird flu became the latest potential pandemic to emerge from Asia, Beijing responded quickly by vowing, in the autumn of 2005, to help other countries develop bird flu early warning systems and to work with international organizations to strengthen quarantines. In January 2006 China hosted a global donors' conference on fighting avian bird flu.

China's growing influence in Southeast Asia, Latin America, and other regions could engender a backlash. As China becomes more powerful, other nations will become more suspicious of its intentions, realizing that despite promises of noninterference, China, like any great power, will satisfy its own interests first. Other countries may recognize that China's supposed dedication to developing nations does not always hold true or that its economic model may prove no more effective than the neoliberal model. Already, China's retreat from socialist principles and incursion into capitalism have alienated some factions in the political left in Latin America and other parts of the world. China's own socioeconomic inequalities are beginning to receive ample coverage in the world media, increasingly exposing some of the failings of China's development scheme. Some scholars even express concerns about the Latin Americanization of China—that is, that China is becoming as economically unequal as Latin America.[63]

China's policies could face backlash in other areas as well. China could overplay its hand, making aid and investment promises that it cannot fulfill, as may have been the case in Latin America during Hu's 2004 visit (see chapter 2 for more on this controversy). Similarly, in Cambodia many local schools complain that aid promised during visits to the country by Chinese leaders never was delivered.[64] Brazil's foreign minister has announced that Brazil has not reaped the new investment from China it expected when it granted Beijing market economy status.[65] As Francisco González explains in chapter 7, China's market penetration also displaces certain sectors of the local economy. Argentine officials have expressed concern about the fact that imports from China are growing at more than three times the rate of exports to China. As a result, Argentina's government has imposed new nontariff barriers on certain categories of Chinese imports.[66] Increased competition from China has also created a dislocation of Brazilian exports to East Asia, primarily low-end, low-technology manufactured goods.[67] According to the Chinese Ministry of Commerce, nearly two-thirds of trade investigations against China in 2005 were initiated by developing countries.[68]

Chinese aid through infrastructure development and business projects lacks transparency. In Cambodia local activists accuse both the Cambodian government and Wuzhishan LS, a Chinese state-owned firm, of forcing hundreds of villagers in a province called Mondulkiri off their land, repossessing the property, and then spraying the area, which includes ancestral burial grounds, with dangerous herbicides. Peter Leuprecht, the UN special representative for human rights in Cambodia, said in a statement, "The government and the company [Wuzhishan LS] have disregarded the well-being, culture, and livelihoods of the . . . indigenous people who make up more than half the population of the province."[69]

Even worse, Chinese aid can contribute to ingrained bad habits in recipient nations. Committed to a new, tough aid model that punishes countries for graft, the World Bank in early 2005 threatened to suspend hundreds of millions of dollars worth of assistance to Cambodia because of Phnom Penh's allegedly rampant corruption. On a visit to Cambodia in April 2006, the Chinese premier, Wen Jiabao, promised Phnom Penh $600 million worth of loans and grants. In the end, the World Bank did not make good on its threat to cut Cambodia off, perhaps because it feared it would then have no influence in the country; it did, however, later suspend several aid projects.

China's poor labor and environmental standards and corporate governance also could trigger a backlash against Beijing, especially when exporting such practices—essentially exporting its own domestic weaknesses. China's Export-Import Bank reportedly declines to sign environmental guidelines commonly adopted by credit providers from most wealthy countries.[70] Such environmental concerns, which have already sparked growing concern in civil society in nations like the Philippines, will soon spread to Latin America, as environmental groups in the Brazilian Amazon, among other places, have begun questioning the environmental practices of Chinese investors.

More generally, the state-led business model China offers to the developing world could undermine the rule of law in Latin America and poorer countries in Asia. To be sure, American, European, and Japanese companies also sometimes abdicate corporate responsibility, and other Chinese companies operate more transparently. But for the most part, Western and Japanese firms have some degree of accountability to their shareholders and boards, uphold at least a degree of corporate responsibility, offer the public information about their environmental and labor practices, and can be sanctioned, whether by America's Foreign Corrupt Practices Act or similar legislation in other countries.

Chinese firms generally do not operate under the same burdens of oversight. And poor corporate governance can lead to labor problems, since companies lacking oversight are less likely to treat their employees well and developing countries have few of the tools necessary to force multinationals to follow labor rules. As mentioned in chapter 4, Shougang International Trade and Engineering, a Chinese state steel company operating in Peru after it purchased Hierro de Peru, is a case in point. Peru's Labor Ministry recorded 170 accidents, including 2 fatal ones, at the mine in one year alone, and Peruvian union leaders claimed to record over 400 accidents a year.[71]

In the long run, Chinese support for fellow authoritarian regimes could also prove detrimental to stability in regions ranging from Southeast Asia to Latin America. In Asia, China's influence can be felt the most in Burma, the region's most backward, politically isolated nation. At important moments in recent Burmese history, when pressure might be applied on Rangoon, China has supported the leaders of the Burmese junta. In May 2003 thugs dressed as monks attacked the convoy of prodemocracy Burmese opposition leader Aung San Suu Kyi on a rural road, leaving seventy or more people dead. The U.S. government believes the junta masterminded the massacre, but China immediately defended the Burmese regime.[72] In recent months, China has continued to defend the Burmese government, though it has worked to help find solutions to Burma's latest crisis.

Similarly, in Latin America the success of the Chinese leadership in delivering continued strong economic growth while retaining political control could serve as an example to some of the more authoritarian leaders in the region. Populist, authoritarian leaders like Hugo Chávez have found their ability to assume regional leadership limited by their dependence on the United States, Brazil, and other democracies for aid and investment. Finding another major source of economic assistance and investment, as the Burmese regime found in China after facing U.S. and British sanctions, would grant actors like Chávez more freedom. Other leaders in the hemisphere will have to make similar decisions about whether to use Chinese assistance as leverage against the United States.

Notes

1. This chapter is adapted, in part, from Joshua Kurlantzick, "China's Charm Offensive in Southeast Asia," *Current History* 105 (September 2006): 270–76; and

Joshua Kurlantzick, "China's Charm Offensive," *Commentary* 122, no. 3 (October 2006): 35–39.

2. David Lamb, "China Works to Improve Ties with Southeast Asian Neighbors," *Los Angeles Times*, November 15, 2000, p. 12. Also author's own reportage from that time period.

3. On the size and scope of Chinese assistance to the Khmer Rouge, see, for example, Ben Kiernan, *The Pol Pot Regime: Race, Power, and Genocide under the Khmer Rouge, 1975–1979* (Yale University Press, 1996). Also see Tom Fawthrop, "Middle Kingdom Puts the Squeeze on Little Kingdom," *Phnom Penh Post*, Commentary (www.phnompenh post.com/ [December 2007]).

4. For polling data on Cambodian views of a potential Khmer Rouge tribunal, see International Republican Institute survey, released March 12, 2004 (www.iri.org).

5. Son Chhay, interview with author, Washington, January 2006.

6. Xinhua, "Chinese President Meets Cambodian Premier, Makes Proposal to Boost Ties," November 13, 2000.

7. Xinhua, "Jiang, Sihanouk Hail Sino-Cambodian Friendship," November 13, 2000.

8. See, for example, Ek Madra, "China Forgives Cambodia Khmer Rouge-Era Debt," Reuters, November 3, 2002; British Broadcasting Corporation, "China Gives Cambodia $600 Million in Aid," April 8, 2006; and Henry Yep, "China's Foreign Aid to Asia: Promoting a Win-Win Environment" (National Defense University, 2006).

9. Paul Marks, "China's Cambodia Strategy," *Parameters* (Autumn 2000): 92–108.

10. Author interviews, Phnom Penh, January 2006.

11. Author interviews, Bangkok, Manila, Phnom Penh, Jakarta, Kuala Lumpur, Singapore, Chiang Mai, Nha Trang (Vietnam), Vientiane, 2005 and 2006. See also Andrew Kohut and Bruce Stokes, *America against the World* (New York: Times Books, 2006); BBC, program on international policy attitudes, annual polling (www.pipa. org); and Office of Research, "Survey on Urban Thailand" (U.S. Department of State, 2005).

12. When in 2003 the Horizon Group polled randomly chosen Chinese citizens, nearly 40 percent picked China as "the most prominent country in the world"; the United States was a distant second. Horizon Group Research, 2003.

13. Erica Downs, Chinese energy specialist, interview with author, January 2006.

14. Michael Richardson, "Japan's Lack of Leadership Pushes ASEAN toward Co-operation with China," *International Herald Tribune*, April 17, 1998 (www.iht.com/articles/1998/04/17/asean.t.php [December 2007]); and Robert G. Lees, "If Japan Won't Help Rescue Asia China Might," *International Herald Tribune*, February 21, 1998 (www.iht.com/articles/1998/02/21/edlees.t_0.php [December 2007]). All currency figures are in U.S. dollars unless otherwise noted.

15. Ministry of Foreign Affairs officials, interview with author, Singapore, January 2006.

16. Michael A. Glosny, "Heading toward a Win-Win Future? Recent Developments in China's Policy toward Southeast Asia," *Asian Security* 2, no. 1 (2006): 24.

17. Ibid., p. 28.

18. Tyler Marshall, "China's Stature Growing in Asia," *Los Angeles Times*, December 28, 2003, p. A1.

19. Glosny, "Heading toward a Win-Win Future?" p. 37.

20. Philippine officials, interview with author, Manila, March 2006.

21. Dane Schiller, "Justice Doesn't Always Translate across Border," *San Antonio Express-News*, April 27, 2004, p. A1.

22. White Paper on Peaceful Development Road of China, State Council Information Office of China, December 22, 2005 (www.china.org.cn/english/features/book/152766.htm [December 2007]).

23. Glosny, "Heading toward a Win-Win Future?" p. 34.

24. Yep, "China's Foreign Aid to Asia."

25. Ibid.; and Associated Press, "China, Cuba Agree on Loan Extension," November 23, 2004.

26. See, for example, Hilary Benn, Secretary of State for International Development, United Kingdom, "China and the UK: Partners in International Development," speech at Fudan University, Shanghai, May 25, 2004 (www.uk.cn/uploadfiles/2005 31011451744.pdf [December 2007]).

27. Thai senator, interview by author, September 2005.

28. Official at Ministry of Foreign Affairs, interview by author, Thailand, September 2005. Also see John Wong and Sarah Chang, "China–ASEAN Free Trade Agreement: Shaping Future Economic Relations," *Asian Survey* 43, no. 3 (2003): pp. 507–26.

29. Bill Guerin, "Indonesia, China Find Love," *Asia Times*, August 17, 2005 (www.atimes.com/atimes/southeast_asia/gh17ae01.html [December 2007]).

30. "Chinese Pose a Trade Threat in Latin America," *Dallas Morning News*, November 26, 2004, p. A34.

31. R. Evan Ellis, "US National Security Implications of Chinese Involvement in Latin America" (U.S. Army War College, Strategic Studies Institute, 2005), p. 5.

32. Thai and Malaysian scholars, interviews by author, January 2006. See also Pallavi Aiyar, "China Hunts Abroad for Academic Talent," *Asia Times*, February 18, 2006 (www.atimes.com/atimes/china_business/hb18cb05.html [December 2007]).

33. See, for example, Xinhua, "Chinese Volunteers to Offer Services in Myanmar," January 11, 2006; and "Communist Capital Flows Downstream: China's Aid to Laos," China Development Brief, February 2006 (www.chinadevelopmentbrief.com/node/454February2007 [December 2007]).

34. Organizer of summits in China, interview by author, Kuala Lumpur, January 2006.

35. Chinese diplomats, interview by author, Washington, January 2006.

36. For more on the Confucius Institutes, see http://english.hanban.edu.cn/market/HanBanE/412360.htm (December 2007); and "NPC Deputy Calls for Promoting Chinese," *China Daily*, March 10, 2006 (www.chinadaily.com.cn/english/doc/2006-03/10/ content_530648.htm [December 2007]).

37. Paul Mooney, "Asian Students Flock to China for Higher Education," *Chronicle of Higher Education*, October 22, 2004, p. 52; and Paul Mooney, "The Wild, Wild

East," *Chronicle of Higher Education*, February 17, 2006 (http://chronicle.com/subscribe/login?url=/weekly/v52/i24/24a04601.htm [December 2007]).

38. See John M. Hubbell, "Immigrants Register before Final Deadline," *San Francisco Chronicle*, April 26, 2003, p. A17; and Jane Perlez, "China's Reach: Chinese Move to Eclipse U.S. Appeal in Southeast Asia," *New York Times*, November 18, 2004, p. A1.

39. Hong Liu, "New Migrants and the Revival of Overseas Chinese Nationalism," *Journal of Contemporary China* 14, no. 43 (2005): 291–316.

40. Western aid worker, interview by author, Vientiane, September 2005.

41. Michael Vatikiotis and Bertil Lintner, "The Renminbi Zone," *Far Eastern Economic Review*, May 29, 2003, p. 24.

42. For more on the idea of a Chinese Monroe Doctrine for Southeast Asia, see Marvin C. Ott, "China's Strategic Reach into Southeast Asia," paper prepared for U.S.-China Economic and Security Review Commission, July 22, 2005.

43. Singaporean diplomat, interview by author, Singapore, January 2006.

44. Agence France-Presse, "China Sees Trade with Asean Reaching 200 Billion Dollars by 2010," April 26, 2005.

45. Jane Perlez, "The Charm from Beijing," *New York Times*, October 9, 2003, p. 11.

46. Laotian officials, interviews by author, Vientiane, September 2005.

47. Ivan Cook, *Australians Speak 2005: Public Opinion and Foreign Policy* (Sydney: Lowy Institute, 2005).

48. BBC World Service and Program on International Policy Attitudes, "22 Nation Poll Shows China Viewed Positively by Most Countries," March 5, 2005 (www.worldpublicopinion.org/pipa/articles/views_on_countriesregions_bt/116.php?nid=&id=&pnt=116&1b=btvoc [December 2007]).

49. Ibid.

50. For more information on student numbers, see Michael A. Glosny, "Stabilizing the Backyard: Recent Developments in China's Policy toward Southeast Asia," in *China and the Developing World: Beijing's Strategy for the Twenty-First Century,* edited by Joshua Eisenman, Eric Heginbothan, and Derek Mitchell (Armonk, N.Y.: M. E. Sharpe, 2007.)

51. "Chinese Teachers Spread the Word to Pass Heritage," *China Daily*, February 1, 2005 (www.chinadaily.com.cn/english/doc/2005-02/01/content_414004.htm [December 2007]).

52. Vinod Sreeharsha, "East Meets West, with an Argentine Twist," *Christian Science Monitor*, September 30, 2005, p. 4.

53. See, for example, numerous mentions of Chinese heritage by Thailand's then prime minister, Thaksin Shinawatra, during visits to China: "Thai PM Seeks Out Roots in Meizhou," *China Daily*, July 4, 2005 (www.chinadaily.com.cn/english/doc/2005-07/04/content_456688.htm [December 2007]); and "Thaksin Pays Visit to Ancestral Family Home," *Nation* (Thailand), July 3, 2005.

54. Lin Che Wei, president, PT Danareksa, interview by author, Jakarta, March 2006.

55. See, for example, Malaysia General News Agency, "Malaysia Bars Ministers from Visiting Taiwan," July 23, 2004. Also Taiwan Central News Agency, "Taiwan Vice President Comments on Indonesian Cancellation of Chen's Trip," December 17, 2002.

56. "Taiwan and Latin America: Another Defection," *Latin America-Asia Review*, July 2005 (http://62.173.71.58/asiaint/ln/lar/lar6628.asp?instance=5 [December 2007]); and Melody Chen, "Divide and Conquer," *Taipei Times*, June 8, 2005, p. 2.

57. Agence France-Presse, "Falun Gong under Pressure over Proposed Thailand Meeting," February 21, 2001.

58. Singaporean diplomats, interviews by author, Singapore, January 2006.

59. Mekong River Commission officials, interview by author, Vientiane, August 2005.

60. Cambodian politicians, interviews by author, Phnom Penh, January 2006. Also see Supalak Ganjanakhundee, "Anti-Thai Riots: House Panel to Probe Violence," *Nation* (Thailand), February 3, 2003.

61. Heather Peters, specialist on human trafficking in Southeast Asia, interview by author, August 2005.

62. Elizabeth Economy, "China's Rise in Southeast Asia: Implications for Japan and the United States," *Japan Focus*, October 10, 2005 (www.japanfocus.org/products/details/1815 [December 2007]).

63. George J. Gilboy and Eric Heginbotham, "The Latin Americanization of China?" *Current History* 103 (September 2004): 256–61.

64. Cambodian journalists, interview by author, Phnom Penh, January 2006.

65. Jonathan Wheatley, "China Dashes Brazil Trade Hopes," *Financial Times*, October 3, 2005, p. 9.

66. Matt Moffett and Geraldo Samor, "Brazil Regrets Its China Affair," *Wall Street Journal*, October 10, 2005, p. A14.

67. Robert Devlin, Antoni Estevadeordal, and Andrés Rodríguez, "The Emergence of China: Opportunities and Challenges for Latin America and the Caribbean" (Harvard University Press, 2006), appendix.

68. Mark O'Neill, "Record Trade Surplus Raises Ire of Foreign Partners," *South China Morning Post*, October 10, 2005, Business p. 2.

69. UN News Service, "UN Official Calls on Cambodia to Cancel Concession on Indigenous Land," July 6, 2005.

70. Ben Schiller, "The China Model" (www.opendemocracy.net/democracy-africa_democracy/china_development_3136.jsp [December 2007]).

71. Robin Emmott, "Peru Miners Feel Oppresed by China's Shougang," Reuters, July 21, 2005; Joel Millman and Peter Wonacott, "For China, a Cautionary Tale—Insularity, Unfamiliar Ways Strain Investments," *Wall Street Journal*, January 11, 2005, p. A18; and Stephen Frost, "Chinese Investments Abroad; Shougang and Labor Protests in Peru," *CSR Asia Weekly* 1, Week 33 (www.csr-asia.com).

72. Richard Boucher, "Anniversary of Attack on Aung San Suu Kyi," statement, U.S. Department of State, May 28, 2004.

CHRIS ALDEN

10

China's New Engagement with Africa

Nowhere in the world is China's rapid rise to power more evident than in Africa.[1] From multibillion-dollar investments in oil and mineral development to the influx of Chinese consumer goods, China's economic influence is redefining Africa's traditional ties with the international community.[2] Two-way trade, which stood at less than $10 billion in 2000, has surged to nearly $40 billion in 2006, while in the same period China's share of Africa's trade has jumped from 2.6 percent to more than 6.0 percent, making it the continent's third largest trading partner after the United States and France.[3] Africa has drawn new diplomatic attention, benefiting from three major tours in the last year by Chinese leaders as well as a summit in Beijing in November 2006. Just a decade ago there was little evidence of China in Africa; today there are hundreds of major Chinese businesses, bolstered by tens of thousands of Chinese laborers, retailers, and tourists.

Coupled with China's willingness to provide direct aid and concessionary loans in African markets is its foreign policy of not attaching political strings; both aspects are tremendously appealing to Africans. As African resources become increasingly important to the health of the Chinese economy, the continent also occupies an important place in China's global ambitions. China's emergence as a key player in Africa, the impact of its presence, and its challenges to traditional Western preeminence in African economies are critical components of this dynamic new relationship.

As Beijing is adamant in pointing out, China's contemporary engagement with Africa is not new but has its roots in policies pursued since the mid-1950s as well as in earlier historical precedents.[4] Not unlike Latin America, Africa during the cold war was seen by Chinese leaders as a terrain for ideological competition with the Soviet Union, the United States, and the remaining European influences. This competition led to Chinese diplomatic and military support in Southern Africa and to aid for liberation movements ideologically committed to Maoist China, not to the Soviet Union. Chinese officials also recognized that, with a numerical advantage in the United Nations General Assembly and with shared anticolonial perspectives, independent African states held the key for the People's Republic of China's desire to occupy the coveted permanent seat on the UN Security Council.

Although the Cultural Revolution in the late 1960s halted overt Chinese political activism on the continent, Chinese overseas development assistance continued. The most notable example of this was the construction of the TanZam railway, linking Zambia to the coastal port of Dar-es-Salaam, breaking its dependency on white-ruled Rhodesia. Apparently the decision to build the railroad grew out of a direct request from Zambian president Kenneth Kaunda to Mao, seconded by his Tanzanian counterpart, Julius Nyerere (who greatly admired Mao's collectivization strategies and applied them in his country). It is true that many aspects of Beijing's current approach to African relations echo the decisions of that era. These include the government's responsiveness to an African priority, the use of state resources and Chinese labor to construct infrastructure projects, and a high-profile, prestigious project to cement relations.

Finally, the saliency of the past for contemporary China-Africa relations is reflected in the degree to which Chinese officials feel compelled to summon it in their dealings with African states. In Sudan, for example, Beijing peppers its bilateral diplomatic events and official communiqués with references to the British general Charles "Chinese" Gordon, who helped suppress the Taiping rebellion in the 1860s. Upon being transferred to the Sudan, he came under siege and was killed by the forces of the Mahdi in 1885. The Chinese claim that this event, which "finally punished" the imperialist, brought the two states closer together. The Chinese government also likes to underscore how African slaves, who escaped from their masters on the Dutch colony of Formosa, fought shoulder to shoulder with the Chinese general Zheng Chenggong's forces in 1664. And the forging of Chinese relations with the coastal states in East and South Africa is characterized as the revival of ties instigated in the late fifteenth century by the Ming dynasty's Admiral Zheng He. As Chinese officials are quick to highlight, the presence of the world's largest fleet at the time did not result in conquest or humiliation of Africans but rather in a brief trading and diplomatic venture. The analogy with the contemporary relationship is never far from the surface.

This chapter examines recent developments in China's new engagement with Africa and seeks to draw useful comparisons with China's growing ties with Latin America. Some key factors that drive both relationships have both economic and diplomatic implications. On the economic side, standing out are the need for energy and other natural resources and the need for new markets for China's burgeoning economy. On the diplomatic front, the driving force is a redefinition of China's diplomatic strategies—for example, foreign aid, South-South cooperation, and strategic partnerships to counter U.S. hegemony and win recognition over Taiwan—as China's global role adapts to a changing domestic and international landscape.

China's New Engagement with Africa

The current phase in China-Africa relations began in the wake of Deng Xiaoping's domestic economic successes and the growing confidence these instilled in the country (for a more detailed account of Deng's policies, see chapters 2 and 3). His successor, Jiang Zemin, toured Africa in May 1996 and presented a proposal establishing the terms of a new relationship with Africa: a reliable friendship, sovereign equality, nonintervention, mutually beneficial development, and international cooperation. The dynamics of the ensuing Chinese reengagement with Africa can be observed in three dimensions: an economic rationale, a diplomatic rationale, and a broader set of concerns linked to China's global ambitions.

Chinese Engagement, African Resources, and New Markets

The need for energy resources remains the most important focus of China's involvement on the African continent, but other natural resources play a critical role as well. With regard to oil, China's overall outward movement strategy of engaging developing countries and locking in resources through government-to-government agreements, which was launched in earnest after 1993, reflects a recognition in Beijing of the dangers of political instability in the Middle East (see chapter 8 for a detailed account of China's oil policies with respect to Latin America). The serious disputes over Iran's nuclear program, the conduct of the Syrian regime, the U.S. invasion of Iraq, and continued violence there have given Africa greater prominence in China's global strategic calculus. As the Chinese economy has expanded, the demand for oil has risen from 3.00 million barrels a day in 1995 to 7.44 million barrels a day in 2006. As Luisa Palacios points out in chapter 8, the growth in China's oil demand is projected to average 3.5 percent annually over the next two decades, reaching approximately 16 million barrels a day by 2030.[5] Currently, just over 30 percent of China's total imports are derived from African sources, and that will only increase with the recent purchase of oil stakes in West Africa.[6]

At the same time, competition for other natural resources (including strategic minerals, timber, and fisheries) and the opening of new markets for its products are diversifying Chinese involvement in Africa. The commodities boom, which has benefited South African and foreign multinational companies (MNCs) working in Africa, has been driven by China's need for raw materials such as nickel, copper, gold, and titanium. West African timber also attracts Chinese investment (60 percent of Africa's tropical timber exports are to China). Chinese companies have quickly become leaders in physical infrastructure development (roads, railroads, and major public buildings) and telecommunications development on the continent. The use of Chinese labor in infrastructure projects, although a growing source of criticism for some Africans, has been crucial for securing contracts against other competitors and the rapid completion of projects. Official figures claim that 82,000 Chinese laborers were working in Africa in 2005, up from 42,000 the previous year; some reports suggest the numbers are higher.[7] Indeed, China's news sources recently suggested that there were 750,000 Chinese living in Africa.[8]

Africa represents a small market for consumer goods, but its trade with China has had a significant impact in two ways. First, China has been able to find a market for its low-value consumer goods (some of which are produced by unprofitable state-owned enterprises). These goods are brought into Africa by Chinese-dominated import companies and sold through a growing informal network of trading posts across urban and rural Africa. In the words of one Chinese trade official, "Chinese products are well suited to the African market. At the moment, China is in a position to manufacture basic products at very low prices and of satisfactory quality."[9]

The second dimension of Chinese economic interests is new investment in industries geared to markets based in the United States and Europe. Using the special provisions allowed through the U.S. African Growth and Opportunity Act (AGOA) and the European Union's Coutanou Agreement, Chinese investors have established joint ventures in the textile and agro-industries whose aim is to export goods to the West at favorable rates. Agricultural investment in Africa has been encouraged by the Chinese government not only for food security reasons but also as a means of circumventing World Trade Organization rules.[10] Chinese construction firms, with lower costs (and, some have suggested, new-found political connections), have been able to outbid traditional Western firms for large road projects in the Horn of Africa and southern Africa.[11] On these, contracted Chinese labor plays a significant role in furthering the penetration of Chinese interests.

While much is made of the Chinese scramble for oil, there is considerable evidence that state-owned enterprises are applying a strategic approach to investment in other sectors as well. One example is the Qingdao municipal government's investment in the textile industry in Zambia's newly created Mulungushi Industrial Park in Kabwe, which is aimed at taking advantage of the AGOA provisions.[12] A joint venture between a Chinese company and a Zambian company to purchase a cotton gin in the country's eastern province seems to echo the vertical integration strategy utilized by China in the energy field.

The Role of Development Assistance and Diplomacy

Symbolic diplomacy, as in the promotion of national representation abroad, plays an important part in China's evolving relations with Africa. A great deal of Chinese economic engagement in African states revolves around the construction of large prestige projects linked to institutional interests in these states. From new foreign ministries in Uganda and Djibouti, to stadiums in Mali, Djibouti, and the Central African Republic, and even to houses of parliament in Mozambique and Gabon, China's material involvement echoes its past endeavors in Africa, such as the construction of the TanZam railroad. Underlying this outlay is a desire on the part of Beijing to demonstrate its ascendancy as a key power on the world stage (or at least on the smaller stage of the African continent) through this symbolic diplomacy. These impulses reflect the Chinese understanding of the imperatives of governance in an impoverished country. Football stadiums or new government buildings provide regimes with tangible signs of power that can establish their legitimacy, even if they do not translate into outright support from the population.

Development assistance, still relatively limited, occupies an increasingly important part of China's relations with Africa. Africa consumes the largest percentage of China's overseas development assistance, which is divided among restricted aid, outright grants to recipients, a limited number of loans, and new mechanisms such as government guarantees for sector investment in the region. In 2005 the Chinese government provided $950 million in assistance to fifty African countries, part of an estimated $44 billion over the last fifty years. This assistance has taken a number of avenues, from the direct funding of the civil service in the Central African Republic and Liberia to providing a substantial loan to an Angolan government reluctant to turn to the International Monetary Fund (IMF).[13] Training programs in technical areas such as hydroirrigation and small-scale agricultural production involving thousands of African farmers have transferred China's expertise to Africa. At another level, China has provided Algeria with a nuclear reactor and modern telecommunications equipment for Ethiopia and Djibouti, along with training to maintain this equipment.

The announcement of debt forgiveness to thirty-one African countries, amounting to $1.27 billion, at the China-Africa Cooperation Forum in 2003 and aid donations to a number of African states are further expressions of this symbolic diplomacy drive. South Africa placed the debt issue on the agenda of the first China-Africa Co-operative Forum in October 2000, much to the consternation of Chinese officials at the time.[14] The decision to forgive the existing debt is as important for its symbolic value (China is responding to a key issue promoted by African leaders such as Thabo Mbeki and Olusegun Obasanjo) as for its substantive impact on payment schedules. This move was supplemented by a decision to exempt duties on 190 export items from Africa's poorest countries. By cancelling debt China places itself in step with the leading foreign powers with respect to Africa.

In terms of military cooperation, the Chinese focus has been on providing training programs, basic equipment, and arms sales. For example, China's arms manufacturing companies have sold fighter jets to the cash-strapped government in Zimbabwe, helicopters to Angola and Mali, and light arms to Namibia and Sierra Leone. During the Ethiopian-Eritrean war, it reportedly sold $1 billion worth of arms to both sides of the conflict.[15] Arms were apparently provided to Congo's Laurent Kabila in 1998, via Dar-es-Salaam, when Rwandan forces appeared to be on the verge of bringing his government down. According to Amnesty International, China has been Sudan's largest arms supplier in recent years, providing helicopters, arms, ammunition, and antipersonnel mines that have turned up in Khartoum's campaign against the Southern Sudanese.[16] Still, Chinese arms sales to Africa are well below those of its leading providers of weaponry: the United States and Russia.

In the humanitarian area, China has broken with its own past to send some 1,200 peacekeepers as part of eight UN peacekeeping missions in Africa, including 600 to Liberia (a country where Taiwan briefly achieved diplomatic recognition). This participation represents recognition of the importance of participating in UN-sanctioned operations that promote stability. China also provided $200,000 in 1999 to combat drought on the Horn of Africa and $610,000 in humanitarian assistance in 2004 for the Darfur crisis. In a dramatic step aimed at countering critics of its role in Sudan, the Chinese government announced in 2006 that it would be providing $3.5 million for African Union peacekeeping operations in that strife-torn region.

It is impossible to separate the Chinese government's new engagement with Africa from its diplomatic campaign aimed at displacing Taiwan's official relations with African countries, as is the case in Latin America. For the Ministry of Foreign Affairs in particular, the diplomatic status of Taiwan remains a critical driver of its Africa policy. The orthodoxy of the past, when Beijing summarily "punished" states that broke diplomatic ties with it by withdrawing foreign assistance and projects, has been replaced with a more flexible approach. It allows for selective involvement of businesses and Chinese provincial representatives, emphasizing the mix of pragmatism and necessity that characterizes China's new Africa policy.

On the diplomatic front, up until 2005 Taipei was able to claim that it held official relations with seven African countries, Senegal (a key state in the Francophone constellation of leading African nations) being the most significant. The diplomatic loss to Beijing of Senegal in October 2005 and of oil-rich Chad in August 2006 reduced Taiwan to the unenviable position of holding diplomatic relations with five of some of Africa's most impoverished fiefdoms, unstable kingdoms, and island nations.

Forging Strategic Partnerships

A key dimension of Chinese foreign policy at the global level is an overriding concern with American hegemony. In part this reflects the U.S. position as the only power with the political will and military means to actively thwart Beijing's interests with respect to the de facto separation of Taiwan from the mainland. On the broader international stage, U.S. ambivalence toward China's emerging status as a world power—reflected in periodic crises such as the Hainan island incident in April 2001 when a U.S. spy plane was forced to land in Chinese territory—and U.S. promotion (albeit selective) of human rights and democracy ensure that a condition of friction exists between the two states.

In the aftermath of the September 11, 2001, terrorist attacks, with the promulgation of the American doctrine of preemptive strikes and regime change, which resulted in the invasion and occupation of Iraq, the Chinese government is deeply worried about Washington's intentions and long-term objectives. As other chapters in this volume illustrate, this concern has led to a search for strategic partners with whom Beijing can make common cause around issues that reflect its core interests and a break with the traditionally aloof Chinese foreign policy. These core interests include mutual respect for state sovereignty as a guiding principle of the international system and nonintervention in domestic affairs of states. China's drive to realize these strategic partnerships is seen in the largely symbolic bilateral cooperation between key global actors outside of the hegemonic reach of the United States.

As a significant player in multilateral organizations, and with its recent ascension to the World Trade Organization (WTO), China recognizes that it needs to court votes in order to protect and promote its interests in these groups. African states make up the largest single bloc of votes in multilateral settings, and as their economic and political interests do not clash with Beijing's interests, Beijing is actively developing partnerships with African states. In the words of Prime Minister Wen Jiabao in Addis Ababa in December 2005, "China is ready to coordinate its positions with African countries in the process of international economic rules formulation and multilateral trade negotiations."[17]

Africa's importance to China was underscored for many officials in the aftermath of the Tiananmen Square crisis, when African states remained a bulwark of support against the Western impulse to pursue punitive sanctions.[18] African votes have been crucial for China in areas as diverse as the International Olympic Committee's decision on where to hold the 2008 Olympics and the UN Commission on Human Rights' resolutions to condemn Chinese human rights abuses. Beijing officials believe this strategic relationship with Africa will give it, at relatively low cost, the means to secure its position in the WTO and other multilateral venues.

Opening Africa: Winning Markets, Hearts, and Minds

While the motives for China's new engagement can be explained with reference to resources, diplomacy, and the search for strategic partners, the question for Western governments and multinational corporations is how China has been able to so quickly penetrate what was once their preserve. The dilemma for Beijing has been its status as a latecomer to investment in Africa as well as its relative lack of experience in developing and managing large-scale extractive projects abroad. In the words of He Jun, a Beijing-based energy consultant, "China does not have a competitive edge over its Western counterparts in an open market. But in a closed market like Africa's, Chinese companies are able to gain from government influence."[19]

Western oil companies and companies in other sectors have been able to build upon generations of engagement, dating back to the colonial period, to secure their investments in Africa. The principal obstacle facing China in the mid-1990s was how to overcome the prevailing structure of economic and political relations to achieve their aims. To break the Western lock on African resources and markets, the Chinese employed a strategy constructed around the following features:

—Competitive political advantage. An explicit willingness on the part of China to work with any state, regardless of their international standing, based upon the Chinese foreign policy precepts of noninterference in domestic affairs in other states. In practice this has meant China has been able to invest in pariah regimes where Western firms are barred from doing business.

—Comparative economic advantage. Utilizing a low-cost bidding strategy, based on lower skilled labor costs and lower managerial costs. The use of low-skilled Chinese labor in projects is one of the key distinctions from traditional Western—and South African—multinational corporations in Africa.

—Symbolic and economic diplomacy. The lavishing of diplomatic attention coupled with support for prestige projects and development assistance (low-interest loans and outright grants) to potential recipient countries by the Chinese government are prominent features of the overall bidding process.

The result of this strategy is that more than 800 Chinese state-owned firms are now active in the African economy, employing tens of thousands of Chinese laborers; bilateral trade was more than $39.7 billion in 2006.[20] Chinese investments have also grown, surpassing $1.18 billion by 2005.[21] The presence of major Chinese multinationals like Sinopec and PetroChina are supplemented by hundreds of small and medium-size enterprises, some no more than a family in a trading shop in the rural interior of the continent. For example, in December 2005 the China National Offshore Oil Corporation (CNOOC) bought a 45 percent stake in an offshore Nigerian oil field for $2.27 billion. It was one of China's largest foreign acquisitions to date, after the 2005 PetroChina acquisition of PetroKazakstan ($4.18 billion).[22] The Nigerian purchase was made despite the fact that industry analysts believed the Chinese had overestimated the potential returns on Nigeria's block 130.[23] China's energy presence is especially strong in Angola and Sudan, states not traditionally aligned with Western powers and that are subject to intense criticism or sanctions for their governments' practices. As China projects its commercial power abroad, strategic competition with U.S. and European interests is increasing.[24]

For insight into the motivation and strategy of Chinese multinationals, it is instructive to look at the much publicized case of CNOOC's failed bid to acquire a controlling stake in a U.S. oil company with large production interests in Southeast Asia. Unocal, the ninth largest American oil firm, had already come to an agreement with Chevron when CNOOC put out its $18.5 billion cash bid in June 2005. CNOOC hoped its much higher, all-cash offer would be more attractive to Unocal than the mix of cash and shares offered by Chevron. The chief executive and chairman of CNOOC, Fu Chengyu, candidly expressed his desire to transform his state-owned company into a multinational player of the first order: "We aim to be a participant in the global industry, like all the international majors, supplying the global marketplace as well."[25] In the end, fears of Chinese control over American corporate interests caused the U.S. Congress to pass legislation blocking the takeover.

Although conditions differ with respect to the veto power of the national legislature over such deals, there are parallels with the conduct of Chinese multinationals in Africa, especially in the oil arena. The case of Angola illustrates some of the key features of the CNOOC offer. For example, the state-owned Indian oil company, the Oil and Natural Gas Corporation (ONGC), thought it had secured a deal with Shell to assume the lease for Angola's block 18, but a last-minute decision by Angola's state-run oil company, Sonangol, gave the rights to China's Sinopec. Crucial to the turnaround was the Chinese government's willingness to provide a $2 billion loan to the Angolan government, freeing it from reliance on IMF sources and the accompanying conditions sought by the financial lending agency. Beijing has gone on to provide additional financing, expertise, and even its own labor force to rebuild Angola's shattered infrastructure, including an estimated $500,000 refurbishing of the Benguela railroad, a new airport in Luanda, and a refinery in Lobito.[26]

In Nigeria the promise of $7 billion in investments, the rehabilitation of two vital power stations, and a sale of arms for use in the troubled Niger delta were part of the package that ultimately secured the deal for CNOOC's oil field.[27] In the Sudan, China began in 1996 a massive program to construct a modern petroleum industry that would serve as both a source of oil for the country and an opportunity to spotlight the China National Petroleum Corporation (CNPC) and demonstrate Sinopec's growing expertise.[28] Chinese military hardware and diplomatic support for the government in Khartoum during its civil war with the South, and now the Darfur region, have played a significant role in sustaining the relationship.

In a more highly regulated environment such as South Africa, Chinese multinationals occupy a very different role than in other parts of the continent. Joint ventures, such as the agreement between Sasol and its Chinese counterparts to establish coal-to-oil plants in Ningxia and Shaanxi provinces, are the product of lengthy and detailed negotiations that, apparently unlike some deals struck in other African settings, are framed in terms that conform to international legal norms and responsibilities. Huawei Technologies has expanded its communications business into thirty-nine sub-Saharan African countries, including an $800 million contract to build the infrastructure for Nigeria's lucrative cell phone market.[29] When Chinese firms do make headway in taking market share or outbidding local firms, their actions are scrutinized and criticized by the media and activist groups.[30] The dispute over the importation of Chinese manufactured textiles, which has erupted in states as diverse as Lesotho and Kenya, with their own established clothing industries, is the most prominent example of this.

For ordinary Africans the most significant impact of Chinese economic activity on the continent is the surge in low-cost consumer goods. Although of variable quality, such goods are available to Africans as never before. Other imports have more value, like "white goods" (refrigerators, air conditioners) and Chinese manufactured vehicles, which appeal to middle-class consumers.[31] Cheap Chinese imports have displaced African workers in industries such as textiles, clothing, and shoes and threaten to displace workers in other sectors, too—like the automotive industry in South Africa. It is in South Africa, with its well-developed industrialized economy, that the most vocal concerns over the impact of China's presence are expressed. Trade unions claim that more than 60,000 workers have lost jobs as a result of the removal of tariffs on textiles and have petitioned the government successfully to persuade Beijing to place a voluntary restraint on exports.[32]

A similar debate is emerging with regard to the Chinese practice of employing its own nationals in African construction projects.[33] The failure to substitute African workers (technicians, unskilled or semiskilled laborers) for Chinese workers employed in the recent flurry of Chinese infrastructure projects is an important oversight, with economic as well as political implications. Construction firms from the West and from South Africa have cried foul with respect to Chinese bidding practices and point out that systematic undervaluation of labor and managerial costs is a key differential in explaining Chinese success. These companies' home countries—where they must comply with labor and environmental standards (from which Chinese multinationals are exempt) and with obligations like hiring local staff—place an untenable burden on them when it comes to bidding against the Chinese. Moreover, the Chinese use of Chinese nationals for labor in construction and infrastructure projects—justified by Chinese managers in terms of their cost, productivity, and cultural affinity—seems misguided in view of unemployment among Africans. For example, the low wages paid to African staff in the mining sector in Ndola, where a Chinese company has reopened an abandoned copper mine, have produced numerous complaints amongst Zambians.

Another example is in the retail sector. The emergence of Chinese retailers across parts of rural Africa has brought new goods closer to the population but threatens to undermine established African retailers. In Namibia, Botswana, Angola, and Cape Verde the influx of Chinese trading shops has been met with a mix of enthusiasm and concern, reflecting the two-pronged impact on the local economy.[34]

Africans Respond to China

The varying responses to China's African venture are illustrated by the following quotations:

—"The US will talk to you about governance, about efficiency, about security, about the environment. The Chinese just ask: 'How do we procure this license?'" Mustafa Bello, Nigerian Investment Promotion Centre.

—"China is both a tantalizing opportunity and a terrifying threat." Moeletsi Mbeki, South African businessman.

—"China provides a new alternative direction . . . the foundation of a new global paradigm." President Robert Mugabe, Zimbabwe.

Overall, Africa has responded with overwhelming enthusiasm to Chinese entreaties, but a significant minority of businessmen, trade unionists, and nongovernmental organizations worry that China is having a negative impact on their areas of interest. Underlying the positive attitude adopted by African governments and society is the recognition that China provides new sources of foreign direct investment (FDI) and development assistance, supports existing regimes regardless of their political orientation, and can serve as an important strategic partner to counter Western influence on the international stage. For those Africans critical of Chinese engagement, however, there are concerns that the combination of Chinese business practices and its no-conditionalities approach is damaging local business opportunities, promoting poor labor practices, and encouraging pariah regimes to ignore human rights.

For African governments, traditional sources of FDI and development assistance dried up in the aftermath of the cold war. The loss was deeply traumatic and had a deleterious effect on their economic prospects. The steady decline in FDI in Africa as a whole, especially when compared to Asia (with China being the leading recipient of FDI), is widely perceived as a major factor in the persistently low level of development on the continent. Coupled with the dramatic fall in foreign assistance after the end of the cold war, the introduction of Chinese FDI is seen as both welcome and necessary for African development. Thus African governments are enthusiastic about providing the requisite licensing for Chinese businesses investing in their countries and the opening of new businesses in neglected areas.

While the focus of the investment boom from China has been on relatively large enterprises, it would be a mistake to see Chinese investments purely in terms of facilitating the growth of government-driven elite networks. African entrepreneurs in small and medium-size enterprises have in the past benefited from the growth of informal and formal linkages with Chinese and Taiwanese business networks outside of government sponsorship. According to one study, African businessmen in Mauritius and Nigeria were able to use contacts with Taiwan (and through them China itself) for accessing information and new technologies and for "facilitating the development of dynamic manufacturing sectors" in these two countries.[35]

In tourism, the rise of a Chinese middle class with spending power and interest in leisure travel has broadened the pool of tourists in an area of great importance to many African economies. The Chinese government has used its policy of promoting officially approved travel destinations as a means of rewarding friendly African governments. South Africa has benefited from this official status, with Chinese tourists in June 2003 alone (3,423 tourists) more than tripling the number in June 2002 (962).[36] In addition to providing a new source of revenue for African states, tourism can throw a lifeline to regimes ostracized by the West. Zimbabwe, for example, became an official travel destination in 2003 and experienced a surge in Chinese tourists, which contributed to a 40 percent rise in tourism from Asia.[37]

The growing Chinese economic involvement has had positive political effects for African governments. Chinese engagement has provided a new source of regime stability in Africa in a number of ways. Pariah regimes in Sudan and Zimbabwe, subjected to a variety of international sanctions for human rights policies over a period of years, have benefited from China's explicit no-conditionalities policy toward the continent. As noted above, when Western oil companies were obliged to withdraw from investment in Sudan, Chinese companies took that opportunity to invest. While Western concern has focused on China's willingness to provide diplomatic succor to pariah regimes (regardless of who designates them as such), this unprecedented level of attention is having an impact on all African governments. The spectacle of the leaders of one of the world's powers regularly visiting the African continent and meeting with African leaders, along with numerous sponsored tours to China by midlevel bureaucrats, local media, and influential researchers, makes a strong impression on African governments and the public at large.

On the broader international front, African governments welcome the arrival of a new strategic partner to diversify their array of external partners or, in specific cases, to counter Western influence. Confronted with the West's prevailing Afro-pessimism and compassion fatigue, African leaders found themselves relegated to the periphery of international politics during much of the 1990s. China by contrast consciously embraced African leaders, feting them in their own countries and during diplomatic visits to Beijing. Africans have taken note of China's growing global economic clout, which surpassed in 2006 the economies of Britain and France, the top two former colonial states and the traditional economic and political influences on the continent.

For African states the importance of multilateralism is undisputed. China's position on the UN Security Council is seen to be crucial to any overall attempt by African countries to protect their domestic interests—and especially by South Africa, with its own aspirations to a permanent seat. The same could be said of the WTO. African countries seem to accept the somewhat paternalistic argument Chinese officials make regarding Beijing's role in preserving these interests. More broadly, China's traditionalist approach to non-interference in domestic affairs accords well with the outlook of even democratically elected leaders in Africa who view the unity of the state as a sine qua non of effective governance. Chinese investment and foreign assistance, in the form of financial aid or in-kind assistance and investment is a welcome alternative to Western sources.

China, a once impoverished country victimized by Western imperialism and later held back by its own pursuit of disastrous forms of socialism, serves as a third world development model for African elites. The Chinese Communist Party provides an example of adaptability to the strictures of the global market economy without sacrificing the interests of its members (who could be seen as prime beneficiaries of any such changes). For leaders and regimes facing domestic instability, the stress of economic restructuring and liberalization, or the pull of democratic transformation, China holds up a beacon of hope that all the gains of office need not be lost in the process.

Against the backdrop of overwhelmingly positive response to China, there are rising concerns among the African business leaders, labor unions, and civil society actors about the impact China is having on the continent. There is the concern posed by the arrival of low-cost consumer goods, which have enabled Africans to purchase basic items formerly beyond their reach but that threaten local manufacturing capacity. More specifically, the conduct of some Chinese businesses (especially but not exclusively small manufacturing enterprises) has caused alarm over labor protections and environmental standards. The death of forty-six Zambian workers at the Chambishi copper mine in an explosion in April 2005, plus the shooting of five workers apparently by company security forces during a strike action against low wages, confirms some of the worst fears of African trade union activists.

More troubling for a coalition of civil society interests is the damage that the no-political-conditions policy is having on the promotion of human rights, accountable government, and transparency. Leaders like Robert Mugabe welcome Chinese engagement as a means of escaping Western-inspired sanctions against his government's systematic violations of human rights and democratic principles. Chinese investments in Zimbabwe and Sudan compensated for dwindling international support elsewhere. Chinese officials do not seem to be fully comfortable with this role, and there are reportedly debates in Beijing about being seen as too close to pariah regimes.[38] Even South African government officials privately voice concern about Chinese policies undermining their flagship program for restructuring the continent, the New Economic Partnership for Africa's Development (NEPAD). Launched in 2000 after much lobbying by Mbeki and Obasanjo of the top industrialized nations, it earned the support of the Group of Eight at the Gleneagles Summit in 2005 with the promulgation of the Africa Action Plan. Accountability and good governance are key features of NEPAD's self-regulating African peer review mechanism. The possibility that lack of transparent practices, promulgated by China, is undermining adherence to NEPAD is a serious challenge to this continental agenda.

China's African Interests: The Challenges of Consolidation

The presence and conduct of China's businesses in Africa is fast becoming one of the permanent features of the African economic landscape. This new development will inevitably excite controversy within Africa and with Western firms. Some of the concerns are part and parcel of the emergence of such a significant player in a liberalized global trading environment based upon market principles.

The controversy over textiles perplexes Chinese officials, who had to restructure their domestic textile and clothing industries in order to join the WTO. They say that since China has abided by the rules of international trade, the market should therefore be allowed to determine the outcome of this matter.[39] The Chinese diplomatic community is aware that unscrupulous businessmen act alongside more legitimate Chinese firms creating a negative impact on their country's image in Africa. Perhaps disingenuously, government officials claim that in China's increasingly free-for-all economy they have only limited ability to regulate independent operators in a third country.[40] Still, there is evidence that Chinese multinationals desire to emulate established global multinationals and are embracing aspects of the corporate responsibility agenda.[41] Even Western critics admit that, if one sets aside the particular cases of Sudan, Angola, and Equatorial Guinea, "the rest of PetroChina and Sinopec activities on the African continent are not especially reprehensible" or at least no more so than their Western counterparts.[42]

The unprecedented publication by the Chinese government of a foreign policy white paper on Africa in January 2006, along with the high-profile African tours by Hu Jintao, Wen Jiabao, and Foreign Minister Li Zhaoxing that same year, underscores the growing importance the continent holds for Beijing. Although China's paper is unusual, the substance in the document merely repeats the framework of relations (the five principles of mutual benefit) that has characterized the official position since 1996 and that summarizes aspects of its implementation over the past decade. More important, this paper was released at a time when China's role in Africa was coming under increased scrutiny both within and outside the continent.

China, after enjoying considerable support within Africa, is experiencing mounting criticism from some African sources and Western governments both for its trade policy (which replicates classic colonial practices of extraction and of dumping low-cost manufactured goods that undermine local industries) and for its political policy (which is uncritical of regimes with poor human rights records). In the face of this criticism, Chinese officials have been anxious to ensure two things: first, that the China-Africa Cooperation Forum held in Beijing in November 2006 would remain a public showpiece of good relations between the two regions; and second, that China can begin to consolidate its economic and diplomatic gains in Africa. At the heart of the consolidation effort are three spheres of contention: trade friction, values friction, and competition with the West. How China manages these issues will be critical to shaping its ties with the African continent.

Trade Friction

The blossoming trade relationship, despite its statistical growth, contains some concerns for African economies. The balance of trade favors China's export orientation. In the South African case, this imbalance has been a topic of contention in ministerial meetings between the two countries for a number of years; local industries and merchant traders have been hit especially hard by the flood of cheap Chinese imports, particularly when these are linked to the setting up of Chinese wholesale and retail shops that use established networks to access goods. Across the continent, from northern Namibia to central Kenya, traditional products and retailers have been edged out by the advent of Chinese businesses. Even in Angola's war-torn region of Huambo, five Chinese retailers have managed to carve out a position since arriving in 2000 that effectively closed down established Angolan suppliers and retailers.[43] Furthermore, the use of Chinese contract labor instead of local people has brought criticism of Chinese-sponsored projects from Ethiopia to Sudan and Namibia.[44] A further cause of friction is bound to be the relative wealth of the Chinese in Africa. For example, in Lesotho the local population has periodically rioted against Taiwanese businesses, which have been operating there since the 1970s.

For African companies in a position to invest in China, the obstacles are significant but not insurmountable, at least in the case of the larger South African multinationals. SA Breweries, First National Bank, Absa, Anglo-American, Goldfields, and a host of medium-size companies have succeeded in establishing themselves in China. The obstacles remain difficult enough to cause figures as diverse as Uganda's president and Nigerian traders to complain about accessing China's market.[45] The growing presence of African wholesale merchants in southern China, including an estimated 100,000 Nigerians alone, has prompted the Nigerian government to ask for the establishment of a "Nigeria town" in Guangzhou.[46]

In South Africa concern over the rapid development of Chinese steel capacity prompted that country's steel manufacturer, Iscor, to caution that Chinese lower cost production may ultimately threaten South African interests.[47] Similar warnings may come from other African manufacturing firms that stand to lose business to China, especially now that China is part of the WTO. The long-standing proposals by China for joint cooperation between Sasol, the coal-to-oil venture, and a Chinese counterpart have been delayed by South African concerns that China's interests lie mostly in absorbing technological innovations for the development of its own industries rather than in a mutually beneficial business venture.

Values Friction

Adopting principles to meet Western concerns about human rights and good governance in restructuring organizations such as the African Union and its subgroups represents a divergence from a key tenet of Chinese foreign policy: nonintervention in domestic affairs. The African Union's constitution explicitly codifies the possibility and the terms of direct intervention by the Peace and Security Council into the policies or actions of a member state if the council finds gross violations of human rights.[48] Also, NEPAD, whose peer review process is based on an independent review of an African country's adherence to good governance criteria, represents another avenue toward adherence to humanitarian norms. The African Commission on Human Rights, although it has had little impact since its creation in 1988, can lend further institutional support for this trend now that African nations are strengthening their links to the commission. The emerging political architecture of

Africa, therefore, has come a considerable distance from the unconditional stance in support of sovereignty as promoted by the African Union.

As expected, this evolving integration of new norms is contested in some African circles. Weak governments and uncertain legitimacy make leaders cling to notions of sovereignty as a legal bulwark against dissent. However, the ideas of human rights and democracy are taking root, albeit unevenly, on the continent, and they challenge the principle of nonintervention. Most troubling for authorities in Beijing is that a bloc of states that could once be counted on to defend the prerogatives of sovereignty in multilateral settings (with the exception of apartheid South Africa) is no longer unequivocally wedded to this position. Thus the Chinese government's involvement with investment decisions, encouraging parastatals to open up trading and man-ufacturing links, will be increasingly problematic. Unlike its Western coun-terparts, which can point to actions by its multinationals as independent of government decisionmaking, China bears responsibility for its multination-als because of their ties with Beijing.

Competition with the West

Beyond the economic rationale and the diplomacy of official recognition, Chinese involvement in Africa has sparked talk of an emerging Beijing con-sensus on the continent that could counter the precepts of the previously unchallenged Washington consensus. The latter involves conditionalities set by the World Bank, the IMF, and donors that include restrictions on macro-economic policy, reductions in public spending, and commitments to trans-parency. In some cases they call for African governments to hold democratic elections. The Beijing consensus, predicated on noninterference in domestic affairs of states and the promotion of sovereign integrity, appeals to many African leaders, who resist Western actions aimed at economic or political reform of their regimes. The Chinese model of development—rapid devel-opment without challenging single-party rule—is another attraction for these autocrats. Thus China is actively encouraging African states to form a bloc that can counter Western interests in such international forums as the UN Human Rights Commission.

In the immediate aftermath of the September 11, 2001, attacks, relations between Beijing and Washington improved. This was temporary, and with the Iraq intervention the two countries returned to a condition of guarded antipa-thy. In the wake of the Sudan crisis, and China's initial refusal to intervene, the American government began to look more closely at the relationship between China and Africa. Two responses are apparent. One, promoted by the Her-itage Foundation, suggests that China's Africa role is undermining Western economic interests and Western attempts to inculcate democratic principles in Africa and needs to be actively countered.[49] The influential Council on Foreign Relations, while also cautionary on certain aspects of Chinese engagement, sees the possibility of cooperation with China in Africa.[50] Beijing's decision to support a hybrid African Union/UN peacekeeping force in Darfur, manifested in the UN Security Council's authorization of UNSC 1769 in 2007, earned the kudos of U.S. and European government officials.[51]

At any rate, U.S. policymakers no longer see Chinese involvement in Africa as outside a broader strategic framework. As a result, the relative freedom of action that China has had in forging relations across the continent is becoming more constrained. An example of this, which is as much a reflection of globalization as explicit interstate rivalry, is the vulnerability of Chinese oil interests to international pressure. Human rights groups want American jurisdiction over companies that list on the U.S. stock exchanges, based on an interpretation of the Alien Tort Claim Act. For example, these groups mobilized a campaign that ultimately led the Canadian oil company, Talisman Energy, to sell its 25 percent share in GNPOC in March 2003. In another example, when China National Petroleum Corporation tried in 2000 to be listed on Wall Street, publicity generated by human rights activists forced CNPC to withdraw its offering and to create a subsidiary, PetroChina, that explicitly promised that none of the capital raised would go to Sudan.[52]

The remarkable economic growth in China has encouraged Western countries, led by the United States, to invite it to participate in the premier club of industrialized nations, the Group of Eight. This gradual incorporation into the G-8 will undoubtedly have an impact upon the economy and policy choices pursued by Beijing. For example, the United States is interested in a further loosening of China's currency peg to the dollar. The British government is anxious to find areas of cooperation with Beijing in Africa, including using the Chinese as an intermediary with the Mugabe regime in Zimbabwe. The end result may be a convergence of interests with the West, with the effect of reducing China's claim to represent the interests of African states.

Conclusion: Future Prospects

At the core of this surge in Chinese interest in Africa remains the overriding need to fuel the unparalleled growth of its market economy. Beijing authorities understand that to successfully expand its diplomatic influence as well as embed itself in the continent, it will need to do more than just promote foreign assistance and greater investment in Africa. Thus China's engagement in

Africa has evolved quickly from a campaign based on meeting energy needs to a broadening range of economic interests, all supported by a diplomatic strategy aimed at appealing to African governments. However, as Africans begin to voice concern about the less positive effects of the Chinese presence, Beijing will be forced to introduce changes to its approach to sustain its position as a preeminent fixture in Africa.

Its leaders have demonstrated that they recognize the importance of devising responses to the challenges of consolidation and are taking concrete steps to address these. For instance, the prospect of trade friction, especially in the area of textiles, has caused the Chinese government, as mentioned earlier, to introduce voluntary restraints on exports with South Africa. Officials are concerned about the conduct of some Chinese businesses and in the case of the Chambishi mining disaster have offered compensation to the Zambian government.

China's active role in promoting UN intervention in Darfur is aimed at showing its support for the regional organization's efforts and for one of its chief concerns. The sense within China of the need to ameliorate the worst features of their rapid economic growth at home, seen for example in the call for greater corporate social responsibility, has its echo in the foreign policy arena. There is a growing public debate on China's role in the world, as the comments of the economist Wang Xiaodong suggest: "We can't be a country that just does business. We must develop relationships besides economic and trade ties with other countries—including stronger military projection. But for the majority of the people, all they want to do is to develop the economy, and for them, anyone who thinks of anything else is foolish."[53]

And finally, there are changes coming with regard to competition with the West. While not reticent in proclaiming its views, China has nonetheless tread carefully with Western governmental interests (if not those of nongovernment organizations) in areas like Zimbabwe and Sudan; it has also shown its willingness to cooperate with Western multinationals in exploiting the continent's resources. The West should show the same level of restraint and concern in assessing China's role in Africa. The reality is that, as Jeffrey Sachs asserts, "The overwhelming feeling toward China (in Africa) is gratitude for support. China gives fewer lectures and more practical help."[54] Westerners too should recognize the limitations that the arrival of China poses for their formerly untrammeled pursuit of their own interests and, where appropriate, look to cooperate with Beijing in partnership with Africans to develop the continent.

In the end the inherent pragmatism of the Chinese leadership—the same impulse that inspired a successful transformation away from socialism to a capitalist system—will enable it to find the means to further develop its position in

Africa. More so than at any other time, the shape that this relationship will take is out of the hands of Africa's traditional partners in the West. Africans and their Chinese partners are forging ties that will form part of the new dynamics of the twenty-first century. Whether Africans are able to leverage this relationship for their own development imperatives remains to be seen.

Notes

1. "China's goal is not to overturn the world order but instead to participate in this order and to reinforce it and even to profit from it." Fu Chengyu, CEO, Chinese National Offshore Oil Corporation, February 2006, cited in *Oil Daily*, February 9, 2006 (www.energyintel.com[December 2007]). This chapter is partially based on material in Chris Alden, *China in Africa* (London: Zed, 2007).

2. "This 21st century is the century for China to lead the world. And when you are leading the world, we want to be close behind you. When you are going to the moon, we don't want to be left behind." Olusengun Obasanjo, president of Nigeria. Cited in Sharath Srinivasan, "Nigeria-China Relations: Expansion and Negotiation as the Rising Great Power Embraces Africa," in *China Returns to Africa: A Superpower and a Continent Embrace,* edited by Chris Alden, Daniel Large, and Ricardo Soares de Oliveira (London: C. Hurst, 2008).

3. All currency figures are in U.S. dollars, unless otherwise noted.

4. For the definitive historical account of Chinese-African relations, see Philip Snow, *The Star Raft* (London: Longman, 1988).

5. British Petroleum, *BP Statistical Review of World Energy, June 2007* (London: 2007), p. 11. Also see Energy Information Administration, *International Energy Outlook, 2007* (U.S. Department of Energy, 2007), p. 22; Ian Taylor, "Chinese Oil Diplomacy in Africa," *International Affairs* 82, no. 5 (2006): 8.

6. British Petroleum, *BP Statistical Review of World Energy, June 2007*, p. 20. Also see David H. Shinn, "Africa, China, the United States, and Oil," *Online Africa Policy Forum* (Washington: Center for Strategic and International Studies, 2007).

7. Chinese International Labor Cooperation, *Annual Report, 2006* (Beijing: 2006). Using country reports from various sources, one can come up with the following: Egypt, 10,000 laborers; Sudan, 4,000–10,000; Algeria, 20,000; Angola, 2,000–20,000; and additional laborers in Ethiopia and Namibia.

8. Howard French, "Entrepreneurs from China Flourish in Africa," *New York Times*, August 18, 2007.

9. Cited in Chris Alden, "China in Africa," *Survival* 47, no. 3 (2005): 32.

10. Domingos Jardo Muekalia, "Africa and China's Strategic Partnership," *African Security Review* 13, no. 1 (2004): 10.

11. There are frequent complaints from locals as to the quality of the roadwork. World Food Program official based in Ethiopia, interview by author, January 2003.

12. *Business Day* (Johannesburg), November 11, 2003.

13. Angolan government official, interview by author, August 2004.

14. South African government (DTI) official, interview by author, May 2002.

15. Africa Program, "Opening a Sino-US Dialogue on Africa" (Washington: Center for Strategic and International Studies, 2003).

16. "Sudan: The Human Cost of Oil" (London: Amnesty International, 2000).

17. Premier Wen, speech at opening ceremony, China Africa Cooperation Forum, December 15, 2003, Addis Ababa (www.china.org.cn/english/international/82534. htm [December 2007]).

18. Philip Snow, "China and Africa: Consensus and Camouflage," in *Chinese Foreign Policy: Theory and Practice,* edited by Thomas Robinson and David Shambaugh (Oxford: Clarendon, 1994).

19. "China: Greasing Wheels in Africa," *Energy Compass*, January 20, 2006.

20. "Fairly Looking upon Sino-African Relations," *People's Daily*, May 16, 2006 (http://english.peopledaily.com.cn/200605/16/eng20060516_266153.html [December 2007]).

21. National Bureau of Statistics of China, *China Statistical Yearbook, 2006* (Beijing: China Statistics Press, 2006).

22. For more information, see chapter 8 of this volume, by Luisa Palacios.

23. "CNOOC Dives into Murky Waters in Nigeria," *Petroleum Intelligence Weekly*, January 16, 2006.

24. "With China Calling, Is It Time to Say Goodbye to US and Europe?" *Nation* (Nairobi), April 14, 2006.

25. Cited in *Oil Daily*, February 9, 2006 (www.energyintel.com).

26. "The Increasing Importance of Africa's Oil," *COMTEX*, March 21, 2006.

27. Ibid.; Vivienne Walt, "China's African Safari," *Fortune* (Asia edition), February 20, 2006.

28. Douglas Yates, "Chinese Oil Interests in Africa," in *China in Africa: Mercantilist Predator, or Partner in Development?* edited by Garth le Pere (Midrand: Institute for Global Dialogue, 2007), pp. 219–37.

29. Walt, "China's African Safari."

30. See, for example, the South African Broadcasting Corporation news broadcast, April 14, 2006.

31. *Business Day* (Johannesburg), April 19, 2006, p. 2.

32. Ironically, it was concern on the part of Beijing, rather than the initiative of the South African government, that caused it to open discussions with Pretoria that ultimately resulted in the introduction of a two-year restraint on Chinese textile exports.

33. Chinese International Labor Cooperation, *Annual Report, 2006.*

34. See, for example, Heidi Ostbo Haugen and Jorgen Carling, "On the Edge of the Chinese Diaspora: The Surge of *Baihuo* Business in an African City," *Ethnic and Racial Studies* 28, no. 4 (2005): 639–62.

35. Deborah Brautigam, "Close Encounters: Chinese Business Networks as Industrial Catalysts in Sub-Saharan Africa," *African Affairs*, no. 102 (2003): 464.

36. *Mail and Guardian*, September 24–30, 2004, p. 18. These numbers must be contrasted with the number of American tourists (21,236) that same month. Americans made up the largest group.

37. "Business Report," *Star* (Johannesburg), April 14, 2004.

38. Wenran Jiang, presentation at the Institute for Public Policy Research, London, June 28, 2006.

39. Chinese ambassador to South Africa, address to African diplomatic corps, Pretoria, January 19, 2006; and Ling Guiru, "China's Trade Stance with South Africa," *Traders* (Johannesburg), no. 24 (November–February 2006): 49.

40. Chinese Embassy official, interview with author, Pretoria, April 18, 2006.

41. See, for example, the websites for Sinopec and PetroChina.

42. Yates, "Chinese Oil Interests in Africa," p. 235.

43. Moise Festo, interviews by author, Huambo, Angola, September 2004 and May 2006.

44. Human Rights Watch, "Report: Sudan and Oil" (www.hrw.org).

45. *Monitor* (Kampala), January 12, 2004.

46. *South China Morning Post*, September 12, 2006.

47. *Business Day* (Johannesburg), April 5, 2004.

48. Jakkie Cilliers and Kathryn Sturman, "Challenges Facing the AU's Peace and Security Council," *African Security Review* 13, no. 1 (2004): 97–104.

49. Peter Brookes and Ji Hye Shin, "China's Influence in Africa: Implications for the United States," Backgrounder Report 1916 (Washington: Heritage Foundation, 2006).

50. Council on Foreign Relations, *More than Humanitarianism: A Strategic US Approach toward Africa* (New York: 2005).

51. For instance, U.S. envoy Andrew Natsios stated in early 2007 that "our policy and the Chinese policy [on Darfur/Sudan] are closer than I realized they were, and I think the Chinese are going to play an increasingly important role in helping us to resolve this." Bates Gill, Chin-hao Huang, and J. Stephen Morrison, *China's Expanding Role in Africa: Implications for the United States* (Washington: Center for Strategic and International Studies, 2007), p. 15.

52. Joshua Eisenman and Joshua Rogin, "China Must Play by the Rules in Oil-Rich Sudan," *Alexander's Gas and Oil Connections* 8, no. 6 (2003): 1 (www.gasandoil.com); and *Drill Bits and Tailings* 6, no. 2 (February 28, 2001; www.survivorsrights international.org).

53. *International Herald Tribune*, August 15, 2005.

54. Cited in Benjamin Robertson, "China Hunts the Big Game in Africa," *Al Jazeera Net*, October 14, 2006 (http://english.aljazeera.net).

PART IV

The United States, China,
and Latin America:
What Kind of Triangle?

11

The U.S.–China–Latin America Triangle: Implications for the Future

A rising Asian giant challenges the United States on not only a global basis but even in Latin America, long considered to be part of the U.S. sphere of influence. The new competitor runs up a huge trade surplus with the United States and buys prominent U.S. companies. In Latin America its thirst for natural resources leads to investment and trade deals in Brazil's iron ore and soy sectors and in Chile's copper industry. Talks are held on how to transport Venezuela's heavy oil to Asia and how to integrate it into plants designed to use lighter grades of crude. Although raw material sectors benefit, industrial firms in the United States and Latin America complain of unfair competition from the new Asian player, and protectionist measures are threatened. Meanwhile, pundits suggest that a new international alliance may be in the making, which would give Latin America a greater say in international negotiations and implant the Asian development model in the Western Hemisphere.

A description of China in the early twenty-first century? Yes, but it is also Japan in the 1980s.[1] For a second time in the last quarter century, Asia and Latin America appear to be joining forces in a complementary process, which could speed up Latin America's economic development while increasing its independence from the hemispheric hegemon. In the earlier case, however, Japan's initial enthusiasm petered out, and Latin America never realized the expected benefits from the relationship. Distance and cultural differences took their toll. Events at home—in Japan's case, the bursting of the economic and financial bubble—demanded greater attention. Resource-saving technologies meant that the search for raw materials became less urgent, and integration with nearby Asian neighbors took precedence over far-away Latin America. In the background, and never forgotten, was the perceived need to avoid alienating Japan's dominant trade and security partner, the United States.

This chapter argues that China's flirtation with Latin America is likely to be tempered by many of these same factors. Granted, there are important distinctions between China and Japan that could create a different situation with respect to Latin America. One of the most important is China's stage of development. As it frequently reminds the world, China is still a poor country. On the one hand, this means that China's rapid growth is likely to go on longer than Japan's did before leveling off, so its resource needs will continue for the foreseeable future. On the other hand, it also means that China's growth, especially in trade, is reliant on foreign investment in a way that Japan's never was. Thus U.S. investment and technology, in addition to the U.S. market, will be crucial. Finally, while the United States is a key economic partner for China, the security relationship between the two is different from that of the United States and Japan. Japan decided to rely on the U.S. security umbrella, rather than building its own defense system, while U.S.-China security relations are more competitive. Overall, it is hard to say ex ante if the differences are more important than the similarities and what this might imply about the U.S.–China–Latin America triangle. We return to this question in the conclusions.

The chapter is divided into four main sections. The first section locates China, the United States, and Latin America in a global context. The second section considers the attractions of a China–Latin America alliance. The third section discusses the problems on each side of the equation. And the final section concludes by asking whether a China–Latin America alliance is likely and, if so, what the implications are for the United States. Intended as a stand-alone analytical piece, the chapter also draws on the volume's other chapters to serve as an overall conclusion to the book.

China, the United States, and Latin America in a Global Context

The U.S.–China–Latin America triangle does not exist in a vacuum. Each leg is grounded in a domestic as well as an international context, and the bilateral relationships are also part of a larger framework, as Riordan Roett and Guadalupe Paz explain in chapter 1. The U.S.–Latin American story is an old one, and it has been widely analyzed in an extensive literature. Likewise, the U.S.-China relationship has been well researched, especially during the last two decades as the connections have grown. The new part of the triangle is the link between China and Latin America, which must be viewed in light of the U.S. presence, given the dominant role that the United States plays with both. Thus the chapter focuses initially on the changing dynamic of a newly resurgent China to determine how it might interact with partners in the Western Hemisphere.

Many experts claim that China will soon displace the United States in the size of its economy and eventually in its economic, and even security, power. In this context, fear has been expressed that a Chinese alliance with Latin America could play a role in undermining the U.S. position and in giving a boost to China.[2] Clearly, China's economic and political status has been rising, but the comparisons vary substantially depending on the issue area and the statistics chosen. Also, China faces a number of problems, some of which are a result of its own success.

The broadest measure of the size of a country's economy is its gross domestic product. Table 11-1 shows three GDP measures for the world's top dozen economies in 2005 (the last year for which full data are available). Some sources state that China is already the world's second largest economy and should overtake the United States in another decade.[3] This interpretation relies on purchasing power parity data, which correct for the cost of living across countries. But the traditional measure of GDP, calculated in dollars at current exchange rates, indicates that the U.S. economy remains nearly six times the size of China's. Japan and Germany are also larger. The two Latin American countries that make the list—Brazil and Mexico—are much smaller.

The main reason that China is expected to surpass the United States is because of its extraordinarily high growth rates. Although the U.S. economy has been expanding fairly rapidly in the past fifteen years, having the highest growth rate among the industrial economies (an annual average of 3.5 percent), China has been growing three times as fast (10.2 percent a year). It is interesting to note that the second fastest growing economy is that of India. The two Latin American countries are in the lower tier in terms of growth as well as other indicators. China's strength is also demonstrated in other parts of table 11-1. As an export-led economy despite its large size, its foreign sales rank third behind those of the United States and Germany. Exports (in relation to imports) are the main contributor to international reserves. Thus it is not a surprise to see that China has the second largest volume of reserves, behind only Japan and way ahead of the United States.[4] All of these characteristics, plus its large population, give China immense potential, now that many of the regulations that were holding it back have been lifted.[5]

Size indicators are very important, especially when combined with information about growth rates, but they are only one part of an attempt to understand China's place in the international system and the implications for

Table 11-1. Indicators of Economic Size, Twelve Largest Economies, 2005

Country	GDP[a] $ billions	Rank	GDP (PPP)[b] $ billions	Rank	GDP growth 1990–2004	Rank	Population Millions	Rank	Exports[c] $ billions	Rank	Gross reserves[d] $ billions	Rank
United States	12,417	1	12,417	1	3.2	3	296	3	1,275	1	188	3
Japan	4,534	2	3,995	3	1.2	12	128	5	678	4	847	1
Germany	2,795	3	2,430	5	1.4	10	82	7	1,127	2	102	5
China	2,234	4	8,815	2	10.2	1	1,304	1	837	3	831	2
United Kingdom	2,199	5	2,002	6	2.6	7	60	9	587	5	44	10
France	2,127	6	1,850	7	1.8	9	61	8	555	6	74	6.5
Italy	1,763	7	1,672	8	1.3	11	59	10	463	7	66	8
Spain	1,125	8	1,179	10	2.7	5	43	11	288	9	17	12
Canada	1,114	9	1,078	12	2.9	4	32	12	428	8	33	11
India	806	10	3,779	4	6.1	2	1,094	2	83	12	138	4
Brazil	796	11	1,566	9	2.6	7	186	4	134	11	54	9
Mexico	768	12	1,108	11	2.6	7	103	6	230	10	74	6.5

Source: World Bank, World Development Indicators (online) for all indicators except GDP growth; World Bank, World Development Indicators, 2006, for GDP growth.

a. GDP = GDP converted to dollars at current exchange rates.
b. GDP (PPP) = GDP converted to dollars using purchasing power parity.
c. Exports = goods and services.
d. Reserves include gold.

the United States and Latin America in the coming years. Within the economic arena, it is also important to understand the characteristics of China's economic growth. While China has an export-led economy, the majority of those exports are produced by multinational corporations.[6] This reflects the enormous amount of foreign direct investment (FDI) that has poured into China in recent years. It is far and away the largest recipient of FDI among developing countries, accounting for over two-fifths of the total between 2000 and 2005, or nearly $50 billion a year.[7] A number of these multinationals are based in the United States, but an even larger number are based in other Asian economies. Japan, South Korea, and Taiwan, for example, have shifted important parts of their industrial capacity to China because costs are much lower than at home. This is especially the case for labor-intensive products, since Chinese wages—although rising, particularly in coastal provinces—are still only a fraction of wages in Northeast Asia. Many of the more complex inputs for the firms relocated in China are imported from the headquarters firm or its suppliers. Some of the goods produced in China by Northeast Asian multinationals are shipped back to their home countries, but most are sold in the United States or in Europe.[8]

This combination of large-scale imports from Northeast (and even Southeast) Asia without compensating exports leads to substantial trade deficits for China with these countries. These have been roughly offset by large surpluses with the United States and the European Union. Thus China itself has had a relatively balanced trade, although this has turned toward an overall surplus in the last few years due, in part, to the vast increase in textile exports after the end of the Multifiber Agreement. In addition, China has increased its exports in other sectors, including some high-technology products. The surpluses have been invested in U.S. treasury securities, partially offsetting U.S. deficits. These imbalances are seen by many experts as jeopardizing the stability of the world economy.[9] Another source of instability is the bilateral trade deficit that the United States has with China, which produces both economic and political problems, including demands for protectionist measures to shield U.S. firms that cannot compete.

It should not be assumed from this analysis of China's large and growing economy, and its successful trade strategy, that the country has no problems going forward. Indeed, a number of potential problems loom, some of them stemming from the very reforms that were responsible for its high growth rates. In the economic sphere, China still has a large number of fairly inefficient state-owned enterprises. These firms have traditionally been supported by state-owned banks, leading to massive nonperforming loans for the latter.

In the last few years, the Chinese government has taken important steps to clean up both financial and nonfinancial firms, but many problems still remain.[10] One of the reasons for the changes is the Chinese government's decision to join the World Trade Organization (WTO), which required China to open its economy to foreign competition. The government has since tried to increase the competitiveness of its firms.[11]

In the social area, both open and disguised unemployment are high and are exacerbated by rapid urbanization. In the last decade China's urban population has increased by some 200 million people, and the migration continues. Partly as a result of the new urban dwellers, unofficial estimates suggest that open unemployment in the cities has reached 11–12 percent.[12] The other main reason for high unemployment is the shedding of workers by state-owned firms, which have declined to about one-third of the total number of firms—although the share of workers still employed by these firms is much higher. The lower number of public sector workers has further increased social problems, since services and pensions were previously provided through the workplace.[13]

Unemployment has contributed to increased inequality in the cities, as has the new requirement that citizens be responsible for much of the cost of education, health care, housing, and pensions. China's Gini coefficient, the most common measure of income inequality, has gone from among the lowest in the world in the 1970s to levels above most Asian countries—and approaching the levels of Latin America, long known as the most unequal region in the world (table 11-2). A larger problem is inequality between urban and rural areas or between coastal and interior provinces. After an initial rapid rise of incomes in the countryside with the abolition of the old collective farm system, rural dwellers have now fallen far behind.[14]

Social problems, in turn, are an important cause of growing political unrest. As a result of their low and declining living standards, rural residents and citizens in western provinces have staged a growing number of protests. These are frequently triggered by local government officials expropriating land with little or no compensation. In addition, government expenditures are far lower in rural areas, and until 2006 agricultural producers had to pay a special tax. But urban protests are also increasing, mainly due to poor working conditions or lack of access to affordable services. Demands for greater political freedom have also resumed after a hiatus following the Tiananmen events in 1989.[15]

These social and political problems bring us back to the topic of this chapter: the importance to China of its relationships with the United States and

Table 11-2. *Indicators of Inequality, Selected Developing Countries, Various Years, 1997–2002*

Country	Survey year	Gini index[a]	90/10[b]
Argentina	2001	0.51	13.71
Brazil	2001	0.59	16.25
Chile	2000	0.51	10.72
Colombia	1999	0.54	15.00
Costa Rica	2000	0.46	9.65
Mexico	2002	0.49	11.87
Peru	2000	0.48	14.60
Uruguay	2000	0.43	7.73
Venezuela	2000	0.42	7.94
China	2001	0.45	n.a.
India	1999/2000	0.33	n.a.
Indonesia	2000	0.34	n.a.
Korea	1998	0.32	n.a.
Malaysia	1997	0.47	n.a.
Philippines	2000	0.46	n.a.
Taiwan	2000	0.24	2.86
Thailand	2002	0.40	5.56
Egypt	2000	0.34	n.a.
Kenya	1997	0.44	6.46
Morocco	1998	0.38	5.33
South Africa	2000	0.58	16.91

Source: World Bank, *World Development Report, 2006.*
a. Gini index = measure that varies between 0 and 1, where 0 means perfect equality and 1 means perfect inequality.
b. 90/10 = ratio of richest decile to poorest decile.
n.a. Not available.

Latin America. Chinese government leaders believe that high rates of growth must be maintained to create jobs and provide government revenue to deal with social problems, build infrastructure, and develop the western part of the country. The low share of consumption in national income means that investment and exports are the key to growth, and they require inputs and markets. U.S. markets, capital, and technology are crucial. But raw materials from Latin America—petroleum, minerals, and agricultural products—are also increasingly important.

Attractions of a China–Latin America Alliance

It is in this context of needing to maintain (very) high growth rates that Latin America has come onto the Chinese radar screen. On paper, a China–Latin America alliance seems attractive for both sides. The most obvious link concerns raw materials. China consumes a large share of the world's commodities, and Latin America is a net exporter of such products. But as this section outlines, there are other attractions as well.

The Chinese Perspective

Approaching the question first from the point of view of attractions for China, this chapter argues that China's main interest in Latin America is related to trade. China clearly needs suppliers of raw materials. In 2004 it purchased over a quarter of the world's tin and zinc, over a fifth of its soy and aluminum, and about a fifth of its copper, numbers that will be much higher by now. As Luisa Palacios states in chapter 8, it has also become the second largest consumer of oil in the world, although it remains a long way behind the United States.[16] China has entered into a competition with other countries for obtaining raw materials, which has driven up prices and brought new countries and regions into the center of world trade.

For its part, Latin America exports a number of products that are crucial to China's continued industrial success. In chapter 6 Robert Devlin provides data showing that the top Latin American exports to China are metals (copper, iron ore, and scrap metal), foodstuffs (soy, sugar, and wheat), and industrial inputs (cotton, wool, and leather). Petroleum is noticeably absent from this list, despite high-profile discussions between Venezuela's Hugo Chávez and Chinese leaders. In chapter 8 Palacios points to a variety of obstacles to greater exports of petroleum to China. First is Latin America's declining production; second is the weak legal framework for investment in many Latin American exporting countries; third are transportation difficulties. Overall, Latin America provides less than 7 percent of China's petroleum needs, and most of this comes from Ecuador, not Venezuela. Palacios does not believe this will change significantly.

While China is only Venezuela's fourteenth largest market, the situation is quite different for some of its neighbors. For example, China is Peru's second largest market (mainly through sales of copper and fishmeal), Chile's third largest (copper), Brazil's third largest (soy and iron ore), and Argentina's fourth largest (wheat and soy). A similar situation exists with some smaller countries. In all cases except Argentina, the United States remains the number-one export destination, but the gap between the United States and China is closing fast. Japan, once very important especially for Chile and Brazil, is fading from the picture.[17]

The other side of the trade story concerns China's exports and their markets. While most large economies have fairly small export coefficients, China's is unusually high at nearly 40 percent of GDP, mainly due to the small share that consumption contributes to output. Latin America also provides a market for China, although it is clearly secondary to its role as a supplier of raw materials. As of 2005 Latin America and the Caribbean purchased 4.0 percent of China's exports, up from 1.8 percent in 1999. The increase (122 percent) was the highest for any region, but the absolute amount (less than $23 billion) remains very small.[18] It is notable that the products China sells to Latin America are quite different from those it buys from the region: textiles and clothing are important, as are telecommunications and other types of equipment (for more than this, see chapter 6).

Probably more important for the long run from China's perspective—and the same is true for many other countries—is access to the U.S. market via Latin America. The web of free trade agreements being signed between Asian and Latin American countries is heavily based on this attraction, and China has begun to join in. It already has an agreement with Chile and is in the process of negotiating one with Peru; others are under discussion. The biggest breakthrough would be an agreement with Mexico because of its close proximity to the United States, but this is unlikely for reasons to be discussed shortly.

What else might China want from Latin America? In chapter 2 of this volume, Jiang Shixue mentions two political aims. One is quite vague and idealistic: "Latin America is a potential partner in China's ongoing quest to establish a just and harmonious world order." Exactly what this partnership might entail is unclear; the main example given is cooperation at the United Nations. The other political goal, by contrast, is very specific: Latin America is the focus for eliminating recognition of Taiwan, since half of the countries that maintain diplomatic relations with the island (twelve of twenty-four) are located in Central America or the Caribbean. As is well known, one of China's principal foreign policy goals has to do with reuniting Taiwan with the mainland, but this is an issue with specific countries, not with the region as a whole.

China has established strategic relations with a number of Latin American countries, including Brazil, Mexico, and Venezuela, according to Xiang Lanxin (chapter 3). But interestingly, Xiang goes on to say that the term *strategic* is much narrower in the Chinese than in the Latin American perception and refers primarily to economic and energy interests. This point reinforces the argument that, despite the attempts of some Latin American leaders to

Table 11-3. *Trade between China and Developing Regions, 2005*

Region	Exports		Imports	
	$ billions	Percent	$ billions	Percent
China's trade with developing regions				
Africa	16.3	2.1	20.0	3.0
Asia	249.7	32.7	250.7	37.9
Hong Kong	124.5	16.3	12.2	1.8
Former Soviet states	37.2	4.9	23.7	3.6
Middle East	24.5	3.2	32.3	4.9
Latin America	22.8	3.0	26.4	4.0
Developing regions' trade with China				
Africa	17.0	7.0	17.5	7.6
Asia	293.7	12.7	271.7	12.5
Hong Kong	130.3	45.0	135.1	45.0
Former Soviet states	20.0	2.6	39.8	5.3
Middle East	28.6	5.4	26.6	6.9
Latin America	19.7	3.4	37.1	6.7

Source: IMF, *Direction of Trade Statistics Yearbook, 2006.*

broaden the agenda, China's main interest in Latin America is trade. It is important to ask how Latin America compares to other sources of raw materials for China—and, more broadly, other partners in the developing world. Two of the chapters in this volume, on Africa and Southeast Asia, provide insights on this question. And table 11-3 provides some comparative data.

Africa is similar to Latin America in that it is distant from China in geographical, cultural, and historical terms. Nonetheless, many indicators show that China is currently more active in Africa than in Latin America. In chapter 10, Chris Alden emphasizes Africa as a source of raw materials for China. While a number of commodities are imported from Africa, petroleum is key: over 30 percent of China's oil comes from Africa, and the figure is rising. Alden also points to Africa's importance as a market, especially for China's low-end goods. In political terms, the Taiwan issue is as important in Africa as in Latin America, but another political goal is also mentioned: obtaining political support in multilateral institutions.

Southeast Asia is a quite different case since it is China's close neighbor. Here economic relations are also important. Trade among East Asian countries has been important for several decades, and recently China has become a key player in these relationships. Currently, about 12 percent of the four largest Southeast Asian countries' trade is with China, and a free trade area with the Association of Southeast Asian Nations (ASEAN) has been signed. Investment has also been booming in both directions. Nonetheless, Joshua Kurlantzick (chapter 9) puts his emphasis on four political goals that China has with respect to Southeast Asia: maintaining peace on its borders, reducing Taiwan's influence, improving its image abroad, and shifting influence away from the United States in the Asian region. This makes sense in that political relations are likely to be more important among neighbors than among distant partners, although the gravity theory of trade also indicates that geographical proximity is important in economic terms.

The Latin American Perspective

Having examined what China might want to get out of a relationship with Latin America—and compared this briefly with China's goals in other regions—the next question of interest is what Latin America's views are on the new relationship with China. The first thing that must be said is that there is no single answer to this question. As Francisco González makes clear in chapter 7, there have been both winners and losers in Latin America. The most obvious winners are important commodity exporters; the losers are those whose exports are geared toward industrial goods. This difference clearly matches the geographical divide between, respectively, southern and northern Latin America. In addition, winners and losers are found across sectors within a given country, where those associated in one way or another with commodities are better off than those in industrial sectors that compete with China. Services have specific winners, losers, and those whose fate depends much more on other factors.

Trade plays a central role. We have already seen that there has been a strong shift toward greater trade with China. This is true even for countries that are not commodity exporters. From the Latin American perspective, however, it is not just a shift in the direction of trade but also a large increase in the overall value of trade. Between 2001 and 2006 exports of goods rose from $352 to $681 billion (in current dollars), while imports grew from $359 to $588 billion, resulting in a $93 billion trade surplus in 2006 (unlike the small deficit of 2001 and a much larger deficit in earlier years). While export volume increased, the major source of the expansion in the value of trade was price rises, where China was an important influence. The current account for the region as a whole has been in surplus since 2003—the first time in decades. As a consequence, international reserves have been accumulating; in 2006 they amounted to $321 billion, or about 10 percent of GDP. Output is booming (GDP growth averaged 4.6 percent in 2003–06, compared to 1.3 percent in 1998–2003), and the unemployment rate fell from 11.0 percent in 2003 to

8.6 percent in 2006.[19] Even those countries that have not been direct winners from trade have benefited to some extent as the perception spreads—especially among investors—that the region as a whole may have turned a corner. China has definitely played a significant role in Latin America's recovery, and most countries see this as a major attraction of the relationship.[20]

Beyond trade, but closely associated, China has also indicated an interest in investing in Latin America. This intention was trumpeted to the world during visits to Latin America by Chinese president Hu Jintao in late 2004 and by Vice President Zeng Qinghong in early 2005. President Hu supposedly promised that China would undertake $100 billion of investment in Latin America over the following ten years. Needless to say, this statement led to high expectations, few of which have been fulfilled. However, in chapter 2 Jiang contends that Latin American newspapers misunderstood Hu's statement, which mentioned the figure of $100 billion only in relation to trade flows. His statement about investment, according to Jiang, discussed the target of doubling the existing value of investment.

Nonetheless, some investments have materialized, although it remains very difficult to put any aggregate numbers on them. Partial evidence identifies some significant projects, especially copper in Chile ($5 billion in one project and $2 billion in another) and steel in Brazil ($1.4 billion). Negotiations are said to be under way for investments in the energy sector (oil and gas) in Argentina, Brazil, Colombia, and Venezuela; minerals in several countries; and infrastructure for export in Argentina and Brazil. Perhaps the most interesting for the region are some high-technology projects between Brazil's Embraer and several Chinese aviation firms.[21]

Some Latin American countries are content simply to strengthen economic relations with China; Chile and Peru would seem to be examples of this approach. Others see the possibility for political or strategic relations as well. Of course, the best known case of a government interest in strengthening political ties is Hugo Chávez's Venezuela. Chávez sees China as an important member of his anti-American alliance, but it is unlikely that China will be willing to engage in such ventures, as discussed later in this chapter. More modest, but more concrete, is Brazil's leading role in the Group of Twenty developing countries in the WTO negotiations; other members of the leadership group are China, India, and South Africa. The G-20, to which a number of other Latin American countries also belong, is striving to get the best deal possible for developing countries in the WTO's Doha Round.

Both Juan Gabriel Tokatlian in chapter 4 and Monica Hirst in chapter 5 discuss the political aspects of the China–Latin American relationship and the implications for the United States. Tokatlian does not foresee China playing a major political role in Latin America, but he does point to Latin America's desire for a diversification of power relations in the Western Hemisphere. While Hirst mentions opportunities for China and Latin America to join forces in the General Assembly to promote projects of mutual interest (for example, in education, health, science, and technology), she also says that in the Security Council China's nonintervention stance has separated it from most Latin American countries.[22]

In summary, a number of complementarities exist between China and at least some Latin American countries. The most obvious are in the trade realm, where China's demand for raw materials has provided a powerful stimulus for the economies of many countries in Latin America. In addition, and often connected to trade through the desire to facilitate the production of raw materials, China has promised funds both for production and for infrastructure. Close political relations between China and Latin America do not seem likely, although tactical alliances may well take place in multilateral institutions.

Problems with a China–Latin American Alliance

The previous section suggests that there are limits on a China–Latin American alliance. We now turn to the problems on each side that may create these limits. They are found in the economic and political spheres and perhaps in the cultural area as well.

The Chinese Perspective

On the Chinese side, a first set of obstacles to a close relationship with Latin America is indeed in the cultural arena. Unlike the case of Japan, which could count on strong local Japanese communities in a number of Latin American countries, especially in Brazil, when it began to expand trade and investment relations, local Chinese communities are much weaker. Thus there is no bridge group that can provide help on issues ranging from language to insights on local customs to connections with local firms and government officials. As the Chinese observer to the Organization of American States (OAS) declared, "Interest is different from an agreement. When the President of China visited South America, he spoke of many things, but much of it was unofficial. . . . Chinese entrepreneurs have very little knowledge of [South America], and when they have begun to invest or explore the possibilities of investment they have encountered difficulties."[23] His main point is that China will be very cautious because Latin America and China are "very different culturally," unlike the situation in East Asia.

The two Chinese authors in this volume, Jiang Shixue (chapter 2) and Xiang Lanxin (chapter 3), also argue that cultural difference is an important barrier to deepening the bilateral relationship. Xiang cites a long list of occasions when China was caught off guard by events in Latin America. "China's rapid emergence in the last decades," he states, "cannot hide its knowledge deficit about recent political events and current trends in Latin America." A related barrier is geographical distance. Distance certainly helps to produce and perpetuate cultural differences. In addition, however, it can also impede trade and investment. Only certain products can be transported in an economically efficient way, placing limits on trade linkages. An obvious example is Venezuela's oil, which has long been a desirable commodity for resource-needy consumers around the world, but proximity has kept the United States with a near monopsony over the product. The long journey between the two continents also poses challenges for investment, since it makes it difficult for executives to keep track of projects. Of course, new communications techniques help to ameliorate the distance factor, but the cultural divide makes personal contact especially important.

Another factor that both Chinese authors in this volume stress is China's perceived need to avoid alienating the United States in the course of expanding its relations with Latin America. Xiang states that "official rhetoric aside, there is no doubt that Beijing's decision at the end of the twentieth century to intensify its engagement with Latin America was largely motivated by the pressing issue of energy security. . . . Yet an important foreign policy dilemma arises from China's new interest in Latin America: simply put, relations with the United States. . . . Clearly, the current regime's main concern in the Western Hemisphere is to avoid any geopolitical consequences resulting from its expansion into Latin America." Jiang, taking a more official stance, states that "China is well aware of the fact that the United States considers Latin America its backyard, and China has no intention of challenging U.S. hegemony in the region."

One of the issues with respect to the United States, as mentioned earlier, is China's reliance on U.S. investment and investment by U.S. allies, especially Japan. More generally, however, China is well aware that the United States remains much more powerful in both economic and military terms, so it wants to avoid direct confrontations. This had led the Chinese government to try to keep a low profile, especially in areas of long-standing importance to the United States. In this light, overtures such as those of Hugo Chávez are especially problematic. China does not want to be perceived as taking sides with groups in Latin America (or elsewhere) that are openly anti-American.

The Latin American Perspective

If the downside of the China–Latin America relationship for China centers on fairly subtle cultural and psychological issues, some of the downsides for Latin America are much more concrete. First, serious economic problems have arisen over the last several years. These come in two varieties. In Mexico and Central America, Chinese competition through low wages is posing a major threat both in export markets and at home. A number of Mexico's assembly plants (maquiladoras) have packed up and moved to China to take advantage of lower costs. Cheap exports are flooding the Mexican market itself and threatening the existence of local firms. And Mexico is losing out in the U.S. market, where China has now displaced it as the second largest supplier.[24]

In South America, by contrast, where exports to China have heightened prosperity, a different kind of concern exists. The fear in South America is that the subregion is being driven back to the old development model of the nineteenth century, whereby it exports commodities and imports industrial goods. This export profile has proved over the decades to have various disadvantages. Prices of commodities have traditionally been volatile and, some would claim, are likely to fall in the long run in comparison to prices of industrial goods. In terms of labor, production of some commodities relies on unskilled labor, which Latin America has been trying to move away from. In those cases where high-technology processes are used, little labor is employed at all. These concerns are magnified by some of the Chinese "investment" proposals, which have turned out to be long-term loans with the requirement that all of the labor come from China.[25]

Latin America also shares some of China's concerns with respect to the United States and its view of the new relationship. While many Latin American countries have long sought more diversified power relations in the hemisphere—this was an attraction of Japan during the 1980s and of the European Union later on—the United States remains the main trade partner throughout the hemisphere as well as the main source of foreign investment. In the last few years, the situation has become more polarized as elections in several countries have returned presidents who have joined in an open anti-American alliance—in contrast to those who want to work closely with the U.S. government and private sector. Of course, there continue to be substantial areas of cooperation with the United States, even among the former group, but the era of good will of the 1990s appears to be over, at least for the short term. This is manifested in the apparent failure of the Free Trade Area of the Americas (FTAA), but virtually no government sees China as a viable substitute for the United States. Thus caution is called for in negotiating new relationships.

Finally, we return to another cultural issue that divides China from Latin America. Despite Hugo Chávez's attempts to muzzle the press and eliminate barriers to indefinite reelection, Latin America in general remains committed to democracy, human rights, and the rule of law in a way that China's government makes no pretense to support. Clearly this does not mean that all Latin American democracies are ideal—nor that the U.S. democracy does not have important failings too—but the entire Western Hemisphere shares a set of values that binds it together.

In chapter 4, Tokatlian puts it this way: values matter. "Latin America shares (and contributes to) the democratic values of the West. . . . Despite clear limitations and inherent internal contradictions, the countries of the region have continued moving forward with democratization. In this regard, China's internal political model is not especially attractive for Latin America." He then goes on to say that China's external diplomatic model is "more seductive," characterized by multipolarism, multilaterialism, noninterference, soft power, pragmatism, collaboration, and persuasion—as opposed to their alternatives. This seems to ignore the fact that China's noninterference policy, in particular, has been roundly attacked as supporting some of the least attractive regimes in the world (for example, Sudan, Myanmar, or North Korea). He concludes that the challenge of the triangle is to combine democratic values internally with new space created by China's greater role on the international stage.

To summarize, a closer relationship between China and Latin America has some disadvantages for both sides as well as some obvious attractions. For China the main disadvantages are geographical distance and lack of familiarity with Latin American culture. Whether greater familiarity would breed more confidence remains to be seen. On the Latin American side, cultural differences are important, but so are concrete economic fears. These vary according to individual country but include worry about unfair competition and about being pushed back toward an undesirable development model. Despite short-term benefits, longer-term problems pose a concern.

Conclusions

The chapter concludes by asking two questions. First, is there likely to be an aggressive China–Latin America relationship in the coming years? Second, what are the implications for the United States of either a positive or a negative answer to the previous question?

The argument here is that it is quite unlikely that either China or Latin America will push for an aggressive alliance, where *aggressive* means a set of policies that would restrict U.S. access to the region. Such a move is neither in China's nor in Latin America's interest. On the Chinese side, various factors stand in the way of such an approach. Most important, China has innumerable problems at home, especially in the social and political spheres. These include rapid urbanization, growing unemployment and inequality, and increasing social protest. The Chinese Communist Party seems determined to maintain power, at least in the medium term, and so must focus on these domestic issues. Environmental problems also weigh heavily on the Chinese government. It might be said that it is precisely because of these domestic problems that China must take risks in Latin America, but this argument does not hold up. Insofar as raw materials are the main attraction in Latin America, alternative sources are available elsewhere (especially in Africa) with lower economic and political costs. A low-key approach in Latin America with some countries—especially Brazil and Chile, perhaps also Colombia and Peru—would be advantageous for China. The players who want an aggressive alliance—especially Venezuela, perhaps Bolivia, Ecuador, Nicaragua, even Argentina—are less attractive.

In particular, there is no evidence that China wants to challenge the United States any time soon, which is what an aggressive alliance would imply. As the *Economist* argues, China will be an Asian power for the foreseeable future.[26] It has many problems to resolve in its home region, and Southeast Asian countries also have natural resources to offer if China plays its cards well. Moreover, China needs the United States and its allies (especially Japan) to provide other inputs for its economy. This chapter focuses on China's need for raw materials, but the large majority of China's imports are industrial goods, both inputs and equipment. It needs high-technology products, which generally come as part of the investment process. These goods can come only from the industrial economies at the present time.

We return, then, to the Japanese example that was introduced at the beginning of the chapter. China's current economic, social, and political situation as well as what it would gain and lose from an aggressive stance in Latin America lead to the conclusion that the Japanese model could be a fairly good predictor of China's behavior. Distance and cultural differences are again important. Issues at home demand full attention. Integration with Asian neighbors is the main foreign policy priority. And the United States, although it plays a somewhat different role vis-à-vis China than it did with respect to Japan, remains a formidable obstacle to aggressive Chinese measures. Last, just as with Japan, new resource-saving technologies are likely to be put in place in China, which will diminish some of the need for raw materials, especially energy.

On the Latin American side, the situation is somewhat more ambiguous, since a few governments seem to want to significantly change the status quo. An alliance with China might be useful in promoting their project, although that can be debated. In the meantime, the South American countries that were so enthusiastic about China in the halcyon days of 2004–05 are reconsidering. They have come to realize that Chinese money also comes with strings—if it comes at all. Most of the initial promises (or what were thought to be promises) have not even begun to materialize. Also, a better understanding of how Chinese investment takes place makes it appear less attractive. As Xiang states in chapter 3, "Chinese trade and investment in the region cannot escape the stigma of a neocolonial pattern, especially given China's very narrow commodity needs." In this sense, a careful study of the African experience would be useful.

Trade relationships, which really have provided copious new resources, are also being questioned. On the one hand is the issue of whether Latin America wants to become primarily a commodity exporter again. On the other hand, even in South America, not to mention Mexico and Central America, there is concern about competition in the industrial sector from a large, low-cost producer. Already barriers are being erected against Chinese exports, which the Chinese feel are unfair (see chapter 2). Clearly, Latin America will be looking for ways to obtain the advantages from the Chinese relationship without the disadvantages. In chapter 6 Devlin has some useful economic suggestions along this line. In chapter 4 Tokatlian presents an equally useful discussion from the political side.

Finally, like China, Latin America must consider the implications of confronting the regional hegemon. The United States is still the main market for most of Latin America, especially Mexico and Central America but South America as well. Particularly important are the industrial exports that the United States buys. Exports to Europe and Asia—including China—are much more biased toward natural resources. Most, perhaps all, Latin American governments realize that China is neither willing nor able to replace the United States. If this analysis is correct and no aggressive alliance is likely, what are the implications for the United States? One possibility is that Washington learns nothing and continues to treat Latin America in the heavy-handed way it has typically done—when it focuses on the region at all. A more useful, if less likely, approach is that the new administration that comes to power in January 2009 takes the Chinese presence as a wake-up call and tries to break the syndrome whereby any U.S. attention to Latin America is soon overshadowed by events elsewhere.

Both Asia and Europe have lessons to offer in how the United States and Latin America could work together to the mutual benefit of both. The Asian example centers on the model wherein less developed countries are incorporated into production chains in an advantageous way. In the case of the European Union, accession countries have been incorporated into the EU model in a way that puts more emphasis on institutions and social policy. The United States appeared to be moving toward a sui generis project in the Western Hemisphere in the mid-1990s with the Free Trade Area of the Americas, but that opportunity has been squandered. Hopefully, a new administration will be able to regain momentum and to find a way to treat China as a partner in the endeavor.

Notes

1. See Barbara Stallings and Gabriel Székely, eds., *Japan, the United States, and Latin America: Toward a Trilateral Relationship in the Western Hemisphere* (Johns Hopkins University Press, 1993); Susan Kaufman Purcell and Robert M. Immerman, eds., *Japan and Latin America in the New Global Order* (Boulder, Colo.: Lynne Rienner, 1992); and Carlos Moneta, *Japón y América Latina en los años noventa* (Buenos Aires: Planeta, 1991). In reality both the history of Japan and China in Latin America began with immigration in the early twentieth century. On Japanese immigration to Latin America, which is better studied, see Iyo Kunimoto, "Japanese Migration to Latin America," in *Japan, the United States, and Latin America: Toward a Trilateral Relationship in the Western Hemisphere,* edited by Barbara Stallings and Gabriel Székely (Johns Hopkins University Press, 1993).

2. See, for example, the prepared statements of the chair of the House Western Hemisphere Subcommittee, Dan Burton, and the assistant secretary of state for Latin America, Roger F. Noriega, for the House of Representatives hearing, China's Influence in the Western Hemisphere, April 6, 2005 (www.foreignaffairs.house.gov/archives/109/20404.pdf [December 2007]).

3. "The World in 2026: Who Will Be Number One?" *Economist: The World in 2026,* p. 62.

4. As of 2006 China surpassed Japan and now has the largest volume of reserves.

5. On China's economic reforms, see Barry Naughton, *The Chinese Economy: Transitions and Growth* (MIT Press, 2007), especially chapter 4; Nicholas Lardy, *China's Unfinished Economic Revolution* (Brookings, 1998); and Nicholas Lardy, *Integrating China into the Global Economy* (Brookings, 2002).

6. See Naughton, *The Chinese Economy,* chapter 17.

7. World Bank, *World Development Finance, 2006,* vol. 1 (Washington: 2006).

8. Guillaume Gaulier, Françoise Lemoine, and Deniz Ünal-Kesenci, "China's Emergence and the Reorganisation of Trade Flows in Asia," Working Paper 2006-05 (Paris: CEPII, 2006).

9. Barry Eichengreen and Yung Chul Park, "Global Imbalances and Emerging Markets," in *Global Imbalances and the U.S. Debt Problem,* edited by Jan Joost Teunissen and Age Akkerman (The Hague: Fondad, 2006). Much of China's trade is carried out through Hong Kong, thus data on Chinese trade are often quite different from those published by its partners.

10. See Naughton, *The Chinese Economy,* chapter 19; and Alicia García-Herrero, Sergio Gavilá, and Daniel Santabárbara, "China's Banking Reform: An Assessment of its Evolution and Possible Impact," Occasional Paper 0502 (Madrid: Bank of Spain, 2005).

11. Lardy, *Integrating China into the Global Economy;* and Supachai Panitchpakdi and Mark L. Clifford, *China and the WTO* (New York: John Wiley and Sons, 2002).

12. C. Fred Bergsten and others, *China: The Balance Sheet* (New York: Public Affairs Press, 2006), pp. 31–32. Official figures are much lower but high enough to alarm the government.

13. Pensions are very important, since China faces a major challenge in its aging population; see analysis in Helen Qiao, "Will China Grow Old before Getting Rich?" Global Economics Paper 138 (New York: Goldman Sachs, 2006).

14. Shubham Chaudhuri and Martin Ravallion, "Partially Awakened Dragons: Uneven Growth in China and India," in *Dancing with Giants: China, India, and the Global Economy,* edited by L. Alan Winters and Shahid Yusuf (Washington: World Bank, 2007); and David Dollar, "Poverty, Inequality, and Social Disparities during China's Economic Reforms," Policy Research Working Paper 4253 (Washington: World Bank, 2007).

15. Susan Shirk, *China: Fragile Superpower* (Oxford University Press, 2007); and Bergsten and others, *China,* chapter 3.

16. For more on this subject, see Daniel Lederman, Marcelo Olarreada, and Guillermo Perry, eds., *Latin America's Response to China and India* (Washington: World Bank, 2006).

17. Data are from International Monetary Fund, *Direction of Trade Statistics Yearbook, 2006* (Washington: 2006).

18. Ibid.

19. Economic Commission for Latin America and the Caribbean (ECLAC), *Economic Survey of Latin America and the Caribbean, 2006–2007* (Santiago: 2007).

20. On the impact of China's trade on Latin America, see Jorge Blázquez-Lidoy, Javier Rodríguez, and Javier Santiso, "Angel or Demon? China's Trade Impact on Latin American Countries," *Cepal Review* 90 (December 2006): 15–41.

21. ECLAC, *Latin America and the Caribbean in the World Economy, 2004–2005* (Santiago, 2005), chapter 5.

22. For an empirical study of the relationship between Latin American countries' trade with China and their votes in the United Nations, see Jorge I. Dominguez,

"China's Relations with Latin America: Shared Gains, Asymmetric Hopes," working paper (Washington: Inter-American Dialogue, 2006), pp. 12–15.

23. Sam Logan and Ben Bain, "China's Entrance into Latin America: A Cause for Worry?" (Washington: Center for International Policy, 2005; http://americas.irc-online.org/am/389 [December 2007]).

24. Robert Devlin, Antoni Estevadeordal, and Andrés Rodríguez, eds., *The Emergence of China: Challenges and Opportunities for Latin America and the Caribbean* (Harvard University Press, 2006); and Enrique Dussel Peters, "Implications of China's Recent Economic Performance for Mexico," briefing paper, Dialogue on Globalization (Berlin: Friedrich Ebert Stiftung, 2005).

25. Devlin, Estevadeordal, and Rodríguez, *The Emergence of China*; and Lederman, Olarreada, and Perry, *Latin America's Response*.

26. "Reaching for a Renaissance: A Special Report on China and Its Region," *Economist*, March 31, 2007, special independent section, pp. 1–18.

About the Authors

Chris Alden is a senior lecturer in International Relations at the London School of Economics.

Robert Devlin is a regional adviser at the United Nations Economic Commission for Latin America and the Caribbean (ECLAC/CEPAL).

Francisco E. González is the Riordan Roett Assistant Professor of Latin American Studies at the Johns Hopkins Paul H. Nitze School of Advanced International Studies (SAIS) in Washington.

Monica Hirst is a professor of International Politics at Torcuato di Tella University (UTDT) in Buenos Aires.

Jiang Shixue is deputy director and professor at the Institute of Latin American Studies (ILAS) and chair of the Latin American Studies Department at the Graduate School of the Chinese Academy of Social Sciences (CASS) in Beijing.

Joshua Kurlantzick is a visiting scholar at the Carnegie Endowment for International Peace and author of *Charm Offensive: How China's Soft Power Is Transforming the World.*

Luisa Palacios is managing director in the Emerging Markets and Energy Group at Medley Global Advisors in New York.

Guadalupe Paz is associate director of the Latin American Studies Program at the Johns Hopkins Paul H. Nitze School of Advanced International Studies (SAIS) in Washington.

Riordan Roett is the Sarita and Don Johnston Professor and director of Western Hemisphere Studies and the Latin American Studies Program at the Johns Hopkins Paul H. Nitze School of Advanced International Studies (SAIS) in Washington.

Barbara Stallings is the William R. Rhodes Research Professor and Howard R. Swearer Director of the Watson Institute for International Studies at Brown University in Providence, Rhode Island.

Juan Gabriel Tokatlian is associate professor of political science and international relations at San Andrés University (UDESA) in Buenos Aires.

Xiang Lanxin is professor of international history and politics as well as director of the Center for China Policy Analysis at the Graduate Institute of International Studies (HEI) in Geneva; he also holds a chair in international affairs at Fudan University in Shanghai.

Index

Accountability: Chinese undermining in Africa, 227; lack in Chinese business dealings, 207–08

Africa: and challenges of consolidation, 227–31; Chinese development assistance and diplomacy in, 217–19; Chinese influence in, 3, 213–35, 248; Chinese living and working in, 216, 221; in competition with the West, 230–31; examples of historical ties with China, 214; rapidity of infiltration, 220–24; response to China, 224–27, 228; strategic partnerships with China, 219–20; and trade friction, 228–29; and values friction, 229–30

Africa Action Plan (G-8), 227

African Commission on Human Rights, 229

African Growth and Opportunity Act (U.S.), 216

African Union, 229, 232

Agriculture: Chinese investment in Africa for, 216, 218; Chinese treatment of rural areas, 126, 244; U.S. policies, 14

Air pollution, 9

ALADI. *See* Latin American Integration Association

Alden, Chris, 3, 213, 248

Algeria, 218

Alien Tort Claim Act (U.S.), 231

Allende, Salvador, 47

Amnesty International, 218

Angola: development assistance from China, 217, 218; energy dealings in, 221, 222; infrastructure aid from China, 222; retail sector in, 224, 228

Antidrug operations. *See* Drug trafficking

Antidumping actions against China, 16, 22*n*40, 34, 38, 99–100, 143*n*2, 153

Antigua and Barbuda, 37

APEC. *See* Asia-Pacific Economic Cooperation Forum

Argentina: exports from, 55, 152–53, 166*n*14; and G-20 policy, 92; oil production and consumption in, 174, 180; Peronist Revolution in, 74; relations with Brazil, 98; relations with China, 255; relations with Taiwan, 96; trade competition with

relations, 42*n*18; visits to Africa, 228; visits to Latin America, 27, 39, 40*n*1, 100, 105*n*12, 153–54, 200, 206, 250; visits to U.S., 42*n*18; on world harmony, 33–34
Humanitarian assistance from China to Africa, 218
Human rights: in Africa, 227, 229–30, 231; in China, 220; in Mexico, 197
Human trafficking, 205
Hun Sen, 194, 204
Hutchison Whampoa, 69–70

IADB. *See* Inter-American Development Bank
IBM, 160
IBSA, 93, 94, 102, 103, 108*n*50
ILAS. *See* Institute of Latin American Studies
IMF. *See* International Monetary Fund
Immigration from China to Southeast Asia, 202, 204
Immigration policy of U.S., 11–12, 201
Imports. *See* Trade policy
India: and BRIC membership, 92; economic growth of, 136, 241; energy needs of, 66; and G-*20* policy, 92; nuclear and space technology, U.S. sharing with, 5; relations with Brazil, 98; relations with China, 102–03
Indonesia, 136, 199, 200, 203, 204, 205
Infrastructure in China, 134
Infrastructure investment in Africa, 214, 215, 216–17, 221
Innovation in China, 133–34
Institute of Latin American Studies (ILAS), 29
Intel, 160, 162
Inter-American Air Forces Academy, 68
Inter-American Development Bank (IADB), 10, 15, 35, 107*n*30
Intermediate states and South-South cooperation, 92, 104*n*8

International Centre for Settlement and Investment Disputes (ICSID) and Oxy lawsuit, 178
International Monetary Fund (IMF), 8, 9, 10, 15, 46
Iraq war: effect of, 219, 230; Latin American participation in, 84*n*24

Jamaica, 37
Japan: economic rise of compared to China, 239–40, 255–56; economic status of, 241, 247; handling of Southeast Asian financial crisis by, 194; oil consumption by, 170–71; relations with Brazil, 98, 247, 251; relations with U.S., 5, 240; shifting of manufacturing work to China, 243
Jiang Shixue, 3, 19, 27, 44, 45, 56, 247, 252
Jiang Zemin, 193, 194, 215

Khmer Rouge, 193–94
Kirchner, Néstor, 15, 38
Kull, Steven, 203
Kurlantzick, Joshua, 3, 4, 193–212, 249

Labor: from China for projects in Africa, 216, 221, 223, 228–29; from China for projects in Latin America, 253; low cost of, in China, 130–32, 243, 253
Lampton, David M., 9
Laos, 197, 198, 202, 203
Latin America: economic advantages of, 139–40; economic reforms, modeling on China, 137–39; new left in, 15; ranking on global competitiveness index, 17–18; relevance of region to international security, 83*n*16. *See also other countries for relations with (for example, China-Latin America relations)*
Latin American Integration Association (ALADI), 35, 97